ALCHEMY AND INDIVIDUATION

The Colors of Transformation

LYNNE EHLERS

ANALYTICAL PSYCHOLOGY PRESS

Oberlin, Ohio, United States of America

Anyone involved with his or her own psychological development is an alchemist.

—C. Conway Smith, MD

THIS BOOK IS DEDICATED TO ALL ALCHEMISTS

IN THEIR SEARCH FOR THE TRUE GOLD

CONTENTS

List of Illustrations

Figures

LIST OF ILLUSTRATIONS (continued)

Sandplay Photographs

LIST OF TABLES

(*Splendor Solis*, folio 26)

Introduction

THIS BOOK STANDS ON three pillars: alchemy, dreams, and sandplay. The three pillars are linked by one premise: that an individual's journey of inner transformation toward psychological wholeness, when looked at through the prism of color, passes through sequential color stages: first black, then white, yellow, and finally, red. Following the path of transformation from black to white to red, we will follow two women's extraordinary journeys toward wholeness. The first is the story of my inner transformation explored through the sequential unfolding of colors in my dreams. The second is an equally transformative journey to wholeness through the colors of the figures the second woman chose in her sandplay. The results of both are an amazing testament to the powerful healing potential of dreams and sandplay.

Our story begins with the alchemists. Their work over two millennia offers us a wide, rich map of the journey toward wholeness. On this map lie many circuitous paths. Our path, through the lens of color, is fairly straightforward. I stumbled upon this path quite

by accident. Nearing the end of my graduate studies in psychology and having spent a year researching the literature on sandplay with the intent of writing a dissertation on the subject, I picked up a book by Marie-Louise von Franz, *Alchemy: An Introduction to the Symbolism and the Psychology.* In it, I came upon a passage by the third-century Greek-Egyptian alchemist Zosimos, who wrote of the material in his vessel turning "first black, then white, and then yellow, and . . . [finally] the *rubedo*—the state of becoming red."[1] Marie-Louise von Franz, quoting C. G. Jung, likened these changes of color to psychological transformation.

Pondering the idea of these changes of color as stages of psychological transformation led to an epiphany: I suddenly remembered a whole series of strikingly black dreams I'd recorded at the beginning of my analysis. Had I also had dreams of white as the predominant color? Or yellow? Or red? I had no idea! But I was intensely curious. As I reviewed the 2500 dreams I'd recorded over the fifteen years I had been in analysis up to that point, I was amazed to discover that I had indeed recorded a series of strikingly white dreams and a series of strikingly red dreams! I had struck gold. Call my epiphany serendipity or synchronicity, it changed the course of my professional career.

The idea of the alchemical black, white, yellow, and red as sequential stages in the process of individuation has been espoused by C. G. Jung and later Jungians (not only von Franz but also Robert Grinnell, Johannes Fabricius, James Hillman, Gerard Astrachan, Edward Edinger, and Joseph Henderson and Dyane Sherwood),[2] but none had presented a case example corroborating or empirically testing this idea. This became my goal. Chi-square tests using residual components were performed on the separate files of "black," "white," "yellow," and "red" dreams in my dream record, yielding remarkable results (see Table 1).[3] Numbers that reached statistical significance are indicated by an asterisk. These results are a strong indication that the ancient alchemists were correct. As shown, the group of

YEAR	TOTAL	BLACK %	WHITE %	YELLOW %	RED %
1974	57	6 = 10.53%	4 = 7.02%	0 = 0.00%	1 = 1.75%
1975	138	5 = 3.62%	3 = 2.17%	2 = 1.45%	4 = 2.90%
1976	37	0 = 0.00%	2 = 5.41%	0 = 0.00%	1 = 2.70%
1977	57	0 = 0.00%	2 = 3.51%	1 = 1.75%	3 = 5.26%
1978	152	10 = 6.58%	11 = 7.24%	2 = 1.32%	9 = 5.92%
1979	82	* 13 = 15.85%	4 = 4.88%	0 = 0.00%	3 = 3.66%
1980	113	* 14 = 12.39%	* 11 = 9.73%	2 = 1.77%	3 = 2.65%
1981	213	* 25 = 11.74%	* 20 = 9.39%	3 = 1.41%	9 = 4.23%
1982	255	23 = 9.02%	* 19 = 7.45%	3 = 1.18%	* 13 = 5.10%
1983	327	19 = 5.81%	15 = 4.59%	1 = 0.31%	12 = 3.67%
1984	321	17 = 5.30%	* 25 = 7.79%	3 = 0.93%	* 17 = 5.30%
1985	250	19 = 7.60%	12 = 4.80%	1 = 0.40%	12 = 4.80%
1986	244	15 = 6.15%	7 = 2.87%	2 = 0.82%	9 = 3.69%
1987	140	12 = 8.57%	8 = 5.71%	0 = 0.00%	4 = 2.86%
1988	166	6 = 3.85%	7 = 4.49%	3 = 1.92%	4 = 2.56%
TOTAL	2542				
AVERAGE		7.24%	5.90%	0.90%	4.09%

Table 1. Evidence for the Sequential Appearance of Colors in Dreams during a 14-Year Analysis, as shown by the average incidence of principal alchemical colors in all dreams, 1974-1988. Statistically significant chi-square tests using residual components demonstrate that the entries indicated with an asterisk occurred in discrete, sequential groups at a frequency greater than chance.

"black" dreams precedes the group of "white" dreams by one year, which in turn precedes the group of "red" dreams by one year. The "yellow" dreams were not numerous enough to be statistically significant. Here was empirical proof that the groups of black, white, and red dreams are sequential, overlapping stages in the process of psychological transformation!

This thesis became the basis of a 330-page dissertation.[4] While empirical proof of my question was a revelation worthy of a dissertation itself, what interested me far more was the psychological meaning of these colors. I had a very good idea about the meaning of the black (*nigredo* in Latin) as it had been such a painful period in my analysis, but of the white (*albedo*), yellow (*citrinitas*), and red (*rubedo*) I had no idea. I turned to the literature on alchemy, full of colorful, interesting metaphorical imagery (for a splendid example of an alchemical text, see Appendix C), but it yielded little insight into the colors' psychological meaning. However, the writings of C. G. Jung and other scholars of alchemy helped me unlock the alchemists' secrets. It is also surprising and exciting to find corroboration for the specific sequence of the alchemical colors in numerous color- and symbol-systems worldwide: for instance, the ancient Japanese medical color system; Hindu cosmology; the colors of clerical robes in the Roman Catholic church; the Chinese *I Ching*, or *Book of Changes*; Indian Kundalini Yoga; modern research on left and right; and Ornstein's split-brain research. I will elaborate upon these in a later chapter.

The analysis of selected "black," "white," "yellow," and "red" dreams from my dream record sheds further light on the psychological meaning of the colors. The meaning of white was particularly difficult to grasp, and the reason why is symptomatic of the fact that in Western culture, with the exception perhaps of depth psychology, spiritual communities, and meditation centers, there appears to be little consciousness of, and even less respect for, what the white represents. By contrast, as I began to fathom the meaning of the colors, red was easy to understand, perhaps because our Western culture is essentially a *rubedo* culture, steeped in the energy and values of the red, as we shall see.

Finally, the completion of a twenty-two year sandplay process by a client called "Christina," whose remarkable story of inner transformation corroborates this thesis of the changes of color over time from black to white to red as stages in the process of transformation, inspired me to put pen to paper at last and turn my life's work into a book.

Although alchemy, dreams, and sandplay appear to be unlikely bedfellows, I feel comfortable bringing these three together in the same volume because all three arise from the same source, the unconscious, as I shall show in Chapter 1, and all share the same language of symbol and metaphor.

Since alchemy is the cornerstone of this book, Chapter 1 looks at it from a historical and cultural perspective. Appendix A and the Glossary, which follows the Appendices, help the reader with unfamiliar alchemical words, and phrases; and Appendix B points out the very real dangers involved with the practice of alchemy *vis-à-vis* the church. Appendix C, a splendid example of an original alchemical tract, focuses on the arcane nature of the alchemical literature, giving the reader an idea of the difficulty in penetrating its secrets when it was rediscovered by three individuals two hundred years after alchemy had been banished to the "trash-heap of history."[5] It is crucial to understand that what the alchemists were trying to achieve in their laboratories was ultimately psychological in nature, although they didn't understand it at the time, and that the colors they saw in their vessels, and the general consensus of the order in which they appeared, from black to white to yellow to red, had profound psychological implications.

Chapters 2 through 6 focus on one of the four colors as a stage in the process of transformation: from black (the *nigredo*) to white (the *albedo*) to yellow (the *citrinitas*) to red (the *rubedo*). The alchemist's writings give us a flavor of what each stage means, but it is through the writings of modern-day scholars of alchemy that the psychological significance and nuanced interpretation of each stage shines through. Each chapter contains corresponding examples of dreams and sandplay illustrative of that stage. Contrary to the alchemists' assertion that red was the final stage (as the three-headed dragon on page xii implies), I was surprised to learn that this is not so. The white and red are actually a pair of complementary

opposites, treated in Chapter 6. The final chapter's Epilogue focuses on the surprisingly different ways in which the balance of white and red was achieved in my life and in Christina's life. Appendix D gathers the pearls of wisdom I've discovered over these many years, offering readers support on their own path of alchemical transformation.

Making the link between the sequential appearance of the alchemical colors in my own dreams over time was an epiphany. And because of my familiarity with the psychological meaning of these colors, tracking the emergence of the alchemical colors in clients' dreams now comes naturally; and when they follow the alchemical sequence, it is both exciting and deeply affirming. But to witness the sequential emergence of the alchemical colors in Christina's sandplay was an astonishing revelation. However, it made sense. Because sandplay, like dreams, can be an expression of the unconscious, the same inner forces pushing for realization described by the alchemists and expressed in my dreams over time would also be at work in the psyche of the sandplayer. Many of us are familiar with dreams and are aware of their healing potential. If you are not familiar with sandplay, however, I invite you to look at the sandplay scenes in this book as dreams and watch the images come to life as they speak to us in the same way that dream images do. I think you will be surprised and amazed at the equally healing power of sandplay and with the poignantly transformative journeys upon which Christina and I embarked.

CHAPTER 1

Linking Color Symbolism in Alchemy, Dreams, and Sandplay

ALCHEMY

ALCHEMY HAS BEEN DEFINED as "a form of chemistry and speculative philosophy . . . concerned principally with discovering methods for transmuting base metals into gold and with finding a universal solvent and an elixir of life . . . a magical power or process of transmuting a common substance, usually of little value, into a substance of great value."[6] The substance of great value is nothing less than the flowering of the human soul and spirit.

The History of Alchemy

The roots of alchemy reach back to the dawn of human civilization. Elements of alchemy are found in metallurgy, ceramics, glass-making, enameling, dyeing and coloring, brewing, and the preparation of drugs, poisons, and cosmetics—crafts well established by 3000 BCE.[7] The roots of alchemy are also found in the magic and ritual surrounding the use of fire, mining, smelting and casting of metals, especially gold and silver,[8] and in the embalming and burial practices of ancient Egypt.[9] These crafts had numinous power for the ancients, who required sacrifices and prayers to the gods before or during their execution. Such practices provide evidence that the practice of alchemy preceded the advent of the word *alchemy* in the written record by several hundred years.[10]

Although there is some controversy regarding the origin of alchemy, the first mention of the word *alchemy* appeared almost simultaneously in China and the Middle East twenty centuries ago: in a Chinese text, the *Ts'an T'ung Ch'i* of Wei Po-Yang, written ca. 142 BCE;[11] and in *Physika kai Mystika,* a book on alchemical matters from Egypt ca. 200 BCE.[12]

Controversy also surrounds the derivation of the word alchemy, although most scholars agree that the word itself is a transcription of the Arabic name of the art, al Kimia. However, the etymology of this word is disputed. Some suggest that it derives from kmt, Khem, or chem, the ancient name for Egypt, the country of the black soil bordering the Nile.[13] Thus, it may mean "the Egyptian art" or "the black art." Others claim that it is derived from the Greek word chyma, meaning to fuse or cast a metal.[14] Still another claims that it is derived from a Chinese phrase, Kim-Iya, that means literally "the juice (or sperm) of gold," one of the Chinese names for the Elixir of Immortality.[15]

Alchemy has been practiced worldwide: in China, India, Tibet, Babylonia, and in the West, where it passed from Greece to Hellenistic Egypt to the Islamic Middle East and thence to Western Europe during the late Middle Ages, Renaissance, and Reformation. Greco-Egyptian, Arab, and Western alchemy, with their linked heritage, are the focus of this book.

The birthplace of Western alchemy is considered to be Alexandria, Egypt. During the eight centuries following its founding by Alexander the Great in 332 BCE, Alexandria was a melting pot and center of learning for Hellenic Greeks, Egyptians, Persians, Syrians, Christians, and Jews. It was from Alexandria and other towns along the Nile delta that the first Western texts on alchemy appeared. In these earliest alchemical texts written on papyrus scrolls, one can find elements of ancient craft traditions blended with Greek philosophy, Babylonian astrology, Egyptian mysticism, Gnosticism, and pagan mythology.[16] Later writers introduced into alchemy elements of Manichaeism, Cabbalism, and Christian theology.[17]

With the fall of Alexandria and the burning of its great library in 650 CE, much of the written knowledge of the ancient world went up in flames. With the subsequent rise of Islam, extant Western alchemical texts, along with texts from China, passed via the Silk Route into the hands of the Arabs in Persia and Syria, where alchemy flowered until about 1250 CE.[18] Great thinkers such as Khalid in the seventh century, Jabir (known to the Europeans as "Geber") in the ninth century, Rhazes in the tenth century, and Abu Ali ibn Sina (known as "Avicenna") in the early eleventh century, absorbed the ideas of the Alexandrian alchemists, introduced the Chinese concept of the Elixir of Life and Philosopher's Stone, and left their own unique imprint as practical physicians and chemists.[19]

When the Islamic empire expanded across North Africa and into Moorish Spain, it brought with it texts on mathematics, zoology, astronomy, astrology, medicine, philosophy, and alchemy.[20] The scholars of medieval Europe knew nothing of alchemy until it was introduced through the great Islamic centers of learning in Cordoba and Toledo in Spain in the twelfth and thirteenth centuries.[21] From there it was translated into Latin and spread quickly throughout Europe, where it flourished until the middle of the seventeenth century.[22]

In the early days of alchemy there were a fair number of female alchemists: from Alexandria, Maria the Copt (also called Maria the Jewess or Maria Prophetissa); another who called herself Isis; another pseudonymously named Cleopatra; Paphnutia the Virgin; and Theosebeia, friend and *soror mystica* (literally, mystical sister) of Zosimos.[23] In the Middle Ages, only Flamel's wife Perenelle,[24] Jon Pordage's Jane Leade, a seventeenth-century English woman, and Thomas South's daughter Mrs. Atwood[25] are mentioned as *sorores mysticae*.[26] In general, though, Western alchemical thought sprang out of a patriarchal paradigm and in its middle and later years was predominantly influenced by males. This influenced the nature of the alchemical literature. I will say more about this in subsequent chapters. (The historical Chronology on pages 10-11 lists major alchemists and alchemical works placed into cultural and geopolitical context.)

The death blow to alchemy came with the publication in 1661 of *The Sceptical Chymist* by Robert Boyle. Boyle's discovery that the four "basic" elements were composed of more basic elements still, struck at the root of all alchemical speculation and ushered in the era of modern chemistry, pharmacology, and mineralogy.[27] With the advent of the scientific method over the next century, interest in alchemy rapidly declined.

As practical alchemy was dying, there arose in the seventeenth and eighteenth centuries a more philosophical and speculative alchemy. The work of Jacob Boehme is a conspicuous example. Other examples include the anonymous publication of *Fama Fraternitatis* in 1614, *Confessio Fraternitatis* in 1615, and *The Chymical Wedding of Christian Rosenkreutz* in 1616 (reputed to have been the work of

Johann Valentin Andreae). The latter launched the "Brotherhood of the Rose Cross" (the Rosicrucians), one of the secret societies that flourished in the seventeenth and eighteenth centuries and out of which Freemasonry evolved.[28] In these secret societies, "theosophical alchemy" was kept alive.[29] What had been a quest for material perfection in substances became a more self-conscious quest for spiritual perfection in human beings.

With this split between practice and theory, alchemy as a generally practiced art ceased to exist. Nevertheless, the numinous aspect of alchemy that had gripped the souls of the old alchemists continued to inspire in later centuries such masterworks as Goethe's *Faust*.[30] In the early decades of the nineteenth century, alchemy was being practiced in the Near East in Egypt, Persia, and Istanbul. And in the remote mountains of Tibet there are alchemists still attempting to turn mercury into gold and to prolong life by drinking small quantities of purified mercury.[31]

The Nature of the Alchemical Literature

Since the alchemical writing of later periods is based on the prototype of alchemical literature produced in the Greco-Egyptian period, it is important to examine more closely the nature and content of the latter.[32] Mircea Eliade divides Greco-Egyptian alchemy into three periods: 1) the period of technical prescriptions; 2) the philosophical period; and 3) the period of alchemical writings proper—the

Apocryphas of Zosimos (third to fourth centuries CE) and the commentators (fourth to seventh centuries).[33]

The texts of all three periods contain a combination of physical and "spiritual" material. For instance, the Leyden Papyrus is an example of the first period of technical prescriptions, collected from a variety of much earlier sources, such as craftspeople's notebooks and scraps of practical information from Egypt,

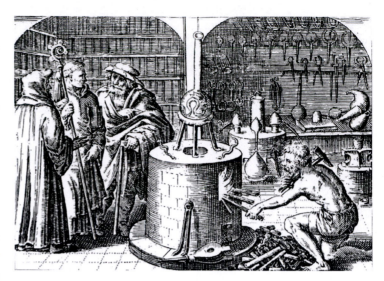

Figure 1. The Two Aspects of Alchemy: Philosophical and Practical *(Michael Maier, "The Golden Tripod," 1618)*

Persia, Babylonia, and Syria.[34] It is a book of medicine and magic, in the form of dialogues and invocations to the gods and goddesses to effect cures for all manner of ills, physical and emotional.[35]

Physika kai Mystika (second century BCE) is an example of the second (philosophical) period. This text is attributed to Bolos de Mendes, variously referred to as "Demokritos," "Bolos Demokritos," or "pseudo-Demokritos." The text is divided into four parts, dealing respectively with the making of gold, silver, gems, and purple. However, the author was really interested in the transmutation of matter, which he believed was indicated by changes in the color of the metals undergoing treatment.[36]

Finally, the book of Ostanes and the visions of Zosimos of Panopolis, Egypt (third century CE), are examples of the third period of apocryphal texts. In the visions of Zosimos, Ion, a

priest of the inner sanctuaries, describes descent into darkness and ascent into light, dismemberment and transformation of body into spirit.[37] These mystical texts may refer to the "death" and "revivification" of metals, or to the death and regeneration of the soul, or possibly both.[38]

Later texts contain some combination of these two aspects of alchemy: the practical and the spiritual. Over time the gap between these two currents grew wider.[39] Some scholars find this gap difficult to understand. According to Eric John Holmyard, "The writings offer us the most bizarre picture of Gnostic theory intermingled with chemical fact, ecstatic visions, descriptions of apparatus, and injunctions to the reader to keep the secret of the Art from the vulgar."[40] However, it is important to remember that from the beginning, alchemy had a twofold nature: the practical laboratory work with furnaces, retorts, and chemical substances, and the more philosophical speculations or "mystical" visions that accompanied the process. The title of the first known Western alchemical treatise, *Physika kai Mystika*, "Concerning Physical Things and Mystical [Spiritual] Things" demonstrates this duality.[41] Both sides are illustrated in Figure 1, a well-known Renaissance etching.

On the right, a half-clothed alchemist is kneeling in his laboratory, stoking the fires of his alchemical furnace, or *athanor*; on the left Basil Valentine, Abbot Cremer, and Thomas Norton are discoursing in a library. These two sides of alchemy have been referred to in a variety of ways: practical and speculative,[42] materialistic and mystical,[43] dogmatic versus hermetic,[44] artisanal and mystical,[45] exoteric and esoteric,[46] physical and philosophical,[47] operational and spiritual.[48] Whatever names are given to these two aspects of alchemy, Jung reminds us that for the early alchemists both sides were one:

> This two-fold work, the physical and the "philosophical," appears to us as two distinct methods, as a double procedure. But to the alchemist it was one and the same … the incomprehensible, mysterious qualities of the substances affected them as a "fascinosum." The … unconscious was thus constellated by, and projected into, the object… therefore the alchemists were under the impression that matter possessed a soul or spirit… a living soul, and as he met this soul everywhere in his experiments, he concluded that at the bottom of all these individual,

physical manifestations, there was a universal, all-permeating soul, an "anima mundi" (soul of the world), which was the cause of every living substance and of its particular form. It is self-evident, therefore, that the alchemistic method had to be a double one, for it dealt with a duality in the object and was therefore bound to be psychical and chemical.[49]

Until the invention of the printing press, alchemical texts were practically inaccessible. For the Greco-Egyptian, Arabic, and medieval European alchemists wishing to read other alchemical texts and to communicate their own discoveries, they needed first to be able to read and write and, in many cases, to travel. In addition, some alchemists may not have been inclined to share their secrets.

There were also problems inherent in the repeated translation and transcription of alchemical texts. The original Greco-Egyptian papyri were translated into Arabic; these texts were later translated into Latin and from Latin into modern languages. The texts had to be copied by hand, which perpetuated and magnified errors made in translation and transcription.

With the invention of the printing press in the fifteenth century, the alchemical literature suddenly became widely accessible. Many of the alchemical tracts were translated into modern European languages. In the sixteenth, seventeenth, and eighteenth centuries, collections of the most famous of these alchemical tracts were printed and widely circulated. (The largest

CHRONOLOGY OF EUROPEAN ALCHEMY

BEFORE COMMON ERA (BCE)

3500	Skilled metalworkers (Sumerian) in Euphrates Valley
3000	Expert goldsmiths in ancient Egypt
1500	Idea of four elements in India and Egypt, five elements in China
ca. 600–501	Historic beginnings of Chinese alchemy
604–531	Lao Tsu, conception of Yin and Yang
540–480	Heraclitus
ca. 400–301	Plato and Aristotle, Theory of the four elements
332	Conquest of Egypt by Alexander, Alexandria founded;* pre-Christian: Hermes Trismegistus, Emerald Tablet
ca. 200	Bolos de Mendes (Demokritos), Egypt, *Physika kai Mystika*
ca. 1–200	Komarios, Instructions to Cleopatra

COMMON ERA (CE)

ca. 101–200	Supposed beginnings of alchemy in India*
250–350	Leyden Papyrus
350–420	Zosimos of Panopolis, *Visions*
3rd–4th c.	*Song of Songs*
410	Synesios, Bishop of Ptolemais, Libya
495–570	Olympiodorus
ca. 601–700	Stephanus of Alexandria
610–641	Heraclius, Byzantine emperor favorable to alchemy*
ca. 650	End of Alexandrian era, rise of Islam*
660–704	Khalid, Damascus, *Secret of Secrets*
722–815	Jabir ibn Hayyan (Geber), Sufi
800	Charlemagne, Holy Roman Emperor*
900	Abu Bakr al-Rhazi (Rhazes), physician, Baghdad

Common Era (CE)

900–960	Muhammed ibn Umail (Senior), *Turba Philosophorum*
1000	Morienus Romanus, Roman hermit in Judea
980–1036	Abu Ali ibn Sina (Avicenna), Persia, Liber Sextus
1099	Capture of Jerusalem by the Crusaders*
1119	Founding of the Order of Knights Templars*
1163	Notre-Dame de Paris construction began*
1193–1282	Albertus Magnus, German Dominican Friar, De Alchimia; Opus
1214–1294	Roger Bacon, Franciscan friar, Oxford, England
1225–1274	St. Thomas Aquinas, Italy
1225–1315	Raymond Lully, Seneschal, Spain, Hermetic Mercuries
1240–1311	Arnold of Villanova, physician, Spain, *Rosarium Philosophorum*
1265–1321	Dante Alighieri, *The Divine Comedy* *
1312	John Cremer, Abbot of Westminster, England
1317	Bull of Pope John XXII against alchemists*
1330	Petrus Bonus of Ferrara, Italy
1330–1418	Nicolas Flamel and Perenelle, French, *A Short Tract*
1345–1400	Chaucer, *The Canterbury Tales* *
1380	Charles V forbids practice of alchemy*
1406–1490	Bernardus Trevisanus, Italian, *Liber de Alchemia*
1440	Execution of Marshal Gilles de Retz, French alchemist*
ca. 1440	Johannes Gutenberg, invention of practical movable type.* It is noteworthy that the world's first movable type for printing was invented 400 years earlier by the Chinese inventor Pi Sheng, 990–1051 CE
1450	Basil Valentine, Benedictine monk, *Practica, The Twelve Keys*

**An asterisk indicates an historical event. Collections of alchemical works are listed in capital letters.

IN HISTORICAL CONTEXT**

Common Era (CE)

1415?–1490 George Ripley, Carmelite, England, *Twelve Gates of Alchemy*

1492 Christopher Columbus' departure from Castile*

1493–1541 Paracelsus, Doctor of Medicine, Basel, Switzerland

1530–1583 Gerhard Dorn, *Ars Chemistica*, and so on

1519 Death of Leonardo da Vinci*

1550–1555 Prophecies of Nostradamus*

1566 **ARS CHEMICA**, Strasbourg

1564–1616 William Shakespeare, England, The Tempest (1611)*

1582 British Library manuscript of the *Splendor Solis*

1593 **ARTIS AURIFERAE**, two volumes, Basel

1602 **THEATRUM CHEMICUM, Vol. I–III**, Ursel, *Turba Philosophorum*, and so on

1603–1638 Henricus Madathanus, *The Golden Age Restored* (1621-22)

1609 Heinrich Khunrath, *Amphitheatrum Sapientiae Aeternae*

1612 Ben Jonson, *The Alchemist*

1613 **THEATRUM CHEMICUM, Vol. IV**, Strasbourg

1614 *Fama Fraternitatis* manifesto of the "Brothers of the Rose-Cross"*

1615 *Confessio Fraternitatis*

1616 *Chymical Wedding of Christian Rosenkreutz* (attributed to Johann Valentin Andreae)*

1617 Heinrich Nollius, *Theoria philosophiae hermeticae*, Hanau

1618 Michael Maier, *Atalanta Fugiens; Golden Tripod*, and so on

1618 Thomas Norton, *Ordinal of Alchemy*

1622 **THEATRUM CHEMICUM**, Vol. V, Strasbourg

1622 Johann Daniel Mylius, *Philosophia reformata* (Balthazar Schwann, engraver)

Common Era (CE)

1625 **MUSEUM HERMETICUM**, Frankfurt, first publication in German by Lucas Jennis, includes Von Lambspring's *De lapide philosophico*, Frankfurt, and Herbrandt Jamsthaler, *Viatorum spagyricum*, Frankfurt am Main, Germany

1637 Death of Robert Fludd, England

1645 Eirenaeus Philalethes, *An Open Entrance to the Closed Palace of the King; Secrets Reveal'd*

1652 **THEATRUM CHEMICUM BRITTANICUM**, London, by Elias Ashmole

1661 **THEATRUM CHEMICUM**, Vol. VI, Strasbourg

1661 Publication of Robert Boyle's *The Sceptical Chymist*

1678 **MUSEUM HERMETICUM**, Frankfurt, first Latin edition, reprinted in 1749

1702 **BIBLIOTHECA CHEMICA CURIOSA**, two volumes, Geneva, by Jean-Jacques Manget

1779 Foundation of Masonic "Illuminated Brotherhood of Avignon"*

1857 Ethan Allen Hitchcock, *Alchemy and the Alchemists*

1893 **MUSEUM HERMETICUM,** Frankfurt, first English edition by A. E. Waite

1914 Herbert Silberer: *The Problems of Mysticism and Its Symbolism*

1944 C. G. Jung, *Psychology and Alchemy, The Collected Works*, Vol. 12

1946 C. G. Jung, *Psychology of the Transference*

1951 C. G. Jung, *Aion, The Collected Works*, Vol. 9ii

1955–1956 C. G. Jung, *Mysterium Coniunctionis, The Collected Works*, Vol. 14

1968 C. G. Jung, *Alchemical Studies* (collection of essays), *The Collected Works*, Vol. 13

and most famous of these collections and the dates of their publication are designated by uppercase entries in the Chronology.)

The publication of alchemical texts into modern language, however, did not aid the reader's comprehension of the material. The elaborate alchemical "language" that developed was baffling, esoteric, and misleading. An array of hieroglyphics came into use: symbols for the four elements, the seven (known) planets, the seven metals, the twelve signs of the zodiac, the twelve alchemical operations or processes, and so on. The elements, planets, metals, signs of the zodiac, and alchemical operations were, in turn, associated with one another. Furthermore, a single substance could be represented by any number of hieroglyphic symbols (see Appendix A). Gold, for instance, was represented at one time or another in more than sixty ways[50] and the Philosopher's Stone in more than six hundred.[51] Also, the terms used often meant different things to different alchemists:

> To add to the confusion, anagrams, acrostics, and other enigmas were introduced, and various secret alphabets and ciphers came to be used by alchemists; in some of these, letters and numerals were represented by alchemical and astrological signs. An additional barrier was erected in the shape of an extensive structure of pictorial symbolism and allegorical expression. Ideas, processes, even pieces of apparatus, were represented by birds, animals, mythological figures, geometrical designs, and other emblems

born of a riotous, extravagant, and superstitious imagination.[52]

Thus, even the alchemists had a difficult time understanding one another. The content of alchemical texts was not only esoteric, but also deliberately misleading. To explain the obscure by the more obscure was common practice, and for good reason. If an adept claimed any success in his work, he could be threatened with very real dangers: attacks on his person to steal the gold,[53] the ransacking of his laboratory and/ or home,[54] and accusations of heresy by the Church, which could lead to death.[55] (For two such edicts, see Appendix B.)

Insofar as alchemy was also a sacred and secret art, there was another important reason for secrecy: to keep the material from the unwise—an attitude of secrecy common to all religious mysteries. For example, Synesios (ca. fourth century CE) wrote:

> The (true alchemists) only express themselves in symbols, metaphors, and similes, so that they can only be understood by saints, sages, and souls endowed with understanding. For this reason, they have observed in their works a certain way and a certain rule, of such a kind that the wise man may understand and, perhaps after some stumbling, attain to everything that is secretly described therein.[56]

Geber, also, declared:

> One must not explain this art in obscure words

only; on the other hand, one must not explain it so clearly that all may understand it. I therefore teach it in such a way that nothing will remain hidden to the wise man, even though it may strike mediocre minds as quite obscure; the foolish and the ignorant for their part will understand none of it at all.[57]

For many adepts the work was clearly an inner as well as an outer experience; it is upon the work of this group that I shall concentrate. However, because of the confusion caused by the need for secrecy and by the obscure and misleading contents of the texts, many misguided souls spent their whole lives and fortunes trying to discover the secret of gold-making or the elixir of life, with little to show for it. There were also charlatans and swindlers—people eager to dupe the gullible and to make easy money in the process.[58]

Thus, given the obscure, esoteric, often incomprehensible nature of the alchemical literature and the bad reputation alchemy came to have, it is little wonder that with the advent of the scientific age, alchemists became the object of "scorn, ridicule and misunderstanding,"[59] their texts rejected as "ravings, superstition and pure nonsense,"[60] "bearing the marks of incipient lunacy."[61]

Even to modern scholars, the alchemical literature appears as "a wild, luxuriant, tangled mass of overlapping images that is maddening to the order-seeking conscious mind."[62] Another says, "All these alchemistic treatises consist of prescriptions, and one becomes more

and more bewildered and has no idea what to make of them. When you read the Latin texts, you fall from one hole into the next. You think you have a glimmer of what the author means, and in the next sentence it is contradicted . . . most of the time one can only hold one's head in despair!"[63]

The Modern "Discovery" of Alchemy

For 250 years after the decline of interest in alchemy, its literature languished on the "rubbish-heap of history."[64] It took the genius of a few individuals to discern the significance of these works for modern times. C. G. Jung is generally credited with the single-handed rescue of alchemy from obscurity. However, in the epilogue to *Mysterium Coniunctionis,* Jung gives the credit to "Herbert Silberer [who] has the merit of being the first to discover the secret threads that lead from alchemy to the psychology of the unconscious."[65] Silberer credits an earlier figure, saying, "The service of having rediscovered the intrinsic value of alchemy over and above its chemical and physical phase, is to be ascribed probably to the American Ethan Allen Hitchcock."[66]

Hitchcock, in his remarkable book *Alchemy and the Alchemists,* published anonymously in 1857, writes,

My proposition is, that the subject of alchemy was Man; while the object was the perfection of Man, which was supposed to center in a certain unity with the Divine nature.[67] . . . The genuine adepts were in pursuit of neither wealth nor worldly honors, but were searchers after truth, in the highest sense of this word . . . whether we call it truth, virtue, wisdom, religion, or the knowledge of God.[68]

Hitchcock goes on to say,

There is undoubtedly an unexplored mass of secret writing in existence, . . . which, if it could be deciphered, would throw a great deal of light upon the . . . nature of man; but to enter this field fully would require both patience and genius.[69]

Fifty-seven years later, Herbert Silberer, an Austrian psychiatrist, published his penetrating study of alchemy called *Problems of Mysticism and its Symbols* (1914)—fourteen years after Freud's publication of *The Interpretation of Dreams*. He delved into the unconscious foundations of alchemy, whose images and motifs closely resembled those uncovered by Freud through his study of dreams. Silberer understood the alchemical symbols as eruptions of repressed unconscious forces, thus discovering in the Hermetic writings the presence of unconscious psychodynamics. By applying the dream interpretation of Freud to the symbolic images and motifs of alchemy, Silberer unlocked their unconscious meaning and translated them into psychodynamic terms. This induced him to view the alchemical opus as "a psychic 'work' . . . a journey of the soul leading the adept to final death and rebirth."[70] Silberer viewed the goal of the opus as that of the alchemist's

attainment of a psychic totality. Because of Silberer's untimely death, his groundbreaking work was not well known.

However, in C. G. Jung we find the patience as well as the genius called for by Hitchcock sixty-nine years earlier. Jung devoted much of the last thirty-five years of his life (from 1926 until his death in 1961) to the study of alchemy. He acquired his own library of original alchemical texts in Greek, Latin, German, and French. With the care of a "philologist . . . trying to decipher a foreign language,"[71] Jung filled notebooks with thousands of notations and gradually was able to unravel the mysteries with which alchemy had cloaked itself for two millennia. Practically every sentence, and in places each phrase, Jung wrote on alchemy is annotated with scholarly references to the Greek and Latin texts with which he was literate. Approximately two thousand pages— more than two-thirds of Jung's voluminous writings—are devoted to alchemy. These include: Psychology and Alchemy (CW 12, 1944); "Fish symbolism in Alchemy" in Aion (CW 9ii, 1951); Alchemical Studies (CW 13, 1968); and Mysterium Coniunctionis (CW 14, 1955-56), generally considered his masterpiece, upon which he worked from 1941 to 1954, finishing in his eightieth year. These works by Jung laid the groundwork for the scholars of alchemy who followed and are the principal source for the ideas contained in this book. Like his predecessors Hitchcock and Silberer, Jung viewed the alchemical opus as a metaphor for the process of inner growth and transformation:

> What they [the alchemists] really discovered, and what was an endless source of fascination to them, was the symbolism of the individuation process.[72] . . . the entire alchemical procedure . . . could just as well represent the individuation process of a single individual, though with the not unimportant difference that no single individual ever attains to the richness and scope of the alchemical symbolism.[73]

This idea that the work of the alchemists is a metaphor for what the psyche goes through in deep long-term analysis underlies the thesis of this book.

Alchemy as a Psychological Process

Edward Edinger, in a public lecture, clarified the psychological meaning of the alchemical opus by drawing a parallel between the work of the alchemist in the laboratory and the work of the individual in psychotherapy or analysis:

> In spite of the confusion generated by the alchemical literature, the basic scheme of alchemy is quite simple: the alchemist or adept was committed to a sacred work, called the opus or grand arcanum. The goal of the work was to create a transcendent miraculous substance, a supreme and ultimate value, symbolized by the Philosopher's Stone, the Elixir of Life, or the Universal Medicine [see the Glossary of Alchemical Words and Phrases]. The first step was to find a suitable material on which to work (the *prima materia*) and submit it to a series of operations. The vessel, vas, curcurbit or alembic in which the operations took place was to be kept well sealed, the equivalent of containment in the analytic process. The attitude to be taken toward the work was one of patience, courage and perseverance. It was considered a sacred work, requiring a prayerful, religious attitude.[74]

Edinger went on to describe the work as highly individual and often lonely; the adept might have one helper, but no more. It was a process started by Nature but completed by the conscious work of men and women. The knowledge gained was a result of direct experience; something each seeker had to discover for themselves, and the result was equated with the creation of the world, which, in psychological terms, signifies the creation of the Self.[75] How color enters into this act of creation is the subject of the next section.

The Importance of Color in Alchemy

From the very beginnings of alchemy, the color of the substances being worked on was of utmost importance. The alchemist Geber wrote, "Truly, the great secret is in colors."[76] And the historian of alchemy, Holmyard, believed that "Color, in fact, to the alchemists was the most important characteristic of a metal, and so we find throughout Greek alchemical literature an insistence on color changes and sequences of color changes that left its mark on all subsequent alchemy."[77]

Heraclitus mentioned four colors: (1) *melanosis* (blackening); (2) *leukosis* (whitening); (3) *xanthosis* (yellowing); and (4) *iosis* (reddening).[78] In the fourfold process (1) *melanosis* was likely caused by the oxidation of an alloy produced by fusing tin, lead, copper, and iron; (2) *leukosis* was a process called "Argyropy," or silver-making, using tin, mercury, arsenic, or antimony—especially effective in whitening copper; (3) *xanthosis* was a process called "Chrysopsy," or gold-making, in which a ferment of golden-colored concoction yellowed an alloy; and (4) *iosis* was a less well-defined process in which the alloy turned purple or violet-red.[79]

Although there was wide variation among alchemists regarding the sequence of appearance of various colors, black, white, yellow, and red became the generally accepted order in which the colors should appear if the process were to be successful.[80]

References to the four colors mentioned in Greco-Egyptian alchemy were echoed throughout the history of European alchemical tracts, including the 13th century text, *Aurora Consurgens*. A look at the linguistic roots in which Western alchemy is anchored provides significant clues to the early symbolic meaning of the colors black, white, and red. In this regard, it is helpful to look at linguists Brent Berlin and Paul Kay's fascinating study of color-terms in 192 languages. In languages with no more than two basic words for *color*, those words are *always* "*black* and *white*" or their equivalents, *dark* and *light* or *dull* and *brilliant*. If there is a third word for *color*, that color is *always* "*red*" (which at this stage of language development includes most of the warm colors: yellows, oranges, browns, pinks, and purples). A language with four color-terms will add *yellow* or *green*; one with five will add the other of the two (that is, if *yellow*, then *green*; if *green*, then *yellow)*; a language with six color-terms will add *blue*.[81] Christopher Rowe, a scholar of antique languages, notes the striking correlation between Berlin and Kay's results for three- to six-term languages and the apparent development of Greek from the eighth to the fourth centuries BCE. Greek in the Homeric period (eighth century BCE) possessed, at most, three color-terms: *black, white,* and *red*. Black and white were limited to qualities of light and darkness, and red to the context of blood.[82] In the fifth and fourth centuries BCE in Greece, Empedocles refers to four primary colors: *black, white, red,* and *ochros (yellow)*; Demokritus: *black, white, red,* and *chloron* (presumably a *yellow-green*); Plato: *black, white, red,* and *lampron*, a term associated with *bright* and *fire*. In spite of the additions of color-terms into Greek, Rowe asserts that only three terms were obviously abstract: *black, white,* and *red*. According to Rowe, light and dark is no doubt the original pair, since it reflected the primal experience of early humans with the dark of night and the light of day. Because of its association with blood, he believes that *red* symbolized life and power.[83]

Overview of the Alchemical *Nigredo*, *Albedo*, *Citrinitas*, and *Rubedo*

As the cover image portends, the Great Work (as the alchemical process was sometimes called) consists of the alchemical *nigredo*, *albedo*, and *rubedo*, pictured as black, white, and red birds tumbling around or fighting in the *Vas Alchyicum*. That is, in the alchemical vessel—or temenos, equivalent to the therapeutic container—the comingled red and white birds appear to be working together to overpower the black bird, on its back with claws raised in defense. That is, in the process of transformation, the activated *albedo* and *rubedo* energies of the psyche, both separately and together, are working to overcome the negative energies of the *nigredo*. In typical medieval fashion, the original four alchemical colors—black, white, yellow, and red—were equated with the four elements, four humors, four planets, four metals, four symbols, and other qualities.

BLACK

As shown in the alchemical woodcut in Figure 2, the first stage of the Great Work, the *nigredo* (or blackness, derived from the Latin root *niger*: "black") was associated with the heaviest element, Earth (symbolized by the downward-pointing triangle—symbolically female—with a line across it; with Saturn and its corresponding metal lead; and with the image of a dark ape-man in the vessel on the woman's head. In the alchemical literature, the *nigredo* was referred to variously as the grave of Osiris, house of the dead, crow, mortification,

Figure 2. The Four Stages of the Opus (Herbrandt Jamsthaler *Viatorium Spagyricum*, 1590.)

chaos, abyss, coal, pitch, a black blacker than black, and many others.

WHITE

The second stage of the Great Work, the *albedo* (or whiteness, from the Latin *alba:* "white") was referred to as the *Rosa Alba* (or "White Rose"), the *Femina alba* (or "White Woman"), the White Swan, White Lily, Luna, Venus, and Sophia. The *albedo* was associated with the second-heaviest element, Water (the downward-pointing female triangle with a dot in the center); with the Moon; with the metal silver; and with the symbol of the White Rose in the vessel.

YELLOW

The third stage of the Great Work, the *citrinitas* (or yellowing, from the Latin *citrus:* "yellow") was associated with the lighter element, Air (symbolized by the upward-pointing male triangle with the line); with the planet Jupiter; with the metal tin; and with a golden-yellow eagle in the vessel. Until the fifteenth or sixteenth century, the *citrinitas* was one of the four principal stages of the Great Work, but gradually the *citrinitas* as a stage fell into disuse. Since there were too few yellow dreams in the study to reach statistical significance, I will cover the *citrinitas* only briefly in this book.

RED

The fourth stage, the *rubedo* (or redness, from the Latin *ruber:* "red") was referred to by the alchemists as the Red Dragon, Red Lion, Red Slave, Red Man, Red Knight, and Red King. The *rubedo* was associated with the most volatile element, Fire (the upward-pointing male triangle with the dot); with the Sun; with the metal gold; and with the lion in the vessel on the woman's head.

In the alchemical Herbrandt Jamsthaler woodcut, one sees a progression from the feminine to the masculine; from the densest element, earth, to the most volatile, fire; from lead into gold; and from a primitive ape-like figure in need of transformation to a lion, the king of beasts, a symbol of the Self. In modern terms, these four are stages in the process of individuation.[84]

Corroboration for the alchemical *nigredo, albedo,* and *rubedo* is found in ancient color and symbol systems worldwide: (1) The ancient Japanese medical color system contains black, white, yellow, and red; (2) in Roman Catholicism, clerics wear black robes, the Pope wears white vestments, and Cardinals' robes are red; (3) in ancient Hindu cosmology, the three *gunas* or tendencies of being, Tamas (black), Sattva (white), and Rajas (red), have color and meaning equivalents remarkably similar to the *nigredo, albedo,* and *rubedo* of alchemy. I'll say more about the gunas in later chapters.

Furthermore, the alchemical *albedo* and *rubedo* as a pair of archetypal opposites have striking symbolic correlates with (1) Yin and Yang in the Chinese *I Ching*, or *Book of Changes*, (2) color symbolism in Indian Kundalini Yoga, (3) cross-cultural research on left and right, and (4) Ornstein's split-brain research. These examples will be discussed in more detail later. Such corroborations across cultures and time make clear that the alchemical colors were not simply figments of the alchemists' imaginations; they were rooted in archetypal patterns and universal physiological processes.

It is important to note that psychologically, the alchemical *nigredo, albedo,* and *rubedo* are common emotional or feeling states experienced in everyday life in a fluid, random way. Among many Jungians and those interested in alchemy and sandplay, this notion is usually as far as it goes. What is unique to this study is the proposition that the alchemical *nigredo, albedo,* and *rubedo*, when considered over the course of many months or years, are also distinct sequential, overlapping stages in the process of individuation.

COLOR SYMBOLISM IN DREAMS: INTRODUCTION TO THE AUTHOR AS DREAMER

I grew up in a small California town where coastal fog rolled over the tops of the hills and down into the valley where we lived. Although I remembered a few vivid dreams from those years, two recurring dreams haunted me. In one, the coastal fog is a giant tidal wave thundering over the top of the ridge, from which there is no escape. In the second dream, as I walk down a deserted road, a huge black truck some distance behind me is bearing down upon me. I try desperately to outrun it but I can only move in slow motion. I didn't know it at the time, but these terrifying dreams were the attempts of my unconscious to break into consciousness.

Those dreams were long forgotten when I began systematically recording my dreams for a dream-study group in 1974. The record of 2500 dreams upon which this work is based spans

Figure 3. *Language of Dreams* (Susan Seddon-Boulet, 1990)

a fifteen-year period, from my late twenties through my early forties. (Table 2, page 22, lists the author's dreams by their alchemical colors and dates, presented in Chapters One through Five.)

When I joined the dream group, I thought my outer life was fine, but I was in for a shock. My dreams told another story. The first two dreams were ominous, and the first fifteen days of recorded dreams, detailed here, revealed such disturbing things about my inner life that I realized I needed professional help.

October 1, 1974. *I dream of snakes in my bed or someplace where I am usually comfortable and unaware of danger. I am not frightened by them as much as surprised—and concerned—to see them moving around so close to where*

I usually am. One, like a cobra, raises its head to eye me. The act of beginning a dream journal had activated my unconscious (the snake) in the place of sleep, dreams, and unconsciousness (the bed). The fact that the snake is a cobra suggests danger. However, if eyes are the seat of the soul, then the fact that the snake makes eye contact with me suggests that the cobra and I are connected at the soul level. My second dream came one week later:

October 8, 1974. I see a stack of logs four to five feet in circumference, eight to nine feet long. I hear the sound of sawing and say, "Prepare a plot for me."

In the context of the dream's words, it appears that coffin-sized logs are being prepared for a funeral. Unaware of it at the time, I was headed for a descent into my depths, a long dark night of the soul and a metaphorical "death" of old patterns and ways of being. Three days later, in a single night, three dreams spelled out, in broad-brush strokes, my problems:

October 11, 1974.
Julie Andrews is *smiling and dancing around.*

❖

I am with another woman. An ex-boyfriend of mine is in the distance, on an island. Water separates us. He is supposed to come by boat to pick us up, but he looks at us, shakes his head, and goes the other way. I feel anguish.

❖

Amelia has a box of jewelry; I, just a handful of jewelry. We agree to look through each other's jewelry, and if we find anything we like, we can take what the other has. My small handful of jewelry consists of hard, dull metal, with many spiky objects. Hers, I discover as I go through her box, contains many soft, round, wonderful-to-touch objects such as amber, and inside some walnuts, I see and feel smooth, creamy-colored alabaster, which shines.

After I entered Jungian analysis and began exploring my childhood, I discovered that my problems were four-fold: I was deeply wounded in the areas of both my inner feminine self (anima) and my inner masculine self (animus). But beneath my depression lay anger, which had been successfully masked under the guise of a smiling, eager-to-please Julie Andrews–like *persona.*

In the second dream of the old boyfriend, we see a painfully thwarted longing for a connection to an ostensibly outer male figure who is distant and rejecting; unconsciously I was longing for a connection to my inner masculine spirit, also distant and rejecting.

Third, I want to exchange my jewelry, representing the dull, spiky, hard-edged aspects of my wounded femininity, for Amelia's jewelry, symbolic of her softer, wiser, stronger inner feminine nature. The fourth problem appears in the image of the walnuts, served at Greek and Roman weddings, symbolizing hidden wisdom as well as fertility and longevity. The smooth, creamy-colored alabaster "eggs" inside the walnuts are suggestive of female ovaries or male gonads. I now understand this reference to the walnuts and alabaster eggs as symbolic of my longing for a connection to my own creativity and generativity, a lack in myself of which I was not conscious for decades.

Four days later, the fifth dream appeared:

October 15, 1974. *BLACK HOLE. I had the feeling some unseen, unheard, unfelt presence was upon me and would suffocate me. I was in bed. For a few seconds the invisible presence was upon me (or so it seemed); it felt as though I had entered a pitch-black hole and could not feel, see, touch,* *hear, or smell anything whatsoever; I couldn't even breathe. I was so terrified at not being able to breathe that I woke myself up with a startled shout.*

My unconscious was trying to tell me that the way in which I was living my life was suffocating. After this dream, the untrained dream-group

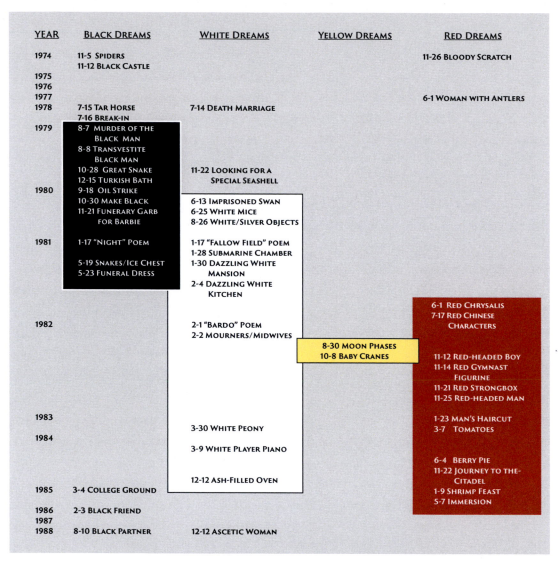

YEAR	BLACK DREAMS	WHITE DREAMS	YELLOW DREAMS	RED DREAMS
1974	11-5 SPIDERS 11-12 BLACK CASTLE			11-26 BLOODY SCRATCH
1975				
1976				
1977				6-1 WOMAN WITH ANTLERS
1978	7-15 TAR HORSE 7-16 BREAK-IN	7-14 DEATH MARRIAGE		
1979	8-7 MURDER OF THE BLACK MAN 8-8 TRANSVESTITE BLACK MAN 10-28 GREAT SNAKE 12-15 TURKISH BATH	11-22 LOOKING FOR A SPECIAL SEASHELL		
1980	9-18 OIL STRIKE 10-30 MAKE BLACK 11-21 FUNERARY GARB FOR BARBIE	6-13 IMPRISONED SWAN 6-25 WHITE MICE 8-26 WHITE/SILVER OBJECTS		
1981	1-17 "NIGHT" POEM 5-19 SNAKES/ICE CHEST 5-23 FUNERAL DRESS	1-17 "FALLOW FIELD" POEM 1-28 SUBMARINE CHAMBER 1-30 DAZZLING WHITE MANSION 2-4 DAZZLING WHITE KITCHEN		
1982		2-1 "BARDO" POEM 2-2 MOURNERS/MIDWIVES	8-30 MOON PHASES 10-8 BABY CRANES	6-1 RED CHRYSALIS 7-17 RED CHINESE CHARACTERS 11-12 RED-HEADED BOY 11-14 RED GYMNAST FIGURINE 11-21 RED STRONGBOX 11-25 RED-HEADED MAN
1983		3-30 WHITE PEONY		1-23 MAN'S HAIRCUT 3-7 TOMATOES
1984		3-9 WHITE PLAYER PIANO 12-12 ASH-FILLED OVEN		6-4 BERRY PIE 11-22 JOURNEY TO THE CITADEL 1-9 SHRIMP FEAST 5-7 IMMERSION
1985	3-4 COLLEGE GROUND			
1986	2-3 BLACK FRIEND			
1987				
1988	8-10 BLACK PARTNER	12-12 ASCETIC WOMAN		

Table 2. Selected Dreams Listed by Color and Date

leader made the ill-advised suggestion that I re-enter my Black Hole to see what came up.

The following night, unable to sleep, I went into an empty room, lay on the carpeted floor, re-entered my dream, and had a terrifying visualization of falling endlessly into a bottomless black abyss. What followed next was an excruciatingly painful experience of lying face-down, arms extended in a cross-form, with the cross of Jesus on my back so crushingly heavy it felt like the weight of the world. I sobbed for an hour. Later, still overcome with grief, I found myself in the Muslim prayer-position, begging for deliverance. My unconscious had shaken me to the core. Fortunately, I had enough ego strength that the experience hadn't triggered a psychotic break.

The experience of falling into the abyss, an undifferentiated primal chaos, is the beginning of the alchemical work and the beginning of deep inner work.

Marie-Louise von Franz says,

Every dark thing one falls into can be called an initiation. To be initiated into something means to go into it. The first step is generally falling into the dark place and usually appears in a negative form—falling into something or being possessed by something. The shamans say that being a medicine man begins by falling into the power of the demons; the one who pulls out of the dark place becomes the medicine man, and the one who stays in it is the sick person. We can take every psychological illness as an initiation. Even the worst things we fall into are an effort at initiation for we are in something which belongs to us, and now we must get out of it.[85]

This dream of the "Black Hole" and the terrifying and painful visualization of that dream—an embodied *nigredo* experience—led me to seek therapy.

In a Jungian analysis over fifteen years, I explored the emotionally painful realities of my childhood and delved into the depths of my unconscious through my prolific and powerful dreams. Selected dreams from each of the four color categories will be presented at the end of each chapter. They are sorted by color and date in Table 2. The areas inside the boxes representing the black, white, and red dreams were separated enough in time to demonstrate that the *nigredo, albedo,* and *rubedo* are distinct, overlapping, sequential stages of development.

Given that I knew nothing about alchemy when I recorded these dreams, the amount of alchemical imagery found in them is astonishing. The dreams also show a remarkable progression from the *nigredo* to the *albedo* and *rubedo* and to the conjunction of the *albedo* and *rubedo*. And as will be seen, dreams with intense, saturated color heralded the beginning, respectively, of the *nigredo*, the *albedo,* and the *rubedo* stages.

Color Symbolism in a Sandplay Process

Sandplay is a powerful therapeutic tool consisting of a sandtray half-filled with sand, water, and hundreds of small figures representing every aspect of life. Children take to sandplay like fish to water. Adults, out of the habit of playing, usually need to be invited to the tray and introduced to the idea that in "the free and protected space" there is no right or wrong way to proceed; they are free to create whatever wants to come out. Some are interested; others are not.

Some prefer to work with the sand alone, sculpting it, shaping it, moving it around; others choose to add figures and to create scenes that tell stories. Some like to talk while they work, although most choose to work with their hands in silence. Since sandplay is essentially a nonverbal activity in which the hands speak, it bypasses the left brain's conscious inhibitions.

It is especially useful for traumatized individuals whose trauma, lodged in the body, is not readily—if at all—accessible to verbal analysis. During the sandplay process, it is vitally important that the therapist not interpret or analyze the tray. This allows the process to live in the symbolic world, where the energies of the client's inner self move teleologically toward healing.

Christina is a woman with whom I worked on and off for twenty-two years. I wondered if the pseudonym she chose was related to the Christa, a sandplay figure she placed in a tray

"Christa" with a Scarab

next to a black scarab during the first phase of her work. The tray, not presented in this volume, was described in my article on the Scarab in the *Journal of Sandplay Therapy*.[86] During her work with me, Christina created fifty-two sandtrays that show a clear progression from the *nigredo* through the *albedo* to the *rubedo* and beyond that to the *coniunctio* of the *albedo* and *rubedo* as the powerful conclusion to her long and difficult journey of transformation.

I will analyze twenty-five of her trays in the following chapters. To all appearances, Christina, adopted at birth, was strong, confident, and tough. Born in the Chinese year of the Fire Horse, she described herself as "fiery and fast-moving." On the Enneagram she was a 7, saying, "Sevens move really fast, but are not feeling deeply." I saw her fiery, fast-moving *persona*—the face we show to the world—as a kind of manic *rubedo* defense against hurt. Underneath her tough Amazon exterior lay profound dependency needs and a vulnerability she found terrifying. For example, when romantic relationships ended, she became panicky, frightened, and obsessed with the abandoning other—signs of abandonment terror, depression, and despair. This was the shadow side of her "tough" persona—the *albedo* part she was unable to own. But for good reason: her adoptive mother had emotionally abandoned, neglected, and abused her, and from the age of seven on, she had been molested by several males in her adoptive family. Her inner feminine and inner masculine sides had both been badly wounded. In order to cope with her painful and traumatic past, she had turned to drugs, alcohol, and promiscuous sex at an early age and had continued the pattern into her mid-twenties.

Christina, then in her late twenties, had spent years searching for her birthmother. She sought therapy with me to deal with the fact that earlier in the week she had heard from the adoption authorities that her birthmother didn't want to be contacted or to make contact with her. As she told me this, Christina appeared matter-of-fact, but as I came to know her better, I realized that the little girl inside of her was devastated.

In our first session she said, "I'm scared to be in therapy; I'm looking for a mother, but I know I can't have one." She wept, then as if surprised, added, "This *never* happens to me! I'm strong, but you seem so caring and sympathetic and understanding that I couldn't help myself." She was so good at "stuffing" her neediness, sadness, and longing that this was a very rare instance when she allowed tears with me in a session, until a huge disappointment halfway through her therapy and a series of disasters late in our work broke down her defenses for good.

Fifteen months into her talk therapy and dream analysis, she related two dreams so painful that she turned to sandplay for the

Phase I	Two years in therapy	9 Sandtrays	*Nigredo* to *Albedo*	7-year therapy break
Phase II	Five years in therapy	21 Sandtrays	*Albedo* to *Rubedo*	5-year therapy break
Phase III	Three years in therapy	22 Sandtrays	*Nigredo* to *Albedo-Rubedo*	End of therapy
Total	**Ten years in therapy**	**52 Sandtrays**	**Transformation**	**12 years of breaks**

Table 3. Christina's Journey to Wholeness: Ten Years of Therapy over Twenty-two Years

first time. She immediately fell in love with sandplay and turned to it often and with relish in the ensuing years. Table 3 is a summary of her healing twenty-two-year sandplay journey.

The sandplay of Phase I (*nigredo* to *albedo* consciousness), created in the first two years of Christina's therapy before her first therapy break, is considered at the end of Chapter 2, "Black—the *Nigredo*." The sandplay of Phase II (*albedo* to *rubedo* consciousness) is discussed at the end of Chapter 3, "White—the *Albedo*." The first tray of Phase III is considered at the end of Chapter 5, "Red—the *Rubedo*," and the remainder of Phase III at the end of Chapter 6 on the union of the *albedo* and the *rubedo*.

Nigredo et lucida   trias partes

Aqua

Caput   Corui

Ipsum similiter Putrefieri est necessarium

Vicunq; color pri nigredine apparebit laudatus est
Dc posita sunt corpa in putrefactoe Arnoldus
et efficiant tria nigra Et tu videbis magis de
nigrari · Gaude · quia principium est digestionis
Comburre ico eis nrm igne scm sit Arnoldus
donec nutriri donec corpa eius constituat et
tinctura extrahat Non aut extrahas ea totum si
mul Sz par et par egrediat omni die donec in
longo impleant tempe Hermes pater phorum
Ego sum niger albi et rubeus albi et citrinus

CHAPTER 2

Black—The *Nigredo*

NIGREDO (LATIN FOR "BLACKNESS") is the original state of matter found at the beginning of the alchemical opus, either as a quality of the *prima materia* (a Latin term meaning "first matter") or produced as a result of the alchemical procedures upon it. The alchemists described it as "darkness," "coal," "pitch," "ashes," "grave of Osiris," "house of the dead," "crow," "mortification," "black blacker than black," to name but a few.

They also called it *Hyle*, the primal substance of which the pre-Socratic Greeks believed the world was made, and *materia confusa* or *masa confusa*—symbolic of the primordial chaos out of which the living world emerged. In this vein, they referred to the *prima materia* as "chaos" (Figure 4), "the abyss," and "beginning of the world." What prompted me to seek therapy was the visualization of falling into an endless abyss, the chaos of my unconscious.

Other names for the *prima materia* were "origin," the "One," the "first being," and the "Philosophical egg." The Philosophical Egg symbolized the chaotic state of matter at the beginning of the world. The egg contained the four elements out of which the world was made: the shell was equated with Earth; the space between the shell and the white of the egg was equated with Air; the egg-white with Water; and the yolk with Fire.

Another alchemical symbol for the *prima materia* is the *uroboros*—the snake that eats its own tail. Neumann calls the uroboros "a symbol of a self-enclosed unconscious psychic situation, of the primal unity." This is the infant's state of psychic unity with the mother. In the history of consciousness this would correspond to the eons before humans developed a sense of an "I" as separate from their experience.

In the individual, Jung likens the *prima materia* to "the original, undifferentiated condition of the unconscious" . . . "an impure substance, a heterogeneous, inharmonious, chaotic mass, where everything is in confusion, and where the . . . constituents are more or less at war with each other." The alchemists projected these dark, warring, unconscious contents onto the matter in their retorts. Jung says, however, "certainly most of the alchemists

Figure 4. The *Prima Materia* as Chaos
(Michelle de Marolles, *Tableaux des Muses du Temple*, 1665)

from which, at the bidding of God, all the wonders of the world may successively emerge."[87]

And for Figulus, "The species or forms of metals cannot be changed into gold and silver before being first reduced to their primary matter."[88] Of these passages, Edward Edinger notes:

> This procedure corresponds closely to what takes place in psychotherapy. The fixed, settled aspects of the personality that are rigid, and static are reduced or led back to their original, undifferentiated condition as part of the process of psychic transformation. The problem of finding the *prima materia* corresponds to the problem of finding what to work on in psychotherapy."[89]

Edinger then goes on to say: "Finding that which needs to be worked on becomes the subject-matter for the novelist or the core problem of the patient in therapy. It is this psychological material which undergoes the color-change."[90]

handled their *nigredo* in the retort without knowing what it was they were dealing with." For the alchemist, it was the *prima materia* that was "tormented, punished, burnt on the fire . . . the whole process a kind of torture."

If the prima materia was not present at the beginning, it had to be found, or the material reduced to its original, undifferentiated state. For the alchemist Edward Kelly, "Bodies quite dry and of a deep black. This is the death of the compound; the winds have ceased, and there is a great calm. This is that great simultaneous eclipse of the Sun and Moon, when the Sea, also, has disappeared. Our Chaos is then ready,

To each alchemist this dark matter was something different, and for this reason it was given a host of names. Ruland's *Lexicon* (1612) gives 50 synonyms for the *prima materia*.[91] Jung claimed to have found 150 synonyms and conjectured that there must be at least 300—a limit set only by the limitations of language itself.[92] By examining some of these names and their context in the alchemical texts, we can begin to arrive at a clearer understanding of the scope of the *nigredo*.

The alchemists believed that Hyle, the original *prima materia*, later differentiated or separated into the four elements: *terra* (Earth), *aqua* (Water), *coelum* (Air), and *ignis* (Fire), which then combined in various proportions to form all matter in the physical world.

The element most closely associated with the *nigredo* was *terra*, also called Earth, our earth, black earth, Adam's earth, carnal earth, stone, and mountain. *Aqua* (Water) was most closely associated with the *albedo*; *coelum* (Air) was most closely associated with the *citrinitas;* and *ignis* (Fire) was most closely associated with the *rubedo*. Edinger likens this separation of Hyle into the four elements to the psychological differentiation of the ego from the unconscious:

Figure 5. Two-Headed Hermaphrodite
(Michael Maier, *Symbola aureae mensae duodecim nationum,* 1617)

> Upon the *prima materia* was imposed, as it were, a fourfold structure, a cross, representing the four elements—two sets of contraries, earth and air, fire and water. Psychologically, this image corresponds to the creation of the ego out of the undifferentiated unconscious by the process of discriminating the four functions: thinking, feeling, sensation and intuition.[93]

Because of its darkness and heaviness, the metal most often associated with the *nigredo* was lead. Psychologically, Hillman calls lead "chronic and dense, a heavy, oppressive and gloomy suffering, without specified focus, senseless and constipative."[94] Because Saturn was the god of lead, the condition of heaviness, darkness, and melancholy was attributed to him. Thus, black was associated with a *Saturnine,* or melancholic, temperament, similar to my state of being at the beginning of my work. The *nigredo* was also personified as man or Adam, the first man, "made out of clay . . . a piece of the original *masa confusa* not yet differentiated but capable of differentiation."[95]

In addition, the *nigredo* was personified as Mercury, god of the beginning and end of the Opus. During the *nigredo* phase, Mercury was encountered as a hermaphrodite, a being not yet fully separated or differentiated into male and female, as portrayed in Figure 5.

Part of the work of the opus was to separate these two, also referred to as *Sol* and *Luna,*

Figure 6. Two Lions Fighting
(Johannes Daniel Mylius, *Philosophia Reformata*, 1622)

Sun and Moon, brother and sister, bridegroom and bride, father and mother. At this early stage of the work, they symbolize what is called the lesser *coniunctio* (Latin for "union" or "marriage"). At the end of the opus, when their separation is complete, these two can be brought back together as King and Queen in a true *coniunctio*, the sacred marriage of the *albedo* and the *rubedo*.

In the animal realm, synonyms for the *nigredo* include cold-blooded, poisonous animals such as the dragon, serpent, scorpion, basilisk, and toad. In milder form we find the salamander and chameleon. Also commonly mentioned are warm-blooded predators such as lions, bears, or wolves, usually depicted fighting, mauling or eating each other (Figure 6).

Jung describes the two lions as "a prefiguration of the royal pair; hence they wear crowns. At this stage they express the passionate emotionality that precedes the recognition of unconscious contents."[96] We see this passionate emotionality at the beginning of Christina's story.

The *nigredo* is also associated with birds of prey or ill-omened scavengers such as the crow, the raven, and the bird without wings—a wingless creature who flies around at night. These creatures from the animal realm depict in graphic form what Jung refers to as "the original, half-animal state of unconsciousness known to the adept as the *nigredo*."[97]

The terms *mortificatio* (Latin for "death," "killing," "mortification"), *putrefactio* ("rotting," "putrefaction"), *solutio* ("dissolution"), *separatio* ("separation") and *divisio* ("division") are connected to this stage. Edinger says *putrefactio* is "rotting," associated with words like *feces*, *excrement*, *bad odors*, the *stench of the graves*, and *worms*.[98] Per Ruland's Lexicon (1612), "It is the property of putrefaction to destroy the old, original nature of a thing, and to introduce a new nature."[99]

"Mortificatio," says Edinger, "is the most negative operation in alchemy. It has to do with darkness, defeat, torture, mutilation, death and rotting."[100] He reminds us of Jung's statement: "The integration of contents that were always unconscious and projected involves a serious lesion of the ego. Alchemy expresses this through the symbols of death, mutilation, or poisoning."[101] In this regard Edinger posits, "the encounter with the unconscious is almost by definition a wounding defeat [for the ego],"[102] but he reminds us that "these dark images often lead over to highly positive ones—growth, resurrection, rebirth."[103]

Thus, unsurprisingly, the *nigredo* is referred to as the "grave of Osiris," "entrance to the West," "land of the dead," and "House of the Dead."[104] At this stage of the opus, the alchemical vessel itself is referred to as a tomb or coffin, Hell and Hades.[105] My "Black Hole" dream, in which I felt I was suffocating, had the quality of a tomb or coffin.

In this image (Figure 7), the alchemical couple (that is, a woman and her animus or a

Figure 7. *Putrefactio*
(Georges Anrach de Strasbourg, *Prætiosissimum donum Dei*, folio 14)

man and his anima) is united, but in this early stage, we could say that, like the bond between mother and infant, the union is a merger; there is no individual separation. Before they can come together in a true coniunctio, they must first become conscious of their individual separateness. For that to happen the two must first go through the nigredo experiences of putrefaction or rotting, destruction, dissolution (the dissolving of old structures) and/or humiliation (learning about our shadow is humiliating).

Thus, the *nigredo* as shadow is also referred to as *limus microcosmi*, the slime or dirt of man, and as *vilissimum*, the vilest, cheapest, most despised thing, the thing rejected as worthless. The author of the *Gloria Mundi* speaks of the Philosopher's Stone in this way; in the beginning, when its value cannot be seen, the Stone is passed by, ignored, or rejected. In my dream in the chapter on the *rubedo,* I pick up an object on the floor of a busy place, ignored or passed by countless others, which springs to life in a wondrous way.

Jung says the *nigredo* corresponds to "the darkness of the unconscious, which contains the cast-off, despised, inferior personality, the shadow."[106] In another place Jung defines *shadow* as "the dangerous aspect of the unrecognized dark half of the personality."[107]

Of analysis, Jung says:

Confrontation with the shadow produces at first a dead balance, a standstill that hampers moral decisions and makes convictions ineffective or even impossible. Everything becomes doubtful, which is why the alchemists called this stage nigredo, . . . chaos, melancholia. It is right that the magnum opus should begin at this point, for it is indeed a well-nigh unanswerable question how one is to confront reality in this torn and divided state.[108]

In this standstill, images of dissolution, dismemberment, decapitation, decomposition, decay, and death appear. In the *Chymical Wedding of Christian Rosenkreutz,* for instance, the Moor is a black executioner who decapitates royalty; in the end his own head is struck off, and a black bird is beheaded.

Five days after I began my dream journal, I dreamed of seeing a human head lying face up on a sidewalk; it is alive, a very handsome male face with a faraway, blank, dull look in the eyes and despair written across the features. It is important to understand this as a symbolic phenomenon, as Jung explains: "Beheading is significant symbolically as the separation of [intellectual] 'understanding' from the great suffering and grief which nature inflicts on the soul."[109]

The enormous list of terms for the *nigredo* indicates that the *nigredo* was quite different for each alchemist, yet to find it was of the utmost importance, because without it the opus was in vain. Thus, the adepts say, "When you see your matter going black, rejoice for that is the beginning of the work."[110] Another exults:

O Happy Gate of Blackness, which art the passage to this so great a change! Study, therefore, whosoever appliest thyself to this Art, only to know this secret, for to know this is to know all, but to be ignorant of this is to be ignorant of all. For putrefaction precedes the generation of every new form into existence.[111]

The following passage by the anonymous author of *Open Entrance to the Closed Palace of the King* conveys a sense of the *nigredo*:

When the Lion dies, the Crow is born. The substance has now become a uniform color, namely, as black as pitch, and neither vapours, or winds, or any other signs of life are seen;

the whole is dry as dust, with the exception of some pitch-like substance, which now and then bubbles up; all presents an image of eternal death. Nevertheless, it is a sight which gladdens the heart of the Sage ... For it is the work of the quickening spirit, which will soon restore the dead bodies to life.[112]

Such passages from the alchemical literature provide us with diverse, sometimes bizarre and imaginative images; nevertheless, as a group they give us strong intimations of the *nigredo*.

I will now turn to modern literature to uncover the *nigredo*'s psychological meaning. Ethan Allen Hitchcock, the first person in modern times (1857) to articulate the psychological meaning of the black color, equates it with humility and "philosophical contrition," close to the meaning of mortification:

The first steps of man toward the discovery of his whole being the alchemists called a philosophical contrition, equated with the black state of the matter, the first color, a sure sign of a true operation ... [involving] the separation of superfluous phlegm and feces from the matter, which then passes into the white state.[113]

Another precursor of Jung's, Herbert Silberer, calls black "the death color."[114] He associates black with the sacrifice of the Lion who kills a part of himself in order to be able to arise renewed and regenerated.[115] That is, the lion as a symbol of the conscious ego-state must be sacrificed temporarily to emerging unconscious

contents for transformation to occur.

Although both of these authors rightly discern the psychological meaning behind the alchemical language, it is the brilliant and definitive work of C. G. Jung that brings alchemy into modern consciousness. Of the *nigredo* Jung has much to say. In general, however, Jung stays close to the original metaphorical material, which is lengthy and difficult to grasp, in an effort, perhaps, to preserve its power and numinosity:

We should not begrudge the alchemists their secret language: deeper insight into the problems of psychic development soon teaches us how much better it is to reserve judgement instead of prematurely announcing to all and sundry what's what. Of course, we all have an understandable desire for crystal clarity, but we are apt to forget that in psychic matters we are dealing with processes of experience, that is, with transformations which should never be given hard and fast names if their living movement is not to petrify into something static. The protean mythologem and the shimmering symbol express the processes of the psyche far more trenchantly and, in the end, far more clearly than the clearest concept; for the symbol not only conveys a visualization of the process but—and this is perhaps just as important—it also brings a re-experiencing of it, of that twilight which we can learn to understand only through inoffensive empathy, but which too much clarity only dispels.[116]

Only occasionally does Jung allow himself to

interpret the material in purely psychological terms:

> The darkness and blackness can be interpreted psychologically as man's confusion and lostness; that state which nowadays results in an anamnesis [analysis], a thorough examination of all those contents which are the cause of the problematical situation, or at any rate its expression. This examination includes the irrational contents that originate in the unconscious and express themselves in fantasies and dreams. The analysis and interpretation of dreams confront the conscious standpoint with the statements of the unconscious, thus widening its narrow horizons.[117]

Figure 8. Slaying the Dragon (*Musaeum Hermeticum,* 1678)

The integration of these two opposites, conscious and unconscious, is the goal of therapy. Jung speaks of the psychotherapeutic process:

> Self-knowledge is an adventure that carries us unexpectedly far and deep. Even a moderately comprehensive knowledge of the shadow can cause a good deal of confusion and mental darkness, since it gives rise to personality problems which one had never remotely imagined before. For this reason alone, we can understand why the alchemists called their *nigredo* melancholia, "a black blacker than black," night, an affliction of the soul, confusion, etc., or, more pointedly, the "black raven." For us the raven seems only a funny allegory, but

for the medieval adept it was, as we have said, a well-known allegory of the devil.[118]

In another place he says:

> It is a bitter thing to accept the darkness and blackness of the *umbra solis* [black sun] and to pass through this valley of the shadow. It is bitter indeed to discover behind one's lofty ideals narrow, fanatical convictions, . . . and behind one's heroic pretensions nothing but crude egotism, infantile greed, and complacency. This painful corrective is an unavoidable stage in every psychotherapeutic process.[119]

Edward Edinger, in his book on alchemy, *Anatomy of the Psyche*, translates the intricacies of the alchemists' work—and Jung's writings on alchemy—into terms more understandable to the modern reader. In the chapter "Mortificatio," he explains that blackness refers to the shadow and alludes to the positive consequences of being aware of one's shadow and of evil.[120] Too great an identification with one side will constellate its opposite. Thus, "dreams that emphasize blackness usually occur when the conscious ego is one-sidedly identified with the light."[121]

"The blackness," Edinger notes, "when it is not the original condition, is brought about by the slaying of something."[122] Most commonly it is the dragon, "a personification of the instinctual psyche" that is slain (Figure 8).[123] However, it may also be the King (who is slain or dismembered), the lion (who, in one version has his paws cut off), the eagle (whose wings are clipped), or the sun (which is eclipsed or which "sinks into the well of Luna"). "King, sun, and lion refer to the ruling principle of the conscious ego and to the power instinct. At a certain point they must be mortified in order for a new center to emerge."[124]

The slaying of the dragon takes on a more personal form in the *nigredo* experience of an alchemist, pictured in the alchemical woodcut shown in Figure 9 and explained in the text that accompanies it:

I am an infirm and weak old man, surnamed the dragon; therefore, am I shut up in a cave, that I may be ransomed by the kingly crown.... A fiery sword inflicts great torments on me; death makes weak my flesh and bones...My soul and

Figure 9. The *Nigredo* Experience of an Alchemist
(Herbrandt Jamsthaler, *Viatorium Spagyricum*, 1590)

my spirit depart; a terrible poison, I am likened to the black raven, for that is the wages of sin; in dust and earth I lie, that out of Three may come One. O soul and spirit, leave me not, that I may see again the light of day, and the hero of peace whom the whole world shall behold may arise from me.[125]

Edinger explains this text:

The infirm and weak old man represents a conscious dominant or spiritual principle that has lost its effectiveness. It has regressed to the level of the primordial psyche (dragon) and must therefore submit to transformation. The cave in which it is shut up is the alchemical vessel. The torture is the fiery ordeal that brings about transformation in order that "out of the Three may come One"; that is, that body, soul and spirit may be unified within an integrated personality. The "hero of peace whom the whole world shall behold" is the Philosopher's Stone, the reconciler of opposites.[126]

The Philosopher's Stone refers to Jung's idea of the Self, the center and core of the personality. In Figure 9, the two winged beings flying out of the old man's mouth are his soul and spirit, which I equate with the *albedo* and *rubedo*. To Edinger, the separation of spirit and soul from the body "is experienced as a death." He quotes this passage from Jung:

> The *unio mentalis*, the interior oneness which today we call individuation, [Dorn] conceived as a psychic equilibration of opposites…a state of equanimity transcending the body's affectivity and instinctuality…But, in order to bring about their subsequent reunion, the mind must be separated from the body—which is equivalent to voluntary death for only separated things can unite.[127]

Edinger believes that "to pay attention to the unconscious does mean to deliberately make oneself miserable in order that the autonomous psyche will be able to function more freely. It has nothing to do with masochism but is rather a conscious participation in the process of actualizing the Deity."[128] Out of the *nigredo*, he says, the Self is born. Surrounding the core words *mortificatio* and *putrefactio* Edinger presents a word-chart indicating the major symbolic connections clustering around

them. These *nigredo* words now carry a ring of familiarity: blackness, defeat, humiliation, suffering, tragedy, King slaying, sacrifice, crucifixion, Dragon slaying, frustration of desirousness, poison, toad, earth, corpse, grave, flesh, rotting, stench, excrement, worms, death, skeleton, skull, vulture, crow, exile, wilderness, sickness, wound, mutilation, castration, impotence, fear.[129]

James Hillman, too, speaks of the *nigredo* in analysis:

> The mind in *nigredo* shows characteristics of downward and backward thinking, an intellect caught in reductive and depressive reasonings and figurings out: past history, materialized fantasies and concretistic explanations. The *nigredo* psyche knows itself as victimized, traumatized, dependent, and limited by circumstantiality and substantiality.[130]

The *nigredo*, then, is not just that which is unconscious, but that which, arising from our unconscious, begs for transformation: feelings of isolation, guilt, melancholy, concupiscence, fear, anger, despair, rage—the list of things belonging to the rejected shadow is endless. Work on any one of these belongs to the *nigredo* phase of psychotherapy.

Stephen Martin, writing specifically about anger, describes this phase:

> In the *nigredo*, the phase of overwhelming darkness, one first confronts the chaos called rage. In therapeutic work, this is the

Figure 10. Alchemical Tree of Life (*Splendor Solis,* folio 15)

time when the patient's persona and defense mechanisms begin to crumble and the wild and shadowy presence that is rage blackens consciousness . . . The patient is captured by the grief and anguish of lost reality-testing and massive projection onto others . . . During this time . . . rage may manifest in a variety of somatic complaints. It may be aimless, unconscious agitation, pervasive muscular tension, cardiovascular irregularities, irritable bowels, hot flashes, pounding head, or pounding fists. Other manifestations may be violent temper outbursts . . . passive-aggressive manipulations, obsessive self-blame, self-righteousness, or even bouts of forgetfulness and somnolence . . . There seems no way out; everything seems polluted and everyone stinks, and not even the analyst can be trusted to fulfill long-deprived wishes or fill the agonizing emptiness. This is the chaos of the alchemical "*prima materia*" which rage so inelegantly deposits on our psychological doorstep. Only when this utter loneliness and outer chaos are faced, accepted, and integrated can any relief take place and meaning emerge.[131]

Psychologically, the *nigredo* is those rejected aspects of ourselves that Jungians call the "shadow" (depression, hungry instinctual desirousness, guilt, fear, rage, isolation, despair). Encountering one's shadow produces suffering. The *nigredo* stage alone would be a bitter pill were it not for the fact that the *prima materia* always contains its opposite, described by the alchemists as "outwardly cold, inwardly fiery; outwardly black, inwardly white . . . a paradoxical substance which contains the seeds of transformation within it."[132]

In a plate from the *Splendor Solis* (Figure 10), the three men wear the alchemical colors black, white, and red, while the birds of sublimation wheel overhead.[133] The white-headed raven signifies that the black, the *nigredo*, is beginning to yield up the white, the *albedo*—a whitening is taking place. In the panel at the base of the plate, this "'whitening" process is mirrored in the four women bathing, washing away the blackness of the *nigredo*.

This transformation of the black into the white is dramatically illustrated in a famous set of ox-herding pictures dating from the Sung dynasty (960–1279 CE). In this series of woodblock prints a raging black ox with menacing horns runs rampant under black storm clouds. With great difficulty at the beginning, an ox-herder captures and gradually subdues the ox, whose color, nose to tail, gradually changes from pure black to pure white. The ox's nature also changes, from menacing and unchecked to placid and self-contained.[134] The black ox may be interpreted as a metaphor for the body and its desires (the id) transformed over time from untamed instinctuality into harmonious self-containment, or as the mind with its racing thoughts gradually stilled into inner peace and tranquility.

Thus, the promise of purification of the *prima materia* and its transformation into the white and the red kept the lonely alchemist at his work.

BLACK DREAMS

At the beginning of my analysis, with my too positive, too upbeat, too "white" attitudes, I was besieged with "black" dreams, the most numerous in the dream record. The sixteen examples I've selected are representative of other black dreams in the record.

Given that I had no knowledge of alchemy when these dreams were recorded, their content is amazingly close to alchemical *nigredo* imagery. In these dreams, there is a clear progression of *nigredo* content from the frightening, primitive, inchoate *prima materia* of the unconscious to more human figures, which represent the alchemical substance in need of transformation—the "core" problem on which I needed to work. These figures, initially terrifying, gradually transformed into positive, helpful figures.

My initial "Black Hole" dream and subsequent visualization of falling into an endless abyss, described in the Introduction, was followed a month later by the following dream:

November 5, 1974. *SPIDERS. I am standing thigh-deep in water, in a river or perhaps on a beach. In the clear water running toward me floats a spider, with its legs wrapped around itself so all I can see is the small peanut-sized shape of its body. I am horrified and suddenly afraid to step on the bottom. Later, I am standing on white sand and begin to see black legs of spiders lurking in the sand, only partially visible. At first, I see just one, but as I look, they seem to multiply until there are spiders practically every square foot! Children are playing in the sand and seem to be unaware*

of them or are not bothered by them, but I see them, and I am too frightened to walk or move.

In the language of the dream, the ground on which I stand is sand, begging the question of whether my "standpoint" or "grounding" is solid. Furthermore, the sand is white, suggesting a standpoint or a viewpoint that is too white, too positive, too un-allowing of the dark *prima materia*—an as yet unidentified problem lurking in the unconscious, but beginning to appear as black spiders, frightening and initially paralyzing. The children playing around me seem not to be aware of the spiders, suggesting that the problem is mine alone.

November 12, 1974. *BLACK CASTLE. I'm floating around in a castle with huge, high ceilings, examining it. Everything is hideously black: walls, ceiling, floors, furniture, even the draperies and fixtures.*

The intense saturation of black as *nigredo* in this dream means that the problems I keep trying to avoid with my "too-white" attitude have hit with full force. Floating also suggests that I am not "grounded" in life. Having given up my teaching career for volunteer work after marriage had left me feeling rootless (floating).

July 15, 1978. *TAR HORSE. I am in a big boat, like an ark. We are loading it with provisions, huge bundles of things, food, grapes, etc. Many people I know are on board: a man I know, his girlfriend, and a male friend of mine. My analyst pops in and out, too. Periodically I dive down under the water. There is a horse down there, oozing tar or something slimy and black, which I recognize and try to avoid.*

After many earlier dreams of leaky, unseaworthy boats, I am now ready to embark on a journey through the waters of the unconscious. There are two couples in the dream. Often in dream analysis they represent a conscious and an unconscious couple; both must connect.

Diving into the waters of the unconscious, I encounter a horse. Given that I was "horse-crazy" as a teen, the horse was related to my instinctuality or libido. But this horse is completely submerged or "drowned" in the unconscious, its powerful energies unavailable for daily life. Depressions will do that: pull the energies normally accessible for daily living into the unconscious.

The horse is oozing tar or "something slimy and black," the stuff of the nigredo. In the dream I try to avoid the slimy black stuff, but I am no longer paralyzed by it, perhaps because horses are evolutionarily and psychologically closer to humans than spiders. In alchemy, the most important operation is to find the substance to be worked on; without it, the work cannot proceed. In a dream the following night, the problem I am trying to avoid breaks through:

July 16, 1978. BREAK-IN. A strange black man breaks away from the crowd and starts running around the side of my house. Suddenly at the back of my house I hear a great crash of rocks and know he has broken in through the back door. I am terrified.

The problem lurking in my unconscious—a negative inner masculine figure—has finally "broken through" into consciousness. A year later I am ready to confront this terrifying figure and deal with him.

August 7, 1979. MURDER OF THE BLACK MAN. A black man stops by a woman's apartment to see her. He is so desperate to see her/kiss her/have sex with her that he goes into the kitchen to find a knife with which to "persuade" her. The dagger is on the counter—an antique sheathed dagger. I become so alarmed for the safety of my friend that I grab the knife and begin to attack the man myself. At first, I just wound him, inflicting small wounds here and there, but finally I become so worked up, so enraged and so alarmed at the threat he poses that I drive the dagger through his heart. He gasps, blood comes oozing out, and he falls over dead.

In this powerful dream I come face to face with the terror lurking in my unconscious—an intensely negative, threatening, possibly murderous masculine figure, who desperately wants to connect with my friend, a part of myself I haven't yet integrated. (From the time I was five, I was terrified witnessing my alcoholic father's murderous rage and domestic violence.)

If we think of the dagger as symbolic of a phallus, the fact that the dagger is antique and sheathed makes it more a symbolic than an actual threat. Until this phallic energy, hitherto projected "out there" onto someone else as threatening, can be acknowledged as my own murderous rage and integrated into my psychic structure, he remains so foreign, hostile, and threatening that I feel compelled to "slay" him.

In slaying him, I am overcoming the dragon of terror inside of myself and coming into my own power. However, he does not die; the following night he reappears.

August 8, 1979. *TRANSVESTITE BLACK MAN. A fearsome black man breaks into a room in my house and demands my clothing so he can disguise himself.*

The black man becomes a quick-change artist who tries to disguise himself in my clothes. He is now someone I must recognize as a part of myself—a dark, shadowy part that must be owned and integrated.

October 28, 1979. *GREAT SNAKE. I look down and open the lid of some kind of container. Inside, just a few inches from my face, I see a great snake begin to move and twist. For some reason it seems "planted" there. I look for bugs (scorpions, black widow spiders, snakes, and so on) but don't find them. Then I see: the snake has grown and is moving. Its head shows. I scream.*

The snake, symbolic of the deepest layers of my unconscious, has begun to "move," to make itself known. Initially this is terrifying.

December 15, 1979. *TURKISH BATH. There is a black woman, nude and corpulent, lounging in and around a small shallow bath reminiscent of Ottoman Turkish baths. She is engaged in conversation and the enjoyable company of a black man, also nude. There are servants or attendants against the far wall, looking on. The couple lounge, talk, happy to see each other again. It seems the man has returned after an absence. I see them in "X-rated" poses, as if I were watching a film that had been sped up.*

In the famous set of alchemical pictures in the *Rosarium Philosophorum*, a fully dressed couple meet; later the couple, nude, enters a bath, where they join in sexual union. Later still, they die and are reborn. In this dream we see a close parallel to the first part of this alchemical series. Although the black man has not yet become a conscious part of my psyche, in the form of a black woman I can meet him in the unconscious, where the initial lesser *coniunctio* can take place. A year later, I strike oil.

September 18, 1980. *OIL STRIKE. At the oil fields, I have struck oil. The black stuff is gushing out and I have no way to control it or pump it uphill as I would like to do. My only choice seems to be to let it flow downhill at its own speed into one of several fields, which, on a map, are colored different shades of purple and lavender, depending on what grade of oil I choose to make, from crude to refined.*

The oil in this dream is similar to the tar or "black slimy substance" oozing out of the horse at the bottom of the sea in a previous dream. However, I can no longer run away from or contain the black substance, which comes gushing out. Nor can I control its direction. In spite of my wish to pump the oil uphill (or "pump up" my too-happy persona?), I must allow it to follow its own course, according to the laws of gravity. That is, I must submit to a process greater than me over which I have no control. However, this oil now has value (oil is often called "black gold"), and I have a choice in what to make of it—from "crude" to "refined." This image offers an insight into color symbolism in dreams: the different shades of oil represent degrees of refinement (that is, differentiation or development). In the following dream one month later, the black takes on a religious or sacred cast:

October 30, 1980. *MAKE BLACK. Ten ways God loves us. The fifth is: Make Black. Do not take the name of God in vain.*

Although at the time I had no knowledge of alchemy, the phrase, "First you must make black" was a common alchemical phrase. Here it appears as a variation of the Ten Commandments, along with the injunction not to take the name of God in vain. My dream appears to be saying that the process of "making black" is sacred spiritual work—a position voiced repeatedly by the alchemists.

November 21, 1980. *FUNERARY GARB FOR BARBIE. I see, laid out before me, some black gauze clothes, which I assume belong to a Barbie doll, even though black seems a strange color for a Barbie doll. They are laid out in the shape of a cross, with the wide sleeves stretched out to form the horizontal axis, whereas the body and legs of the outfit form the vertical axis.*

Here, what is dying is not something masculine, but something from my wounded feminine side. As my relationship to the previously threatening inner masculine began to change, so did the relationship to my inner feminine, which in this dream is associated with a Barbie doll now dressed in black, her outfit in the shape of a cross. That is, from the dream I might infer that I am ready to give up my Barbie doll persona. The result feels like a death, as the poem in my journal two months later attests:

January 17, 1981

> "Night"
> night
>   where is your light?
>   where is the bright?
> dark the far, dark the near
>   dark the center, dark the fear
> death
>   of life?
>   of husband? wife?
>   endless strife
> black the dread
>   heavy like lead
> a ghastly bed
>   to Hades wed
> deep the dark, dark the deep
>   why do you weep?
>   fear ye the leap
>   of faith, or lack of sleep?
> slow the dying
>   heavy the sighing
>   bitter the crying
>   fear of flying

This poem is filled with alchemical *nigredo* imagery: night, darkness, fear, strife, the heaviness of lead, dying, and grief. I feel "married" to Hades, god of the underworld—the realm of the dead (and the dying parts of my *persona*).

May 19, 1981. *SNAKES ON THE ICE CHEST. I am one of two lifeguards at a swimming pool. A box about the size of a large ice chest is at the edge of the pool. I look in it and see filth—the stuff the filter has caught: bits of junk, unchewed or undigested food, garbage. On top of all this are two black snakes with large heads. They seem to be guarding the garbage.*

There is a parallel here between me as one of two lifeguards guarding the swimmers in the pool and the two snakes guarding the garbage in the box or ice chest. What is inside the chest (what is "on my chest") is the "stuff" of the *nigredo*—the *prima materia* or raw material of the unconscious: garbage, filth, junk—that which is undigested or indigestible to the conscious standpoint—dredged up from the pool, symbolic of the personal unconscious. Thus, there is more *nigredo* to be processed, which I am still holding onto or "guarding." But a swimming pool is more contained and of manageable proportions (that is, more personal), than the vast, impersonal, collective ocean of my earlier dreams.

May 23, 1981. *FUNERAL DRESS. I go outside and see everyone dressed in black—not just ordinary black, but ink black, jet black. Obviously, someone of great importance has been killed or has died. I do not know who! How could I not know? It's very important for me to find out.*

As old, familiar aspects of the psyche are given up, the result always feels like a death. It is important for me to find out what or who has died, so that the loss can be properly mourned and buried.

Four years later, after the alchemical white, yellow, and red have been activated, the following two black dreams show a resolution to the problems posed by the earlier dreams of the "oil" and the "black man":

March 4, 1985. *COLLEGE GROUND. I'm on a hill overlooking a broad valley. Through the center of the valley runs a road. On the right side of the road are the beginnings of what will become a men's college campus. It is all laid out, with a fountain in the middle and roads going out from it like the spokes of a wheel. The rest is bare dirt. Nothing has been built yet—just the plan laid out and the roads in place. Directly across the road, on the left, is what will one day be the site of a woman's college. Now it is a farm in operation, and we are standing in the road in front of it. I see some old wooden buildings—barns, sheds, perhaps a farmhouse, and near the road, a farmer working to irrigate his orchard. Circling the base of each tree is a kind of donut-shaped pump, giving water to each tree. As the farmer works, one of the pumps pierces the ground and a thick, black crude oil comes oozing out of the ground in a lava-like flow until the farmer is sitting in it, up to his waist. He does not seem at all unhappy, knowing that oil money will help build the quadrangle at the center of the women's college.*

The broad, open valley, which will one day house two colleges—places of higher education and learning—is a farm, and the farmer watering the trees and working the land may be a now more earthy, grounded, embodied, yet generative aspect of my inner masculine. The circular pumps surrounding the trees and giving them water is curiously similar to a *yoni* and *lingam* (vagina and phallus). The two together are a Hindu symbol of the archetypal masculine and feminine, Shiva and Shakti, in divine embrace—a profound *coniunctio* image. Their coming together pierces the earth and leads to the discovery of oil. However, the oil gushing out of the ground is no longer something to be avoided like the tar oozing from the horse; the farmer sits in it, reveling in it, for it represents riches—the basis of what will become a pair of educational institutions: a women's college on the left and a men's college on the right. The ground plan for the men's college forms a mandala: a circular fountain with roads leading out from it like the spokes of a wheel; the plan for the women's college has a quadrangle at its center. That is, in the center of the women's college sits a more "masculine" square; in the center of the men's college is a more "feminine" circular fountain. Like the Yin/Yang symbol,

each contains a piece of the other, forming a symbolically integrated whole. This symbolic *coniunctio* takes more personal form in the following dream a year later:

February 3, 1986. *BLACK FRIEND. A black man talks to me and I, to him. I am attracted to him, but we are able to communicate with each other without a shred of flirtatiousness.*

White female and black male, mortal enemies years earlier, have made their peace. That is, within my psyche, the previously threatening, over-eroticized, and unconscious relationship of inner male and female elements appears to have been neutralized and transformed into a pair, now able to relate to each other as friendly equals.

August 10, 1988. *BLACK PARTNER. A young, energetic black man asks me if I would like to be partners with him. I say "Yes." He holds out something and asks me to grasp it. I do and pull him towards me.*

Within my psyche, male and female are now ready to be joined in a conscious, harmonious way.

Reflections on Selected Black Dreams

Although making generalizations based on only seventeen dreams is difficult, the content of the selected black dreams is remarkably similar to alchemical *nigredo* imagery. For example, the chthonic, subhuman spiders and "horse oozing something slimy and black" are the inchoate

prima materia. When this *masa confusa* becomes recognizably human (as the black men who break in and threaten), it becomes clear that the fearsome, negative inner masculine in myself is the *nigredo* substance or "core problem" in need of transformation. These dreams reveal the painful struggle involved in bringing my shadow problem into consciousness and integrating it—a mortifying dark night of the soul. The content of the selected dreams is full of fear, strife, heaviness, break-in, torture, death, dying, and grief—a close parallel to the images of the alchemical *nigredo*.

Although black dreams with negative content (present almost exclusively in the first half of the dream record) continued, not all the black dreams were negative. For instance, in 1985, the year after the end of the *rubedo* phase, the black crude oil in "College Ground" is no longer something to be avoided or controlled but welcomed. And the "Black Man" dreams in 1986 and 1988, which show him in a positive light as an inner partner, contain resolution to my earlier *nigredo* problem with the black man as a highly negative masculine figure. Likewise, my earlier Julie Andrews and Barbie doll personae had to die in order for me to enter into partnership with a transformed inner masculine, no longer projected "out there," but comfortably integrated into my psyche.

CHRISTINA'S SANDPLAY—PHASE I: *NIGREDO* TO *ALBEDO* CONSCIOUSNESS

This section covers Phase I of Christina's journey, which lasted two years before she took her first break from therapy. Fifteen months into her talk therapy she related two dreams. In the first, she says, *"I am lying in a bathtub and I see a 'black mass' in my vagina."* I asked her to reenter the dream with me and find out what was in the black mass. "It's dirty, disgusting, full of anger and pain," she replied. In another dream at this time, *"A woman slapped me in the face, saying 'you're worthless and unlovable.'"* At this point in her analysis, Christina was beginning to uncover the inexpressible pain and suffering of her childhood and was ready to face the wordless mystery and horror, anger and pain embodied in the "black mass"—the very stuff of the *nigredo*. Given the power of sandplay to heal through the wordless shaping of sand, placement of figures, and optional addition of water, it seems no surprise that to give voice to the inexpressible, Christina turned to sandplay. She was drawn to it like a fish to water. In the ensuing five months, before she took leave of therapy for the first time, Christina created nine sandtrays. We'll look at six.

Tray 1. My Life as I See It

Christina picked up her first figure, a large black tree, and placed it in the very center of her tray, saying, "This is the Tree of Life; my favorite is a weeping willow." Since my own inner tree has always been the weeping willow, I felt an immediate limbic resonance, although the lifelessness of this tree suggested a burnt, barren blackness at her core.

The two tall figures at the back left of the tray she described as "Two women, my ancestors, from a time when women were strong and powerful and great." These two figures are the positive mothers she wishes for. However, they are neither human nor personal; they belong to the archetypal realm. It should be noted that the tall brown figure she called a "mother" figure on the left is actually a male phallus, suggesting that she unconsciously may also be looking for a positive father as well as a positive mother.

But hiding behind the tree are two witches: "my adoptive mother and her sisters." The pewter knight in front of them she explained as "my old self, defended, with a suit of armor." The female graduate "is me, after my BA degree, with new life possibilities." Of the turtle breaking out of its egg she said, "I always liked turtles; they just 'go along.' I can crawl back inside my shell when I want to." True, but she was now sticking her neck out and coming out of her shell.

Diagonals in sandtrays often hold important opposites. If we follow the diagonal from the graduate (and maybe the turtle at the back left of the tray) to what Christina called "my ideal house" placed in the front-right corner of the tray, we see that she cannot get "home" to her authentic Self without first encountering and integrating the *nigredo* of her traumatic past, symbolized by the black tree and the two witches hiding behind it.

In the front-left corner of the tray lies "the bridge to my new life." This bridge points directly toward where I sat, which I took as a sign that she was ready to get closer to me (perhaps as a positive mother-figure?). However, the bridge as the transcendent function holds the tension of opposites.[135] Under the bridge lurk an alligator and two snakes—primitive, cold-blooded reptilian creatures—while two more snakes lie on the bridge, suggesting that attachment, especially to a mother figure, is dangerous.

In the far front-left corner she placed what she called "a dancer." The dancing god is Shiva, who, in Hindu mythology destroys the old world, which he holds in dreamtime until the new world is ready to come into existence.

Again, following the diagonal from the front-left corner to the back-right corner, we see the arc of a rainbow mirroring the arc of the bridge. In Greek myth, the rainbow is Iris, bringer of change. Perhaps the rainbow is a symbol holding out hope that the dangerous bridge can be crossed.

On the positive right-hand side of the tray

Tray 1. My Life as I See It

is a mysterious black snake with a mammalian-looking head raised and looking ahead. The snake, crawling on its belly, is a creature of the earth. On the Myers-Briggs Typological Inventory Christina was an extraverted sensate type, very much in her body.

As I got to know her better, I learned that she was a gifted *clairsentient*—able to pick up intuitive knowledge of things through her body, in the same way a clairvoyant is intuitively able to "see" into the collective unconscious lying outside of common awareness.

I analyzed Christina's first tray using Kate Amatruda's method of focusing on Problems (or Obstacles), Resources, and Solutions: [136]

Problems: Visually what strikes me is the literal black of the *nigredo* all over the tray, and there are problems everywhere: in her

Tray 1, detail. Two Witches

armoring, her turtle shell as defended, the dead tree as her burnt core, and the witches as negative mothers. If attachment is dangerous, I wonder about abandonment and the tree as a dead inner child.

Resources: She is a college graduate with a

keen intellect; she has a warrior inside of her; there is safety inside her turtle shell; the two archetypal "women" appear powerful enough to deal with the two witch-mothers; the dancer is her male spirit; a rainbow holds the hope of something better; the black snake may be her inherent earth-based or body-based wisdom.

Solutions: Christina has hope; a willingness to come out of her shell, stick her neck out, cross the dangerous bridge into the arms of a secure attachment figure; a powerful male spirit to guide her; and a vision of an ideal home within, the Self.

After this first tray, Christina's sandplay took off.

Tray 2. The Story of My Life

Christina's second sandtray was created one month later. Her poignant life story, telling where she's been, where she is now, and where she's going[137] follows a counterclockwise arc from a pregnant woman in the left-back corner of the tray to a woman holding the hands of a toddler at the top of the tray. The pregnant woman is Christina's birthmother. She said, "I want a picture of her before she had me. It would be nice to go back that far. This woman is full of confusion, anger, sadness, and despair. She doesn't know what to do. It would be scary to have this baby and raise it alone, with no support from the Other person who made the baby." The next three figures—mother and child, the slightly hidden baby in a manger, and the woman walking out of the tray—tell her birthmother's story: "She has the baby in the birth clinic, leaves the child, and walks on." Christina was abandoned at birth.

The crawling baby, reaching its hand up to the drunk couple on the bench says, "But who am I?" "This crazy woman (the woman on the bench) gets this baby without doing any of the footwork to be prepared for it." In fact, the couple left Christina in bed with a drunk uncle known to be a child molester while they went out to buy diapers, formula, and all the things needed to support their new infant. Worse, this family with an eight-year-old son was woefully unequipped to handle any child. The adoption was not completed until Christina was five years old. Christina's adoptive mother—and all seven of her siblings—had been molested as children. She was a partyer, obese, addicted to food, alcohol, sex, and prescription drugs. She had married her husband to be a positive father but never a lover and turned to other men for sex.

Christina remembers her as a pill-addict, saying, "She was usually passed out every morning, so I fed and dressed myself every day . . . With a butcher knife, mother would threaten to kill the whole family for her pills. She would shake me to tell her where my father hid her pills; I'd have to tell."

Christina was severely neglected and abused

by her adoptive mother. With no good memories of her, Christina was glad when her adoptive mother died of an overdose when Christina was seven.

Given the emotional abandonment by both mothers and the toxicity of her adoptive mother, Christina's attachment was to her adoptive father, a factory worker with an eighth-grade education whom she described as a sweet, religious, but passive, ineffectual man, who, when not at church, was glued to his television set. Their

Detail, Tray 2. Upper left corner

Tray 2. The Story of My Life

standard dinners were takeout food. After her adoptive mother's death, Christina slept in the same bed with him until puberty, often asking him in a plaintive tone, "Do you love me?" He always answered, "Yes."

Thus, in the tray, it is poignant to see the little girl with a doll in a triangular enclosure seated directly between the birthmother walking out of the tray and the tombstone. She had been abandoned by two mothers. To hear from her birthmother that she did not want to make contact or to be contacted by Christina must have been a devastating blow.

Christina said of the little girl with a doll: "She's always taking care of it, but even before mother died, she started putting a wall around herself. It was very small, just around me."

Donald Kalsched has described how, in cases of severe psychological wounding, people develop a protective "Self-Care System" to shield themselves from further wounding.[138] This fence, created when Christina was very small, is the beginning of her "Self-Care System" to protect her small, vulnerable, and wounded self from further threat. From alchemical symbolism, a downward-pointing triangle symbolizes the feminine.

Later in her analysis, Christina dreamed of a deep, bloody cut on her skin directly over her heart, in the shape of a downward-pointing triangle. I suggested that the wound to her feminine soul had become conscious enough that she could now "see" and feel it.

The next figure in the tray is the knight in full body-armor, "My old defended self." And here we see why: after her adoptive mother's death, Christina was sent to an uncle's every summer, where her older male cousins molested her into her teens.

The knight symbolizes her adopted persona as "tough," defended and self-reliant. The bottle in front of the knight (unfortunately, my early sandplay collection lacked a bottle of hard liquor) stands for alcohol and marijuana that Christina began using from the age of eleven on. At thirteen, she became sexually active, and like her adoptive mother, Christina became addicted to alcohol, drugs, and promiscuous sex, having her first abortion at age fifteen.

In her strict Catholic school, Christina, a high-spirited girl by nature, felt very much out of place. After high school, she left home and joined a circus group, who, behind the scenes, were drug dealers, one of whom raped her. During the next seven chaotic years, between a series of relationships with dysfunctional men, she supported herself waiting tables.

At the ends of relationships, she would fly into a rage and break everything, including doors and a car windshield. But panic would throw her into the next relationship. Thus, it's not surprising to see the dark slouched figure, which she described as "me, sometimes, in my shell like the turtle," both figures symbolizing her abandonment, abuse, and despair.

Despite this history of almost unimaginable trauma, Christina's intelligence, self-sufficiency, and enterprising nature led her to enter college at twenty-three. At the age of twenty-seven, she joined Alcoholics Anonymous and Narcotics

Anonymous, really worked the program, and got clean and sober.

The next figure, a kneeling woman embracing a child, represents Christina's first AA sponsor. Through her, Christina learned that she was a Borderline personality. The three children, Christina said, "Are about leaving, going to school and playing." Given their place in the sequence of her life story, they seem poignantly out of place and very small, but perhaps the maternal love of her sponsor allowed the inner child in Christina—sealed off when she was so small—to crawl out of her shell and back into a life that now could include some innocence, hope, and play.

The next figure shows Christina, now twenty-eight, as a college graduate. Through AA, Christina met Joe, a recovering alcoholic just out of a failed marriage. After her graduation, she moved across the country to California to be with him. Because she was having relationship difficulties with him at this time, he is not in the tray. Instead, Christina placed the large black-and-red figure of Kali in front of the graduate, calling it "A beautiful goddess image."

Kali is actually a hideous goddess of death and destruction—one of the darkest goddesses on the planet. So, on the one hand, Christina is facing her demonic shadow. But on the other hand it's important to know that Kali kills demons in the service of restoring peace, so Christina is really facing a powerful female archetype strong enough to subdue her own powerful destructive tendencies. She is one of only two people in my practice ever to put Kali in their tray. This tray appears in my article on Kali.[139]

The last figure she placed in the tray was the woman holding the hands of a toddler, saying, "I'll show you how." I wondered if this was her hope, that I could help the little girl inside her? And was it also a portent that an internalized good-mother imago would one day allow Christina to nurture herself? Later, as I studied all of her trays, I noticed that Christina often placed figures of great importance at the center back of her trays. I came to call these figures the "ruling principle" of the tray. If so, then the negative witch-mother is the ruling principle of Tray 1, and its opposite, the wish for the good mother is the ruling principle of Tray 2.

Overall, this tray attests to the fact that Christina had been living out the undifferentiated rage and addictions of *nigredo*-consciousness. But the fact that she's taken the time here to pause and reflect about her life—which is what depth psychotherapy allows—is the beginning of *albedo* consciousness. The objects in this tray form a circle. If one were to stand in the center of the circle and follow the progression of the timeline, one would be moving to the left. Symbolically, movement to the left in sandplay is a movement toward the unconscious, so her sandplay will be carrying her more deeply into the depths of her unconscious. After she finished the tray, I suggested she make up a myth or story of her life, which she did. Her myth became the focus of Tray 4.

Tray 3. *Nigredo* and a Dawning Consciousness

Tray 3, created two weeks later, is the first of several trays in which every figure is pewter. What does pewter represent? In a famous experiment by Harry Harlow, infant monkeys, reared in a cage and fed through nipples attached to "mother" monkeys fashioned from bare wire, grew up anxious and fearful.[140] So we might interpret pewter, in general, as the hard, cold metal mother, without warmth of feeling—perhaps symbolic of Christina's "tough cookie" persona. The black, barren "tree of life" surrounded by pewter figures make this the epitome of a *nigredo* tray. Christina needs dragons and fantasy power-figures, which are archetypal. The three dragons represent untamed aspects of the primordial psyche, the "id" or *nigredo*. Of the fierce warrior women in the tray (see Tray 3, detail), she said, "All these powerful women are me now." The one male in the tray, the tall figure to the right of the tree, is "A haggard old soul; this is how I feel. I need a solution for this man." He is Saturnine, who, like the god Saturn, holds on, afraid to let his children be born. This is someone who works hard, doesn't laugh or sing, and doesn't allow the child-spirit to live and breathe.

Christina is living in Kalsched's archetypal defenses of the Self, but not feeling it. A child's raw feelings must be mediated and human-ized by another human—the child's parents or caregivers, a therapist, or a loving Other. With the exception of her father and first AA sponsor, Christina had never had that. However, there is cause for hope: the mother kneeling with the child at the base of the tree expresses her longing to connect to her birthmother and with her own abandoned inner child and the woman with a crystal she called "a mother-type." Of all the figures in my collection, this one, which came to me in a dream, is the one with which I most identify—another example of the limbic resonance between us. But the most poignant figure in the tray is the smallest: Gollum, seated at the feet of the armored knight, back left. "That's me, small and vulnerable," she said. Being able to reach below her "tough cookie" persona and see herself as small and vulnerable is the beginning of albedo consciousness.

It should be noted that the presence of water in a tray, whether real water applied directly to sand or into a container, or imaginal water unearthed when sand is moved aside to reveal the blue of the tray bottom, suggests a client's ability to reach down into the unconscious and access feelings. Until now, Christina has not touched the sand or applied water. There is a bridge in Tray 1, implying the presence of water, but Christina did not even run her finger through the sand to hint at water underneath it.

Tray 3. *Nigredo* and a Dawning Consciousness

Tray 3, detail. Warrior Woman

Tray 3, detail. Gollum

Tray 4. Shamanic Journey

A week later Christina came in. Out of the myth or story I suggested she write about her life, she announced excitedly, "Last week I went on a shamanic journey!"

I call my dog, but he doesn't come; instead, a dragon pops in! I say, "I'm not afraid of you! C'mon, let's go!" I hop on its back, over lush green, a great distance. I see a huge castle with a moat and drawbridge that draws down as I approach. There are little robed figures standing around, but they all scatter and disappear as I approach. The castle is deserted. I walk in and explore all the rooms. There's a bedroom with the bed made up. I go up a winding staircase to the top of the castle and see all around. It is beautiful, but there is no one here except that I know one person is down in the dungeon. I'm afraid to go there for fear I'll find people tortured, bloody, mutilated, etc. but I go anyway, and find only one person: Chrissie! [Chrissie is the little girl or inner child, traumatized since birth, still living inside of Christina. In order to survive her childhood, Christina needed to close the door on painful memories and move on, leaving her wounded infant self and child-self locked away and abandoned in the dungeon of her defended psyche.] She's chained to a wall. I go get her bread and water and unchain her. She's angry at me, asking where I've been and why I didn't come sooner? I tell her to calm down and sit and hold her and rock her and rock her. I feel what she's feeling and what I'm feeling, and it's confusing.

Tray 4 is fairy-tale-like. It represents a huge shift in her trays to date. Here we see water in the tray for the first time, a beautiful greening and a centering in her psyche—a premonition of the appearance of the Self.

She says, "The landscape is lush green with mountains and trees everywhere." Christina has placed the castle in the very center of the tray, in place of the dead tree. Surrounded by "big, thick walls," a moat, and a drawbridge, at first sight it appears phallic-looking, closed-up, and defended. The figures outside the castle are unfeeling pewter too: the robed figure on the left is Death; on the right Galadriel (one of J. R. R. Tolkien's *Lord of the Rings* characters, an Elf queen of surpassing beauty, knowledge, and power) is standing arms open, ready to receive; and there are three dragons—one small, one flying above the castle, and one large, with Christina on its back. Dragons are fierce aspects of the *nigredo*, but in the context of centering, which this tray represents, the trauma can be integrated with her core.

In Christina's myth, the drawbridge opens to allow her inside. This opening of the once-defended castle suggests that the castle and everything in it has become a symbol of the greater Self. Joe Henderson says, "Whenever the Self appears, the Shadow is right there."[141] The Shadow is not necessarily bad; it's what's unconscious. Everything inside the castle, including Chrissie, her abandoned child, has been lying in the shadow, unconscious. Because Christina couldn't feel her feelings, she had acted them out through the *nigredo*

Tray 4. Shamanic Journey

of addictions and rage. But writing her own myth and re-creating it in the sand has shifted that into *albedo* consciousness.

In this tray, Christina is bridging the defended, unable-to-feel ego pieces (metal) with the deepest parts of herself and her inner world, including Chrissie, her abandoned inner child. Now she has an ego-connection to powerful archetypal parts of herself. This connection represents the beginnings of an ego-Self axis, the living connection of the ego with the greater Self. Christina had to work hard at making that bridge. And it took huge courage for her to go down into the dungeon and face what was there. It's important to remember that the goal of sandplay is not the appearance of a Self-tray but to work with the defenses to integrate the trauma.

Tray 5. Integration

Christina began her session the following week on a lively note saying, "I'm really good at what I do! I want to create my life as it is today in all its facets." In this tray we see further evidence of centering and integration.

The defended castle in the center has been moved aside; the tray's center is now transformed into the more human, relational aspects of herself at her core. Of the two women, left to right, she says, "I'm coming out, ready to learn"; "I feel connected, with stuff to give"; so she's beginning to see herself in a more positive light. On their right sits the Gollum, facing the dancing couple. So she's integrating the inner child into her consciousness and allowing herself to feel how "small and vulnerable" she feels, especially in relation to Joe.

The radial design, beginning with the figures at the top of the tray and moving clockwise, features the following:

Back center: The archetypal black goddess, Ganesh, and Garuda.

Back right: The woman smoking on a bench is "my old addicted self, very far in the background." The clear glass beads, as her addiction, are "a dangerous bridge, slippery," but the dancer Shiva is destroying the demons.

Center right: Dancing couple: "She's what I do, over in there, Joe and I, doing that little dance." The red glass beads "are separated, because Joe and I are not even connected anymore."

Front right: The house and children are "the shelter and my kids at the shelter where I work."

Front center: The bridge leads to "graduate school" represented by a female goddess. Perhaps in graduate school she will find her inner goddess.

Front left: The shell with food represents "a table, with all these people coming to eat! And I'm going to serve them!"

Center left: Green beads circling the hula dancer are "about healing and growth." The green beads also extend from dancer to castle because "there's more than one way to get here."

Back left: The Tree of Life, the castle, her dog, and the mother kneeling with the child, "Me, when I go to see Chrissie in the dungeon." She's beginning to integrate the positive mother in herself. Buddha sits partially hidden by the tree. She said, "It's through this kind of healing that I achieved that: a bridge—a long, long way back to those buried feelings."

With all these bridges and paths, Christina is not trying to bridge; she is bridging. "But," she says, "I need something for *me.*" Encircling the three central women with white pearls, she murmured, "circled by white light." The white light is the full-blown emergence of the *albedo,* the deep interiority, which really began with the water in the last tray, when she entered the castle and found Chrissie.

As she stepped back and looked at her tray, she said, "What I've been looking for— my connection to my personal mother—I've found, through my connection to all these Goddesses! And their roots go down, beyond

Tray 5. Integration

this sandtray, to the Source; the connection is that deep." As she began to feel the depths of her own sacred spirituality, and a connection to a real mother, her words gave me great hope.

In this tray, the eight radial arms are connected to a precious "center." Pratibha Eastwood calls the archetype of eight "The Auspicious Double Quadrinity," manifesting positively as "balanced energy in personal life; rearranging personal reality by living symbolically, not just materially," and negatively as "Inflated view of power; struggling with the dark side of power, money, sex, control and recognition."[142] Although this tray as a whole speaks to the positive aspects of the Double Quadrinity, Christina's three central figures are still pewter, making me wonder about the negative aspects of the number eight in her psyche.

Tray 6. Neural Integration

A month later, Christina constructed the last tray of Phase I. This tray shows the split in her psyche coming together as a neural integration.

On the left, we see the *nigredo* of the old neural pathway with its defended pewter figures, all aspects of her personality, who, because of the hurt, couldn't feel. They are standing on the icy cold path of the "slippery slope" of addiction in Tray 5. The exception is Christina (the colorful smoking woman on the bench at the back left), perhaps now more of an observing ego sitting back and taking in the whole scene. The fact that she is in color suggests that the greening and centering of the two previous trays have infused her ego with color and new life.

On the right is a symbolic representation of a new neural pathway with dark blue stones—a spiritual color—paving the way. This pathway is more human, with warmth of feeling in the flesh and blood figures. The crawling baby "Chrissie" and her growing attachment to the positive mother figures on the right suggest a growing Mother-Child unity in the therapy—the stuff of the albedo.[143] But she has not yet integrated the negative mother.

The two paths meet with two women—a pewter woman on the left and a flesh-and-blood woman on the right—each holding a small child in her hands. Christina has internalized enough of the good mother at this juncture that she is ready to leave therapy and strike out on her own. The path away from

therapy holds a kissing couple that she called "a melding together, marriage, something to look forward to." Here is her first step into the *rubedo*, a coming out into life and into relationships. For partnerships, Christina had always looked to men as the connection to her *animus* (her inner masculine spirit): her father, her boyfriends, and as we shall see later, a husband—all safe father figures.

What Christina didn't know is that it would take many years and many tears to integrate the negative mother-wound and the negative *animus* inside of her to find a true *coniunctio*. If the blue glass beads behind the couple represent water and the red glass beads before the couple, fire, we see that she is trying to bring the opposites of water and fire together. The hoped-for result is the unified personality, the Self. This couple portends an inner marriage of the positive feminine and the positive masculine (*albedo-rubedo* consciousness) in herself. This inner marriage is the true *coniunctio*. The bridge to the future, headed toward me in Tray 1, is now headed away from where I was seated, and away from me.

Christina stopped therapy for seven years. In our first two years together, she did a tremendous amount of inner work. Six months into her therapy with me she said, "I've always 'reacted' to everything everyone said or did; now I'm starting to get outside myself." Ten months into our work together, after a meeting of her women's group, she remarked, "It feels

Tray 6. Neural Integration

so different! Before, I was full of anger and rage! Now I'm calmer and more in control." And after one of the many breakups with her boyfriend, Joe, she said, "This is the first time in my life I've ended a relationship on a good note."

Reflections on Phase I of Christina's Sandplay Process

In Phase I, Christina lived out the *nigredo* through her reactivity, rage, anger, and undifferentiated feeling. Evidence of the *nigredo* in the sand is seen literally in the blasted tree, the pewter figures as archetypal defenses against feeling, and in the lack of blue (water) in Trays 1, 2, 3, and 5. Evidence of the *albedo* in Phase I is found in the presence of her deep reflections on her life, in the water at the castle, in finding and connecting with the inner child Chrissie in Tray 4, and in establishing the beginnings of the Mother-Child unity with me.[144] This became evident when she told me shyly one day that she wanted to "crawl into my womb."

During the seven years that she was gone, Christina married her boyfriend Joe two years after she left therapy; she put herself through graduate school and completed an advanced degree in the helping professions; and through her intelligence, industriousness, and ambition, began a highly successful career. We will look at Christina's sandplay, "Phase II: *Albedo* to *Rubedo* Consciousness" at the end of the next chapter.

Rosa · Alba

Albū trans

survura

pa̅ ꝑfecta

mine̅ra

Melius qua̅̅ nͦ

Elix̄ album

Andrei ꝑs

argͭ

Calbate latone. et reponite libros Arnoldꝰ
...ne corda vr̅a corrūpa̅t̅ qz res nr̅a le̅uis est
et leue indiget subsidio q̅m dealbauit me · ille
faciet me rube̅ ꞇ Albū et rube̅ ex ȳna radice ꝑ
cedit Quod fit in albo · fit in rubeo Arnoldus
Gitur fili ph̅ice oparis et dealbas · et minu
In ipo ꝉpe transce̅dis Beatꝰ eris Hoc si su
bito videris · admi̅ratio timor et terror tibi eueiet
Oque ta̅re reitera et ne tedeat te Speculū
reiterare. quia̅us totū opꝰ sit longiqui · qz
ꝑ longa decoctȯez fit �̅ꝺ Speculū

CHAPTER 3

White—The *Albedo*

A PASSAGE IN THE *Bibliotheca Chemica Curiosa* says, "the color black is succeeded by the white." In alchemical texts the white phase was called by many names: the *albedo* (Latin for "whiteness") or *dealabatio* (Latin for "whitening"), the *tinctura alba* ("white tincture"), the *femina alba* ("white woman" or "white queen"), the white rose (opposite page), white swan, white dove, *luna* ("the moon"), *anima* ("soul"), Venus, Sophia, *terra alba foliata* ("white foliated earth"), *lapis albus* ("white lapis" or "white stone"). All are feminine terms, pointing to the fact that from the beginning of alchemy, the color white was associated with the ancient feminine principle—also associated with the moist (as water, falling dew, "mercurial water," the sea, sea water, the ocean, a "viscous subtle fluid," and humidity), the heavy, the cold, the metal silver, ash, and salt.

In the alchemical literature, passages such as the following convey something of the quality of the *albedo*. For example, in association with the moon, the alchemist Dorn says, "Luna is the counterpart of Sol, cold, moist, feebly shining

or dark [that is, as the hidden new moon], feminine, corporeal, passive . . . She is the sister and bride, mother and spouse of the sun."[145] And in the Rosarium: "this luna is the sap of the water of life, which is hidden."[146]

Zosimos and the Alexandrians of the third century CE called this feminine principle "animated Quicksilver."[147] Because quicksilver is silvery-white and can turn other substances, especially copper, white, the alchemists associated the color white with mercury (another name for quicksilver) and with the metal silver.

Another association to the *albedo* is with ash. Stephanos of Alexandria writes: "If you see the All becoming ash, know that it has been well prepared. For the ash is full of power and virtue."[148] In *De Chemia*, Senior says, "The white foliated earth is the crown of victory, which is ash extracted from ash."[149] Jung explains ash as "the calcined and annealed substance, freed from all decomposition."[150] That is, the impurities of the *nigredo* have been burned away, and what remains is ash. Senior, in the same passage of *De Chemia*, tells us to

"Sow the gold in the white foliated earth." This curious phrase is interpreted by Hillman to mean, "Inside the silvered ['*albedo* conscious'] mind, let the sun ['*rubedo* consciousness'] shine in."[151] Ash appears in my dreams.

Regarding salt, Jung notes the following: "Salt as much as ash is a quality of the *albedo* and, according to Mylius, is identical with 'the white stone, the white sun, the full moon, the fruitful white earth, cleansed and calcined.'"[152] For Jung, alchemical salt refers to feelings and to Eros.[153] For other properties of salt as the arcane substance, I refer the reader to Jung's *Mysterium Coniunctionis*.[154] James Hillman, in his essay "Salt: A Chapter in Alchemical Psychology," elucidates alchemical salt's more psychological aspects: salt is "sharp, stinging, acute, burning in on itself with wit and bite, corrosive acrimony, self-accusation and self-purification."[155] To Hillman, salt is the "ground of subjectivity"; "its nature is to fixate, correct, crystallize and purify"; in this sense salt is "holy, cleansing and bitter,"[156] but taken to extremes "becomes puritanism, fanaticism and terrorism."[157]

The *albedo* stage is also associated with dismemberment and a death-like state, as seen in this illustration and text from the Sixth Parable of *Splendor Solis*:

Rosinos relates of a vision he had of a man whose body was dead and yet beautiful and white like Salt. The Head had a fine Golden appearance, but was cut off at the trunk, and so were all the limbs; next to him stood an ugly man of black and cruel countenance, with a blood-stained double-edged sword in his right hand, and he was the good man's murderer. In his left hand was a paper on which the following was written: *I have killed thee, that thou mayest receive a super-abundant life, but thy head I will carefully hide, that the worldly wantons may not find thee, and destroy the earth, and thy body I will bury, that it may putrefy, and grow and bear innumerable fruit.*

Figure 11. Dismemberment
(*Splendor Solis,* folio 20)

The gruesome plate shown in Figure 11 is descriptive of the psyche during the *albedo* phase. Carrying over from the *nigredo*, analysis continues to feel like a real torture, a dismemberment, or a "coming apart at the seams." In a dream presaging this period in my analysis, *I saw, lying on a sidewalk, a disembodied man's head (still alive),* and later dreamed *that a woman who swam in a swimming pool with a whale* (the energies of the Self) *was decapitated.*

The association of death with the *albedo* phase is described in this magnificent passage on the *albedo* by the English theologian and alchemist John Pordage, a pupil of Boehme:

> Therefore, if the human will is given over and left, and becomes patient and still and as a dead nothing, the Tincture will do and effect everything in us and for us, if we can keep our thoughts, movements, and imaginations still, or can leave off and rest. But how difficult, hard, and bitter this work appears to the human will, before it can be brought to this shape, so that it remains still and calm even though all fire be let loose in its sight, and all manner of temptations assail it![158]

This passage reminds me of Evelyn de Morgan's painting *SOS* (Figure 12), illustrating that *albedo* consciousness is yielding, receptive, Yin. However, yielding does not mean passively falling victim; it means allowing, receiving, taking in, not fighting against. This actually takes a great deal of strength—like a Taekwondo master who is yielding but powerful.

Later in this same passage quoted above, Pordage goes on to say:

> The artist must wait until he sees the Tincture covered over with its other colour, as with the whitest white, which he may expect to see after long patience and stillness, and which truly appears when the Tincture rises up in the lunar quality: illustrious Luna imparts a

Figure 12. Evelyn de Morgan, *SOS*

beautiful white to the Tincture, the most perfect white hue and a brilliant splendour . . . This is the . . . water, blood, and heavenly dew of the Divine Virgin Sophia, . . . made white and pure, like brilliantly polished silver. And all uncleanliness of the blackness, all death, hell, curse, wrath, and all poisons which rise up out of the qualities of Saturn, Mercury, and Mars are separated and depart, wherefore they call it their separation, and when the Tincture attains its whiteness and brilliance in Venus and Luna they call it their sanctification, their purification and making white.[159]

The rapturous quality of this passage conveys the quality of the *albedo* as if it were the final goal of the opus. As Jung says, "The *albedo* was highly prized . . . by many alchemists as if it were the main goal."[160] In this passage, Venus and the Divine Virgin Sophia are images of Pordage's *anima* (soul). Jung notes that the alchemists often called the *anima* the *anima mundi*, the soul of the world, which they believed was imprisoned in matter. The goal of the opus was to free the *anima* (soul) from her state of imprisonment in matter. This soul was set free by means of washing (*ablutio, baptisma*) or cooking.[161]

This washing is not just physical; it's symbolic of cleansing and purification. According to Marie-Louise von Franz, "The *Nigredo*—the blackness, the terrible depression and state of dissolution—has to be compensated by the hard work of the alchemist and that hard work consists, among other things, in constant washing."[162]

Edinger defines the washing, ablution, or baptism in psychological terms:

> Baptism is basically a purification ritual that washes one clean of dirt, both literal and spiritual . . . Psychologically, the dirt or sin that is washed away by baptism can be understood as unconsciousness, shadow qualities of which one is unaware. Psychological cleanliness means not literal purity, but awareness of one's own dirt. If one is psychologically clean, one will not contaminate one's environment with shadow projections.[163]

Cooking is another image belonging to the *albedo*, often found in the dreams of individuals in therapy. In Michael Maier's *Atalanta Fugiens* we read: "When you have obtained the white lead, then do women's work, that is to say: COOK."[164] What is being "cooked" in therapy is the indigestible raw material of the unconscious into something digestible to the ego.

Using the alchemical imagery of the moon, Jung describes the *albedo* in metaphorical terms:

> [After the *nigredo*] the situation is gradually illuminated as is a dark night by the rising moon. The illumination comes to a certain extent from the unconscious, since it is mainly dreams that put us on the track of enlightenment. This dawning light corresponds to the *albedo*, the moonlight, which in the opinion of some alchemists heralds the rising sun.[165]

This gradually dawning light Jung likens to "daybreak," but he says, "not 'till the *rubedo* is it sunrise."[166]

Erich Neumann's essay "On the Moon and Matriarchal Consciousness" is a superb description of the *albedo* stage in psychological terms. "Matriarchal Consciousness" or "Moon (Lunar) Consciousness" describes not only a stage in the historical development of human consciousness, but also a psychological stage (that is, the type of consciousness experienced during the *albedo* phase of therapy), a religion, or a neurosis, and it can exist in men as well as women.[167]

Neumann calls this "the phase in which ego-consciousness is still child-like, . . . dependent in its relation to the unconscious . . . possessing no free, independent activity of its own; it waits passively, attuned to the spirit impulse carried toward it by the unconscious . . . In other words, it is dependent upon mood, upon harmony with the unconscious."[168] This he likens to a "psychic situation in which the unconscious [the *albedo*] is dominant, and consciousness [the *rubedo*] has not yet reached self-reliance and independence."[169] This situation is never divorced from the unconscious, for he says, "it is a phase, a spiritual phase, of the unconscious itself."[170]

Neumann likens what emerges from the unconscious, "when, where, and how it will" to the act of conceiving, pregnancy, and birth: "It must wait for time to ripen, while with time, like sown seed, comprehension ripens too."[171] He continues:

Only when the time is "fulfilled" does understanding come as an illumination. Similarly, in woman's primal mysteries, in boiling, baking, fermenting, and roasting, the ripening and "getting done," the transformation, is always connected with a period of waiting. The ego of matriarchal consciousness is used to keeping still till the time is favorable, till the process is complete, till the fruit of the moon-tree has ripened into a full moon; that is, till comprehension has been born out of the unconscious.[172]

Here Neumann makes a distinction between patriarchal and matriarchal consciousness. For matriarchal consciousness, understanding is not an act of the intellect; rather, it has the meaning of a "conception" that must first "enter" matriarchal consciousness "in the full, sexual, symbolic meaning of a fructification" and then "come forth" like "a seed which has sprouted."[173]

This . . . involves the whole psyche, which is now permeated through and through with the full-grown perception that it must realize, must make real, with its full self, This means that the conceiving and understanding have brought about a personality change. The new content has seized and stirred the whole being.[174]

Neumann says this "understanding" means "realizing," "to 'bear,' to bring to birth; it means submitting to a mutual relation and interaction like that of the mother and the embryo in pregnancy."[175] This is why the alchemist's *curcurbit*, or retort, is so often referred to as "mother" or "womb."

The moment of conception is veiled and mysterious . . . without any awareness on the part of the head-ego; . . . growth needs stillness and invisibility, not loudness and light. . . it is in the cool reflected light of the moon, when the darkness of unconsciousness is at the full, that the creative process fulfills itself; the night, not the day, is the time of procreation. It wants darkness and quiet, secrecy, muteness, and hiddenness.[176]

This describes, also, the analytic hour. In this respect, Neumann thinks matriarchal consciousness is more concrete, closer to actual life, in the heart rather than the head.[177]

He says it is essential to bear in mind that the processes of matriarchal consciousness "have their relation to an ego and can therefore not be described as unconscious."[178] Further, "The comparative passivity of matriarchal consciousness is not due to any incapacity for action, but rather to an awareness of subjection to a process in which it can 'do' nothing, but can only 'let happen.'"[179] It is more interested in the meaningful than in facts and dates; it is oriented teleologically to organic growth rather than to mechanical or logical causation.

Neumann makes an important point about psychotherapy and inner change:

Since the process of cognition is a pregnancy and its product a birth…its "knowledge" cannot be imparted, accounted for or proved. It is an inner possession, realized and assimilated by the personality but not easily discussed, for the inner experience behind it is scarcely capable of adequate verbal expression and can hardly be transmitted to anyone who has not undergone the same experience.[180]

For this reason, he says, simple masculine consciousness finds this "knowledge" of matriarchal consciousness "unverifiable, willful, and … mystic … It is the same kind of knowledge," he says, "which is revealed in the true mysteries and in mysticism; it consists not of imparted truths but of experienced transformations, and so necessarily has validity only for people who have passed through a similar experience."[181]

The moon-spirit bestows culture, too. From the "watery depths" come prophecy, poetry, wisdom, and immortality.[182] This wisdom, he says,

is a wisdom that is bound and stays bound to the earth, to organic growth, to ancestral experience. It is the wisdom of the unconscious, of the instincts, of life, and of relationship bound to fate, and to living reality. Its illusion-less view of actuality may shock an idealistic, masculine mentality, yet it is related to this actuality as nourisher, helper, comforter, and lover, and leads it beyond death to ever-renewed transformation and rebirth. The moon-wisdom of waiting, accepting, ripening, admits everything into its totality and transforms it, and along with it, its own being. It is always concerned with wholeness, with shaping and realizing, that is, with the creative. [183]

But Neumann points out the dangers inherent in matriarchal consciousness. It can be unaware of being dominated by the unconscious. Inner realization can get concretized in outer reality, so that no transformation is possible. In both an historical and personal context, Neumann is right when he says:

When mankind is forced to come to patriarchal consciousness and to break with the unconscious, matriarchal conscious-ness . . . becomes something negative . . . the spirit of regression . . . the terrible mother . . . a witch . . . This negative moon [becomes] . . . a symbol of the devouring unconscious. Especially as the dark moon, it becomes the blood sucker, the child-murderer, the eater of human flesh; it symbolizes the danger of inunda-tion by the unconscious, of moodiness, lunacy, and madness.[184]

Neumann then points to the positive value of matriarchal consciousness:

Moon-consciousness or matriarchal conscious-ness is creative and productive at the beginning and end. Moonlight is the first light to illumine the dark world of the unconscious, whence it is born and to which it remains bound; and all things that are child-like, growing, creative, and feminine remain faithful to their relation to the moon-spirit.

But as development goes on, that which was a progression out from the unconscious comes to be a holding fast to unconsciousness. Only in later periods of development when patriarchy has fulfilled itself or gone to absurd lengths, losing its connection with Mother Earth, does individuation bring about a reversal.[185]

The "matriarchal consciousness," or "Lunar consciousness," which Neumann elucidates so brilliantly, is also an accurate description of the *albedo* stage of therapy. Men as well as women need to experience this *albedo* or "lunar" side of their natures in order to experience wholeness.

For other examples of the psychological meaning of the *albedo* I turn to scholars of alchemy, to modern poets, and to writers. Hitchcock thought the whitened state meant "purified affections."[186] For Silberer, the white symbolized "the wise man who knows how to resist all seduction."[187] However quaint, simplistic, or puritanical Hitchcock's and Silberer's ideas may sound, freedom from compulsion rather than "purity" in the puri-tanical sense may be what they were trying to express. Hillman warns that the white of the *albedo* is not the white of naïveté and inno-cence, but is, rather, a quality of being or feeling that characterizes the *albedo* stage in analysis:

This *albedo* whiteness, achieved after the soul's long exile in *nigredo*, must be distinguished from the primary white of the materia prima, the candida of innocence . . . In analysis, this *albedo* whiteness refers to feelings of positive syntonic transference, of things going easily and smoothly, a gentle sweet safety in the vessel, insights rising, synchronistic connec-tions, resonances and echoes, the dead alive on the moon as ancestors who speak with internal voices of the activated imagination—all leading to the invulnerable conviction of the primacy of psychic reality as another world apart from this world, life lived in psychological faith. In this tepid and shadowless lunar light, every-thing seems to fit . . . The mind in *albedo* more likely dreams. Receptive, impressionable, imag-istic, self-reflective and perhaps comfortably magical … No problems, except the vast generalized abstractions of spirit—for spirit and soul are unified.[188]

An aspect of the *albedo* emphasized by Hillman is "the primacy of psychic reality as another world apart from this world." T. S. Eliot says the same thing in "Burnt Norton":

> At the still point of the turning world.
>   Neither flesh nor fleshless;
> Neither from nor towards; at the still
>   point, there the dance is,
> But neither arrest nor movement. And do
>   not call it fixity,
> where past and future are gathered.
>   Neither movement from nor towards,
> Neither ascent nor decline. Except for the
>   point, the still point,
> There would be no dance, and there is only
>   the dance.
> I can only say, there we have been: but I
>   cannot say where.
> And I cannot say, how long, for that is to
>   place it in time.
> The inner freedom from the practical
>   desire,
> The release from action and suffering,
>   release from the inner
> And the outer compulsion, yet
>   surrounded
> By a grace of sense, and a white light still
>   and moving.[189]

In these lines T. S. Eliot has captured the quality of the *albedo*—a kind of empty space in a teeming universe, more easily described by what it is not than by what it is: the still point, time out of time. For those used to a life of action and conscious reason, the initial psychological impact of the *albedo* can come as a shock. Jack London describes this experience in "The White Silence":

> Nature has many tricks wherewith she convinces man of his finity—the ceaseless flow of the tides, the fury of the storm, the shock of the earthquake, the long roll of heaven's artillery—but the most tremendous, the most stupefying of all is the passive phase of the White Silence. All movement ceases, the sky clears, the heavens are as brass; the slightest whisper seems sacrilege and man becomes timid, affrighted at the sound of his own voice. Sole speck of life journeying across the ghostly washes of a dead world, he trembles at his audacity, realizes that his is a maggot's life, nothing more. Strange thoughts arise unsummoned, and the mystery of all things strives for utterance. And fear of death, of God, of the universe comes over him—the hope of the resurrection and the life, the yearning for immortality, the vain striving of the imprisoned essence—it is there, if ever, man walks alone with God.[190]

It is clear from this passage that London had been gripped by the numinous experience of the unconscious; in it are echoes of Pordage's words: "the human will . . . becomes patient and still and as a dead nothing." James Kirsch describes this *lunar* side of London's soul as the "non-rational quality of the Unconscious," warning that "We cannot afford to maintain an attitude of contempt, hostility or loathing against the . . . non-rational quality of the Unconscious. We would do better to accept it as it is, a world of images and of mysterious life."[191]

Stephen Martin, describing the *albedo* phase in therapy, carries this idea further. He says *albedo* consciousness creates a shift away from the fiery instinctuality and "unconscious acting out or acting in" of *nigredo* impulses, toward a recognition of the symbolic meaning concealed within them. During the *albedo* phase, he says, "proto-imagery takes shape; . . . these images are healing, and the interaction with them permits the patient to achieve a vital sense of psychological interiority." This, in turn, leads to what he calls the creation of "symbolic consciousness . . . By embracing and integrating the compellingly real imagery, whether through dream, fantasy, thought or idea . . . isolation gives way to erotic relatedness, first between patient and analyst, then between patient and self."[192] Finally, the *albedo* words, "to remain still, wait, hold, sense, rest," from a poem read at Marion Woodman's memorial, capture the essence of her lifelong work with the wounded feminine in Western culture.[193]

In cross-cultural comparisons, we find parallels to the alchemical white. For instance, in Hindu Tantric art and philosophy, white is the still point, "the nucleus of Being."[194]

In the American Navaho tradition, white is the moon's color in sand paintings and the color of the Spirit Land (that is, the land of the dead).[195] White in Slavic lands and Asia is associated with the absolute stillness of death and mourning and with birth to the new life beyond.[196] Similarly, in Christianity, the priest's white linen robe is the garment of death, first communion, and baptism.[197] And in Buddhist doctrine, the White Tara is "the highest spiritual transformation through womanhood, she who leads out beyond the darkness of bondage," the Mother of all Buddhas.[198]

The color white in alchemy was associated with the moon, the metal silver, the element water, with dew, ablution, baptism, salt, ash, white earth, and with images such as the white swan, white rose, white lily, white woman, a girl clad in white, luna, Venus, Sophia, and so on. The white of the *albedo* was also associated with the activities of cooking, baking, and washing, and with the quality of patient stillness and waiting—all qualities associated with the archetypal feminine principle—applicable to both men and women.

In psychological terms, the quality or essence of the *albedo* is difficult to capture. It has been referred to as "an abstract, ideal state . . . reflecting the primacy of psychic reality" as opposed to outer reality. It is nonrational; it meditates, dreams, and prophesies. Existentially, it is experienced as mysterious, ghostly, silent, still; as "deadness," and as a sense of our smallness and utter aloneness in the universe. However, within the principle of waiting and keeping still, a conceiving and ripening is taking place, so that what may emerge is prophecy, poetry, music, dance, and the wisdom of the instincts, the heart and the body, and release from inner and outer compulsions.

Although many alchemists believed the achievement of the *albedo* was the "crown of victory," the final goal of the opus, as described so poetically by John Pordage, Jung reminds us that it is not: "In this state of 'whiteness' one does not live in the true sense of the word . . . In order to make it come alive it must have 'blood'; it must have what the alchemists call the *rubedo*."[199] Hillman argues that the bridge to the *rubedo* is via the yellow, *citrinitas*. But first, let us look at dreams and sandplay characterizing the *albedo* phase.

WHITE DREAMS

During the *albedo* stage of my analysis, I was enthralled with my dreams (recording three to five dreams a night, many very long) and with my analysis (which increased from one to three times a week). I was so absorbed with my inner world I couldn't wait for my next analytical appointment. During this time, pursuing anything in the outside world paled in comparison with what was happening in my inner world.

The content of my white dreams is more varied than the other categories, although many white dreams contain *albedo* imagery strikingly similar to the alchemical images.

The shift in color from black to white and the change of quality in the white as it progresses is expressed perfectly by the anonymous author of *An Open Entrance to the Closed Palace of the King*: "the body that has to be cleansed is intensely black. While it passes from blackness to whiteness, . . . [it is not] at once perfectly white; at first it is simply white—afterwards it is of a dazzling snowy splendour."[200]

In sharp contrast to the utter blackness of the *nigredo* dreams, my early white dreams are the pre-*albedo* white of innocence and naïveté. Later white dreams herald the dazzling white of the true *albedo*. With white dreams also, there is a progression from negative to highly positive content.

Importantly, my initial "black" dream (November 5, 1974) was also an initial "white" dream. The sand on which I stood was white; that is, my initial conscious standpoint was white. But this is not the white of the true *albedo*; it appears closer to the pre-*albedo* candida of naïveté, purity, or innocence of which Hillman warns.

The following dream, one year after the beginning of therapy, is a classic *albedo* dream of death and rebirth.

July 14, 1978. DEATH MARRIAGE. I am on an island. After many adventures I find myself in a tunnel next to a little man. As we are about to leave the tunnel, his relatives arrive and torture us (mainly him) for days, until he is exhausted and ready to die. For some reason I was chosen to watch over him, even though there was nothing I could do to prevent the torture or aid him. It was terrifying. Those relatives kept jumping at us, threatening us with knives and daggers, and choking us with dust. I wanted to run and hide, but I couldn't. At the moment he is ready to die, suddenly white-haired although his skin is still young, we are taken out of our torture-chamber and led to a little room, where my companion goes through some kind of rite before he dies. His left hand is pricked, blood oozes out, and suddenly he comes over and presses that hand against mine. He has chosen me in marriage, after which we will both go to our deaths. It is a solemn and sacred ritual. I am not sure I am ready for it, but as we are walking along, surrounded by all the relatives and tribespeople, there is an air of festivity and great rejoicing. I join in the mood, skipping and dancing along. We enter the church to be married and the next thing I know, we are outside. I feel my head and notice a crown with white lace on it.

Here, my tortured inner masculine has suddenly become white-haired, close to death; he has chosen me in a marriage sealed by (red) blood, after which we will both go to our deaths. In alchemical terms, when white Lunar mercury and red Solar sulfur unite before their impurities have been burned away, the result is a mortificatio. Psychologically, a premature *coniunctio* or coupling is always mortifying—an experience that feels like death.[201] Paradoxically, the death-marriage procession is joyous because this ritual death also holds the possibility of rebirth. The white of the tortured man's hair later reappears as a crown of white lace on my head—a good prognosis for the transformation of my negative inner masculine. But first the two must die.

This dream bears a striking resemblance to the archetypal marriage-death-and-rebirth motif of the *Rosarium Philosophorum* series, and to its alchemical text, in which the white and the red, Sol and Luna, are conjoined and then must give up their lives for the sake of their royal son (the Self).[202] Figures 7 and 20 in this book and the sixth plate in the *Rosarium* series illustrate this motif. This dream of the premature *coniunctio* is an example of white and red in their raw, unrefined form. The true white of the *albedo* is still to come.

November 22, 1979. LOOKING FOR A SPECIAL SEASHELL. I am with a group of people dividing up the property. I receive some seashells, but the one that is most important to me, a small, round pearly, silky-soft, and satin-smooth white one is not among them. I am looking for it and know it's around but cannot find it.

The quality of the seashell in this dream is like a pearl, akin to the Chinese Pearl of Great Price, or Pearl of Wisdom. The dream infers that I am looking for something representing true *albedo* consciousness (that is, my own true femininity) but have not yet found it.

June 13, 1980. IMPRISONED SWAN IN PLASTER-OF-PARIS POT. I am in a garden or park. A gardener has been planting things in pots. I notice a flower in a basket.

As I look closer, I realize it is not a flower at all, but a long-necked white bird (a swan?) disguised as a flower. Its head is hidden by the head of the flower, and its body is hidden under a plaster-of-Paris mold, used to anchor the bird in the basket. The only part of the bird I see is its neck. Then it moves, rising up out of the basket and making small attempts to fly. But it is heavily weighted down by the plaster-of-Paris ring around its neck. Twice it rises up, making efforts to fly, as if trying to show me or tell me something.

The bird in this dream is a part of my own nature, trying to break free, to "fly." But it is so weighted down or imprisoned by the plaster-of-Paris mold (that is, by social or collective "convention") that it can hardly move, much less fly.

This dream has its direct corollary in alchemy, whose aim or goal was to free the anima mundi or soul of the world, which the alchemists believed was imprisoned or enchained in matter. It is also reminiscent of Jack London's "vain striving of the imprisoned essence."203 So the albedo is a death-like or pupa-like state, as if the soul were waiting to be born, or, as Richard Tarnas says, "Who we are before we even think about who we are."204

June 25, 1980. *WHITE MICE. I hear mice chewing away at a wall. I peek down a tube of fabric and see two tiny white mice. I find D-con and sprinkle it down the hole. Later when I come back to inspect, I notice the corpses of two large white mice, then in another spot, see a dozen or more corpses of mice, rats, even rabbits, all white, all eerily "frozen," as if in mid-track.*

I spot and try to poison what I infer are the rodents that have been chewing away at the walls of my defenses. The helpful little white creatures become "corpses." But unlike *nigredo* imagery, they are neither black, nor are they even dead, just temporarily "frozen" in mid-track, similar to the *albedo* imagery of waiting and keeping still.

The following poem from my journal, with its frozen white landscape, is similar in feeling-tone to the eerily "frozen" mice in the dream:

January 17, 1981

"Fallow Field"
fallow field
 barren
  empty
 mute
icy winds gust, howl over you,
 ragged,
 jagged
where is the warmth
 of sun rays and shiny days
  the gentle wind of yestermonth?
tender days are gone, lost
 to lonely winter white
 night—is there no end?
pale moon glow
 distant on cold snow
  hoary hide
 covers a deeper dark
  blacker night
  smell of rot, decay
where is the light?

```
    seek not
spring has its own season
    reason why
curse not the sacred
    now eternal
        waiting
    waiting
regenerating
```

My poem is an apt metaphor for the early feeling state of the *albedo*: barren, empty, mute. The setting is night, moonlight on cold snow; the feeling, one of barren loneliness and eternal waiting. Although we think of death, rot, and decay as a *nigredo* experience, von Franz reminds us that the difficulties continue into the next stage: "In alchemical literature, it is generally said that the great effort and trouble continues from the *nigredo* into the *albedo*; that is . . . the hard part, and afterwards everything becomes easier."[205] The white snow covers the blackness and putrefaction of the *nigredo*. However, like the gushing oil of the earlier *nigredo* dream, the rotting, decaying earth becomes the fertile soil of regeneration from which the flowers of Spring (the *rubedo*) may emerge. This poem reminds me of the passage in "The White Silence" by Jack London, with its frozen white landscape and eerie silence—our subjective experience of the *albedo* when the reality of the unconscious first strikes with full power, as it does in the following dream:

August 26, 1980. *WHITE/SILVER OBJECTS. Dazzling sequence of white or silver objects:*

First: *a white container, such as the one I use as a planter*

Second: *a bunch of carrots, which are silver-white*

Third: *a white unicorn.*

This archetypal dream *appeared just two months after the "White Mice" dream. The color of the objects is not just white, it is dazzlingly white, heralding the true albedo. Objects not usually white have become white, as is the unicorn. Symbolically, a container is a feminine vessel: perhaps simply a planter in which to plant the seeds of future growth, or perhaps it is the analytic container, the temenos, which "holds" the client's emerging material during the important albedo stage of the work. The silver-white carrots are a strange image; are they the promise on the end of a stick that draws the unicorn forward into unknown psychic territory?*

In alchemy, the unicorn was related to the lunar feminine principle (the solar lion its male counterpart). Although the principal color of the unicorn is white, it is interesting to note that a Greek fifth-century BCE historian describes the unicorn's horn in the alchemical colors black, white, and red.[206] In Greco-Roman symbolism, the unicorn was an attribute of all virgin moon goddesses, especially Artemis/Diana, the goddess with which I most identify. Thus, what is emerging appears to have something to do with a lunar feminine consciousness within me.

On the other hand, in Christian iconography, the unicorn was associated with chastity, purity, virginity, and perfect good, images of both Mary and Christ.[207] In the famous unicorn tapestries in the Cluny Museum in Paris, the unicorn, as a symbol of Christ, is sacrificed. What is being sacrificed in analytic work at this point is my too white need to maintain an appearance as perfectly good, chaste, pure, naïve, and innocent. Thus, the unicorn in the dream may represent both death and resurrection or rebirth.

The *dazzling* white of the unicorn, carrots, and container appears again in the following three dreams spaced just a week apart:

January 28, 1981. *SUBMARINE CHAMBER. I leave a party. As I walk across the lawn, a vicious black dog races out at me, snapping and snarling. Just before he reaches me, I haul myself over a fence and enter my car, a white Ford. There are two keys like safe-deposit keys in the door. As I enter the car the pale blue interior becomes a white chamber. Sunlight is flooding down into it. I climb down a ladder to get in; when I get down inside, I feel as if I am floating in water. At the far end of the chamber, above the water, the air is stale, so I go back to the entrance where the air is fresh.*

In this dream, a vicious black dog of the *nigredo* (that is, my fierce negative mother and/or father complex) is still "hounding" me. I flee to the old family car—which I drove after college. Paradoxically, the safe-deposit-like or submarine-like white chamber of the car is also a classic image for the analytic container or *temenos* during the *albedo* stage of the work: a safe place in which I could feel contained and suspended in time, as if floating, in order to work on my unconscious—from which I am trying to flee. If we are too oblivious of our

shadow, the *nigredo* lies in wait, ready to pull dreamy *albedo* consciousness back into the unconscious.

January 30, 1981. *DAZZLING WHITE MANSION. I am headed for a dazzling white mansion on a hill, but the path on which I am riding my bicycle leads into a lake and starts getting deeper. I try to keep the bike up, but I sink down. For a moment I am afraid I will submerge, but on my left appears a telephone pole with a shelf to stand on.*

February 4, 1981. *DAZZLING WHITE KITCHEN. I see a woman (the recently deceased mother of a friend of mine) standing in a kitchen softly singing a Swedish folk song to herself while she scrubs, first the floor, walls, and ceiling of the kitchen, and later the room adjacent to the kitchen. I am surprised that both rooms are dazzling white, without another speck of color in them.*

The "dazzling" bright white light flooding my consciousness in all three dreams is an image of the archetypal light, symbolizing perhaps growing consciousness and hope—in stark contrast to the absence of light characterizing the *nigredo*. These dreams also contain water-imagery, a symbol of the unconscious, also associated with the *albedo*. In two dreams, I am floating or about to be submerged; in the third, the scrubwoman is washing (another *albedo* activity). The fact that the scrubwoman was no longer living gives her a ghost-like quality. These images of ghosts and floating are reminiscent of Dorn's image of spirit and soul floating upward, after they have left the body—suggesting that the *albedo* is a kind of disembodied consciousness—"the dead alive on the moon" as Hillman puts it.[208] As with the poem "Fallow Field," another of my poems, below, speaks to this theme of disembodied consciousness, death-like stillness, and eternal waiting:

February 1, 1982

> "Bardo. Tartarus. Acheron's Delta."
> Between life and death in no-life land
> Wander shades of pale gray
> No sun, no moon nor day nor night
> To break the endless gray of day
> No cloud, no storm, nor breath of air
> To fresh the stale atmosphere
> No bird, no beast, nor blade of grass
> To move the silent emptiness
> Prison of my soul,
> let wind blow/ light glow/ spirit grow/ life
> flow

These poems capture the essence of the *albedo* as a stage between the *nigredo* and the *rubedo*, to be found in the following dream as well:

February 2, 1982. *PROFESSIONAL MOURNERS?/ MIDWIVES? I am about to die or give birth. Two professional mourners or midwives come into my room, where I am lying in a bed, to help aid me through the process. The first one comes in wearing a long white gown. She looks like Mother Teresa, and after she enters, she stands near the wall saying,"Mea culpa, mea culpa; may you go quickly and well." Then the second woman enters, dressed the same, and she, too, starts chanting and praying.*

Death and gestation belong to the *albedo* stage, and what is born, to the *rubedo* stage. Although it is unclear whether I am dying or giving birth, typical of dreams touching the core wound or the core of the process when paradoxical opposites come together, I am more likely both dying *and* giving birth. The two white-robed women, either mourners or midwives, or more likely both mourner and midwife, are present to facilitate the passage. The two women pray and chant. The first woman's chant, "*Mea culpa,*" is puzzling. How could someone chanting "My fault," "I am to blame," or "The guilt is mine" be of help? Perhaps the first mourner, as a part of my own psyche, is taking responsibility for the pieces of myself that need to die before the second woman, as midwife, can aid in the birth. Both dying and giving birth can be slow, painful processes. However, both also hold the promise of joyful release—the promise of the new child (as the *rubedo*) to come.

Nine months later—the period of a full human gestation—I experienced a burst of *rubedo* dreams: "The Red-Headed Boy" (November 12, 1982); "The Red Figurine" (November 14, 1982); "The Red-Headed Man" (November 25, 1982). I will analyze those dreams in Chapter 5. Four months after these red dreams, the following *albedo* dream appeared:

March 30, 1983. *WHITE PEONY. From my own garden I have a large, multi-petaled white flower—a peony? Someone standing on my right is admiring it. I tap it to coax it open, and almost as if by magic it springs open into full bloom. It is so magnificent that there is a hushed* chorus of "Oohs!" as it opens. *The center of the flower is black, with a whole group of black stamens rising from its center. The black contrasts with the light white of the petals, which have veins of pink or rose running through them. I reverently show it to the several people near me who saw it open and came over.*

In Buddhism, the flower of the Self is a thousand-petaled white lotus—rising from the muck of the lily pond—in the center of which sits the Buddha, a symbol of the Self. The awe and magic that surround the opening of the large white peony in this dream herald it as something very special, perhaps the birth of the Self. Just as white is the color of illumination gained through suffering, and just as the Self contains the paradoxical opposites of dark and light, the peony's center contains the black of the *nigredo*. Its white petals, with veins of pink or rose, are whispers of the *rubedo* to come. One year later, another remarkable *albedo* dream appeared:

March 9, 1984. *OLD WHITE PLAYER PIANO. In a broad meadow overlooking the ocean several families have stored their belongings in what appear to be long, low sheds or shacks covered with plastic or tarps. The appearance of the scene is of an abandoned or neglected outdoor warehouse or junkyard. I have some connection with the family whose belongings are here. I don't know why I am here, except that there is something purposeful about my being here. I go in, not knowing what I will find, and come across a most unusual old white piano. It is an upright, square in shape. I put my fingers to the keys and play some notes. The sound that comes out is exquisite: pure, deep, resonant tones as rich and wonderful as those produced on a Stradivarius violin. I realize the richness and beauty of the tone is enhanced by the wood of which the piano is made: perhaps oak? I am enchanted with this piano. Not only is it an unusual color, but the decoration on it is unusual also: small, flowery, carved decoration and motifs around the oval window, almost baroque or rococo, as if the piano had come out of the seventeenth or eighteenth centuries. And when I begin to play it, I realize that it is practically playing itself, and that my part in it is miraculously effortless. Suddenly I realize that this is indeed the case; that what I have before me is an antique player-piano. As I look inside the oval window of this piano and let go of the keys, the piano begins to play in earnest. Although it is out of tune because it has been sitting unused for so long, the tone is magnificent, and the music being played is equally full, rich, and magnificent: classical music from a classical age. I am fascinated as I watch the inner workings of this piano producing its complex, rich harmonies, and realize that the music emerging from the piano is not autonomous; I can influence its course and sound by pressing pedals with my feet, and that in order for the music to continue, I must help out. Thus, there is a highly interactive quality between the piano and myself; I can influence the final sound of the music as much or as little as I choose. Although this piano is not originally mine, my deep absorption with it makes me feel as if it belongs to me and I belong to it. I cannot imagine it not being mine and resolve to make it so.*

Just as the alchemists said the Stone of the Philosophers (the alchemical gold) was to be found lying in the streets or on dung heaps, so, too, the piano is found in an abandoned, neglected junkyard. The degree of fascination, the sense of the miraculous or the magical surrounding the piano allude to the numinous quality of the Self, to which my ego, as I am playing the keys, plays a subordinate yet reciprocal role. This dream is a beautiful example of the relationship between ego and Self: neither is autonomous. Although the player piano can generate its own sound, it needs the attention and cooperation of the pianist, in a reciprocal dialogue and interaction. The newly opened white peony of a year earlier, here in the form of a piano, now comes into "full play."

Two more alchemical albedo dreams, this one nine months after the piano dream, are further developments of inner *albedo* consciousness.

December 12, 1984. *ASH-FILLED OVEN. A very small group of us need a place to meet or to do something or to live. The man in our group finds an abandoned church and during a time when the rest of the world is sleeping or not around, he takes us to the church. He has procured a huge old key to the church and takes it out to open the door as we climb the steps. Through some dark windows near the door I sense the presence of someone inside this old "abandoned" church and become frightened, but the man with us opens the door and in we go. Once we are inside, the "presence" rushes out of the shadows at us and closes the door behind us. I am startled and frightened, but the man is not out to harm us; he seems more like a guardian for the church, who doesn't want "just anybody off the street" coming in. He doesn't seem to mind our being here; in fact, he acts as if we were expected or welcome. We go in and explore, and toward the back of the building we come to a room through the doors of which I see a huge beehive-shaped stone or rock or brick oven—like the kind used to bake bread in ancient times.*

It is filled to the brim—even up into the chimney—with ashes, which I assume is normal. But when the man takes the boards off the vent, ashes fall out like so many forgotten items out of Fibber McGee's closet.[209] *I realize that it has been filled with ashes beyond its capacity, and it now needs to be cleaned out. Somehow cleaning it out seems important, and I take on the job to do it. I am holding a large plastic sack, almost as tall as I am, watching a thin stream of ashes flow into the sack, almost like a stream of water. I think at this rate it will take forever to empty out, but I feel a lot of energy and enthusiasm for getting the job accomplished and imagine taking shovels and carts and barrels and whatever we can find to get the job done. Then I am sitting and the ashes are on my lap. I run my fingers through the fine white ash and realize this, for the most part, is white oak ash, which is good for fertilizing the soil, and wonder where we could give it—especially this quantity—so that it can be put to good use.*

The setting of this dream—an old, abandoned church—is a spiritual place, a place of prayer, stressed by the alchemists as necessary to the progress of the opus. The fact that it's abandoned suggests I have not been attending to my spiritual life. The beehive-shaped oven inside the church building is astonishingly similar to the oven-like heating apparatus used by the alchemists (Figure 13). This oven is overflowing with ash, an alchemical substance associated with the *albedo* and with the alchemical operation called *calcinatio* or calcination, which has to do with fire and burning to ashes or powder. Perhaps now, eight years after therapy began, the bitter salt of tears and the fires of analysis have burned at the *nigredo* in my psyche until there is only ash left to clean out. I take it upon myself to empty the oven. "Ash extracted from ash is the crown of victory" proclaims Senior.[210] And Stephanos of Alexandria writes: "If you see the All becoming ash, know that it has been well prepared. For the ash is full of power and virtue."[211] As seen in earlier dreams with the black oil and the rotting soil, my unconscious wants to put the ash to good use. This would indicate that in psychological work, inner change creates the potential for generativity, for passing on the gift.

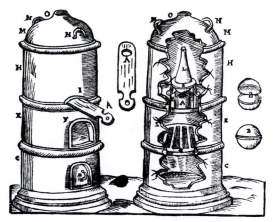

Figure 13. Alchemical Oven
(Allison Coudert, *Alchemy: The Philosopher's Stone*)

Four years later, to the day, another *albedo* dream appeared. In this dream, the body of the woman becomes a metaphor for the alchemical oven.

December 12, 1988. *ASCETIC WOMAN. On the white tiles of a bathroom floor, I see a woman lying on her back, naked. She is nothing but skin and bones, although she is also very much alive. When she breathes in, every organ in her body becomes plainly visible. I stand in fascination and awe before her. Is she a yogini?*

In Buddhist art one sometimes encounters the figure of the Fasting Buddha (Figure 14), all skin and bones, seated in the lotus position. The woman's body is remarkably similar to this image. She, too, is in a deeply interior world, reflective of the *albedo*'s quality of interiority, reflection, and stillness.

However, unlike the Buddha, the woman in the dream is lying naked and prone on the white tiles of a bathroom floor. Like the ashes in the alchemical oven, perhaps the inner impurities in her psychic body have emptied themselves out. Here the work of the alchemist Dorn comes to mind: the goal of the work is to establish a spiritual position "supraordinate to the turbulent sphere of the body,"

Figure 14. Fasting Buddha

so that "the affectivity and instinctuality of the body no longer has a disturbing influence on the rationality of the mind."[212] The dream appears to be a metaphor for this process. It is unfortunate that some individuals take this highly symbolic material literally. In extreme form it could become anorexia or fanaticism.

Reflections on the White Dreams

It is difficult to generalize on the basis of fifteen dreams and two poems. Nevertheless, the content of the selected white dreams clearly contains alchemical imagery: white associated with passive stillness, waiting, and death-as-frozen-life, or death-as-precursor-to-birth; water as snow, washing, immersion; and ashes. White is also the color of the new soul, free of the body. These images correlate highly with *albedo* imagery.

As with the black dreams, the content of the white dreams shows a movement from negative to highly positive, confirming the transformative nature of the opus. The white sand of my first dream, "Spiders" (1974), suggests that my conscious standpoint is the pre-*albedo* "white" of innocence and naïveté. "Death-Marriage" (1978) is a premature or lesser *coniunctio*. In it, my tortured inner masculine must die and is not seen again until the *rubedo*. In the remaining *albedo* dreams, content related to my feminine self emerges. The search for the "Special Seashell" (1979) may be a metaphor for what I have been looking for in myself—something softer and more natural than the dull, spiky jewelry of my earliest dreams. The "White Swan" as my feminine soul is imprisoned in matter and cannot fly. In the dreams of the "White Mice" (1980) and the poem "Fallow Field" (1981), movement is frozen; the world eerily still, deathlike. In "The Submarine Chamber" (1981) and the "Dazzling Mansion" (1981), I am submerged in the unconscious, but after the absence of light in the *nigredo*, dazzling white light floods my consciousness. White-robed Mourners/Midwives (1982) help something to die so that something new may be born. What is born is my feminine Self, my *anima*. The dream of the "White Peony" (1983) bursting into full bloom may be a description of the Self blossoming as inner strength and beauty, and the "Old White Player Piano" (1984) as inner and outer energies working in reciprocal harmony.

CHRISTINA'S SANDPLAY—PHASE II: ALBEDO TO RUBEDO CONSCIOUSNESS

After a seven-year absence, Christina returned to therapy for another five years. During Phase II she created twenty-one sandtrays, very different from her sandplay during Phase I. Here, we will look at nine trays. They span her psychological development from deep immersion in *albedo* consciousness to the gradual emergence of *rubedo* consciousness.

In the first session after her return, Christina told me that she had found some information online about her birthmother and had sent a letter to her via her birthmother's brother. The morning of our first appointment, she dreamed that she received a letter from her birthmother. The dream was prescient, for the very next day she received a message from her birthmother on her answering machine, saying she would like to talk to Christina. We were both amazed and thrilled. At long last, her birthmother was ready to make contact with the child she had left behind.

Tray 7. Lost Childhood and Innocence

One month later, however, Christina still hadn't heard anything from her birthmother. She said, "I'd love to do a sandtray today." Working silently, she carefully swept the sand aside to create a large lake. With the exception of the moat around the castle in Tray 4, this is the first time that Christina has opened up to the blue-as-water at the bottom of the tray. The meaning of the blue will become evident when we look at the meaning of the figures in this tray.

In the back-left corner stands a pregnant woman with two babies flanking her. Christina buried the two babies in the sand under the two crosses, saying, "These were my two abortions." I wondered if the buried babies might also be her inner infant self, "thrown away" twice by her birthmother (at birth and again now, with no contact).

At the back-right corner of the tray is a little girl with a flower, which Christina poignantly described as "My lost childhood and innocence." I wondered if this might also be her inner child Chrissie's loss of hope that her birthmother would call. Of the woman carrying the child she said, "That's me; this is what I wish for." I silently interpreted this not as a wish for a child of her own, but as a longing for her birthmother to call so she could be back in the tender, loving embrace and welcoming arms of her birthmother, or perhaps mine.

As she placed the birth-giving mother in the front right of the tray, she related two dreams she'd had about brown-skinned babies: in the

Tray 7. Lost Childhood and Innocence

first, *she's giving birth to a dark-skinned baby but says, "I'm not ready for it";* in the second, she says, *"I've given birth to a dark-skinned baby, but maybe the dark-skinned baby is the darkness in me I need to embrace."* So, with all these figures, we see Christina opening to her feelings of grief, hurt, loss, and abandonment.

These figures make clear that Christina's uncovering the lake in the center of the tray is an opening to her own depths—the well of her unconscious—and to her feelings. Of the whale in the water Christina said, "I *liked* it." The whale is a symbol of the Self. And in feeling her feelings as deeply as she is, she has formed a connection to the Self. The reader will recall my dream, presented in the section on the *nigredo*, of a woman swimming in a

pool with a whale. The woman is decapitated by the whale. To lose one's head means that the conscious dominant (that is, the dominance of the conscious ego) is lost; Christina is now in the world of the body, with all its feelings. The poignant sadness of this scene made me want to weep.

This tray represents a huge shift in her sandplay from the *nigredo* pewter of no-feeling and the unconscious acting-out of violence and rage, to the *albedo* world of deep interiority, connected to feelings. Her world is now much less defended. The pewter figures of the archetypal world have been exchanged for living human figures, carrying feelings of loss, grief, and death.

Christina was now willing to go deeper into

her mother issues of attachment and abandonment. The deep sadness, loneliness, rejection, and pain she felt regarding her birthmother's silence was mirrored in how she felt in her marriage, which came out in her next tray (not covered). I saw a parallel process between her birthmother's rejection of her and Christina's rejection of her husband.

Tray 8. "The Darkness in Me I Need to Embrace"

Three months later, still waiting for a call from her birthmother, Christina entered the therapy room and her eyes misted up. "It's sweet and sad to be with you again," she averred, "but then I feel myself suck it back in." This was another example of Kalsched's Protective Self-Care System, trying to protect her from getting too close to me, another mother figure, for fear I might hurt her the way her birthmother had hurt her in the past and was hurting her now by not calling. It was a call, heartbreakingly, that was never going to come.

Again, Christina hollowed out the sand to make a lake, smoothed it with a brush, and placed the birth-giving mother in the same place as the whale in Tray 7, saying, "Me, on my soul's journey." "The darkness in me I need to embrace," as she called it in Tray 7, is now front and center. Also front and center is a turtle in a shell. "You told me they birth themselves and make their own way to the sea," she recalled. Sadly, this thrice-abandoned, thrice-motherless child, feeling so alone and abandoned was being forced to birth herself and make her own way into life.

At the back of the tray behind the birth-giving woman lurks the ruling principle of the tray—the bad mother in many forms: A witch-mother mask, which she said represented her birthmother. In front of the mask lies a skeleton—perhaps the dying wish for her birthmother to call; to the left of the mask is Edvard Münch's *Silent Scream*: "How I feel," she said. To the right of the mask, she said, "The crouched-over figure feels like depression" (and also perhaps early maternal deprivation); the witch with a broom further to the left "was my adoptive step-mother, hard on the girls but easier on the boys; the old woman in the rocker behind her is the way I see her now; she's dying." The themes of death and what feels like endless waiting are also aspects of the *albedo*.

She asked herself, "Is there anything else related to feelings about my birthmother?" She picked up a volcano (her rage), placed it in the back-right corner of the tray, and partially buried it with the shovel, adding, "I'll just put it [the shovel] in the tray, too." The partially buried volcano and the shovel as a tool suggests that she is now better able to manage and control her rage instead of unconsciously acting it out.

Tray 8. "The Darkness in Me I Need to Embrace"

In the front-left corner stands a Day of the Dead couple, representing her marriage to Joe. Christina said Joe was like her adoptive father: passive, weak, depressed, and unable to commit. By contrast, she described herself as strong, controlling, dominant, and manipulative. She admitted, "My marriage is on the rocks. At home I am a rage-a-holic, engaging Joe in all-night battles." Again, the diagonal from the buried volcano to the Day of the Dead couple contains the polarities of buried rage at her birthmother and the acting out of her birthmother trauma with Joe.

"Divorce?" She asked. "I'll give it one year. If Joe can't change, then I'll divorce." She also said of her sex life that she was "Tired of always being the initiator" and that she and Joe had not been intimate for four months—the same length of time she had been back in therapy. Clearly, her energies had shifted from the outer world toward her inner world. Next to the Day

of the Dead couple she half-buried a pregnant woman, saying, "If I divorce at the age of forty, I will have less chance for a baby."

The group of figures in the center right of the tray—mostly hidden by the butterflies—relate to her early beginnings, seen in the Phase I trays: the drunk couple on a bench, "my adoptive parents"; the two cans of beer, "Very sweet! You found them!" (referring to the fact that seven years earlier, my sandplay figure collection lacked any bottles or cans of alcoholic beverages); a woman wearing a blue cape with stars "is kind of seductive"; and the pewter woman with open arms "is open and vulnerable; I'm not there yet."

The group of figures in the right-front corner of the tray are all images of the good mother. For example, Glinda, the good witch, whom she said, "is my aunt, a 'good mother,'" stands diagonally across from the bad witch-mother in the back-left corner of the tray; to her right, the woman holding the hands of the toddler "is my AA sponsor who showed me unconditional love. We're still friends." The seated little blond girl "is me now, more vulnerable." And the butterflies "are a symbol of transformation and change. How much I've changed and grown!" she exclaimed.

Two things are happening. In opening up to the blue waters of her unconscious, Christina is really beginning to feel at a deep level the pain, sadness, and rage at her rejection and abandonment. She is now feeling this more keenly with her husband as well. She is also beginning to feel and acknowledge her smallness and vulnerability, hallmarks of the albedo, and the beginnings of the Mother-Child unity espoused by Dora Kalff[213] The two pairs of diagonal opposites in the tray (buried versus acted-out rage and bad-mother versus good-mother) also suggest that she is now able to hold the opposites in consciousness—a large step on the journey toward psychological maturity.

Tray 9. Marital Conflict

For the next six months, Christina's trays focused on her unhappiness with her marriage. This tray was representative of many of them. In this session Christina was sad, saying, "Joe's parents are here; I'm pulling away from the caretaker role." She was angry at Joe's passive, depressed father who had been a poor role model for Joe. In one of her women's groups, she had cried through the whole check-in.

With a powerful sweep of her two hands, Christina opened up the sand in the center to blue in the shape of a perfect heart, but the shape is not complete. I would call it a half-hearted heart, which matched her mood. But the blue is the place where she can go down inside herself to meet shadow qualities. The alchemical *solutio* of tears or the dissolving of our defenses allows us to grieve to integrate our trauma. In the center of the lake she placed the same barren *nigredo* tree we

Tray 9, detail. **Silent Scream and Wounded** *Animus*

saw at the beginning of her sandplay process, and directly in front of it she placed the black figure crouched over in grief or despair. In the sand directly in front of the black figure, in exactly the spot where the point of the blue heart would be, she placed a Day of the Dead couple. Christina added nine snakes: four in

Tray 9. Marital Conflict

the water, four wound into the branches of the tree—as if it were the head of the Medusa—and a black snake, which she carefully wound around the death-marriage couple.

On the diagonal from the back-left corner to the front-right corner we see a man and a woman shooting at each other. At this stage of her development, to bring the masculine and feminine together would be death (the alchemical *mortificatio*). On the diagonal from the back-right corner to the front-left corner are two people on stretchers. In the outer world, both she and Joe were being wounded by the fighting, but Christina's own inner masculine and feminine were also wounded. They are, however, being cared for.

Hidden behind the black tree are two figures: a slumped-over nude male and

Münch's *Silent Scream*. Was the male Joe? I wondered. Or had she projected onto Joe her own wounded masculine? Christina's wounded *animus* arose because of the deep wounds to her feminine soul.

When she finished, I asked her with which figures she most identified. She said, "The shooters, the wounded, but the crouched-over figure is also me, and that tree is how I feel when I'm really down." This last admission was a startling reversal of her reference to this same black tree as "the Tree of Life" in her first tray. This suggests that she is now getting into her core wound and really feeling it.

The *nigredo* is seen in the reappearance of the all-black tree and the primitive reptilian snakes—creatures with little differentiation or feeling. But the *albedo* overshadows even the darkness of the *nigredo*, as seen in Christina's ability now to reach down into the blue well of her feelings and to suffer the outpouring of grief, anger, disappointment, and despair. Compared to previous trays, the opposites of her wounded masculine and wounded feminine show more differentiation. Her experiencing her wounded self is the key to bringing her inner masculine and inner feminine together.

Tray 10. Differentiation of *Anima* and *Animus*

On the left side of Tray 10 are a group of female figures; on the right, a group of male figures; and in the center of the tray, a dancing couple. The female figures include the smoker on the bench (her addict), her pewter Warrior Woman, a Zorro-like woman on horseback, Glinda the longed-for good mother, a peasant woman holding a child, a mother holding the hands of a toddler, the open-armed pewter woman, and a sunbathing woman. Christina said, "These women I know! They're very familiar to me!"

Of the group of male figures on the right side of the tray Christina said, "I don't know any of these! The men . . . [she hesitated] I don't know . . . " Her voice trailed off. Then she pointed to the tall, phallic male (which she mistook for a female figure in Tray 1), the drunk man, the pirate brandishing a sword, the red devil with horns, and the brown slumped-over male, and said, "This is the area of the rapist. The man holding a lamb and the man lying down is my adoptive father—gentle, nice, but passive, asleep. And the man out in front comes out of *GQ* [*Gentleman's Quarterly*

Magazine]. I picture him as a man in a suit, but at a party with a martini, a big ego and a trophy wife, who looks at porn at home."

In Tray 10, Christina is further differentiating her masculine and feminine sides. The female figures are internalized. She recognizes all of them as different aspects of herself. Her inner masculine, however, has always been projected onto men "out there." Christina said, "I've never had a male role model and no real male friends. I've had lots of women friends, but no men-friends." That is to say, her inner masculine is split into the sexualized, aggressive male; the egotistic male; and the passive, weak, sleeping/unconscious male. Because she had no role model for a healthy male, Christina has no relationship to a healthy inner male figure either. However, in the middle of the tray the dancing couple feels like a connector between these two sides of herself. In this dancing couple, a union is trying to happen. It's dynamic, it's dancing, and Christina is working with it.

Tray 10. Differentiation of *Anima* and *Animus*

Tray 11. Feeling Vulnerable

Three months earlier, Christina's adoptive older brother had died. And the month before this session, I had come into the session wearing a body cast. I had been in a car accident and had broken my back. When Christina asked me what happened, I made the mistake of saying too much. She was not able to return to therapy for a month. In this session after her return, Christina said, "My [AA] sponsor touched on a truth: when I feel vulnerable, I 'go away.' After my adoptive brother's death, I didn't call my father for nine days. With you, too: when you told me about your accident, I 'went away' for a month." Because of her attachment to me and this sudden news that my life, too, was vulnerable, it was hardly a surprise that the week previous to this session, Christina had dreamed of longing for her birthmother.

Silently but energetically Christina cleared away a central lake, holding her deepest feelings. In the center of this lake, two surgeons are doing open-heart surgery on a child. The surgical table sits atop a purple heart in a blue pool of grief. In the military, the Purple Heart is awarded to soldiers wounded in battle. So after the news of her brother's death and the fact that I, too, could have been killed, the surgery figure suggests that, symbolically, her heart has been ripped out—a very early feeling-injury to her little girl self: the same feeling-injury she may have been carrying about her birthmother as well as her adoptive mother.

This hypothesis seems to be borne out by the ruling principle of the tray: the evil witch-mother standing on a raised mound at the center back of the tray. At her side stands a caveman carrying a huge stone on his back (the trauma she has borne since birth). And further to the right stands her obese adoptive mother, who abandoned her through her addictive behavior all through Christina's childhood and abandoned her forever through her overdose when Christina was seven.

From around the edges of the tray Christina scooped up sand to create a high protective embankment around the lake. At the back of the lake on the embankment, Christina smilingly placed "a real bird's nest!" Inside of the nest she placed a large white egg, with a chick hatching from it. A colorful feathered bird sits on the egg. But just off to the right of the nest, an alligator crawls out of the water with a similar colorful bird in its jaws.

What is going on here? Is the bird in the alligator's jaws Christina's dead brother, snatched out of the nest? Or, if the two colorful birds represent the nesting parents tending the hatching chick, is the father still there while the stepmother was carried off in the jaws of her addictions? It's also true that Christina was feeling crushed by the lack of a call from her birthmother, and the news of my having been nearly crushed in my car may have dragged her deeper into her core wound. We don't know. Both the stone and the alligator are primitive. The nest is no longer safe.

Tray 11. Feeling Vulnerable

At the back left of the tray, the Three Little Pigs stand in an open straw hut. Behind the hut stands the big, bad wolf, who will, in Christina's words, "Blow the house down," meaning the wolf (as death) is always at the door; it's not safe in the world. Christina's core wound is experienced as Kohut's "unnamable dread."[214] That dread is made visible in the form of the Grim Reaper who stands on the left at the top of the ridge, surveying what is going on in the lake.

In the front left of the tray, a Native American woman on a horse with a travois heads out of the tray, "going away," and in the front right of the tray, an old-fashioned Western woman walks away from a man (perhaps Christina leaving her husband Joe).

The vulnerable part of Christina copes by leaving all attachment figures. But her fierce Warrior Woman *animus* is out in front, standing guard to protect her.[215] She said, "The more vulnerable I feel, the more *she* comes back in."

With her tray finished, Christina returned to the couch, her persona stripped away, and sat in silence, looking at me, small, sad, and teary. A shy smile crossed her face. I mirrored her feelings in silence. "This is really hard to do," Christina murmured.

"It takes a lot of courage to let your vulnerable feelings show," I replied.

"I think I'm ready to write my birthmother again and tell her more (about me) and tell her I was disappointed when she didn't call me back." I encouraged her wish.

Tray 12. Feeling Small and Vulnerable

Christina's next sandplay two months later was based on the same theme: feeling small and vulnerable. Christina was tearful as she told me over the holiday break her sponsor had "flaked" and she still hadn't heard from her birthmother.

Tray 12 is remarkably similar to Tray 11, with a few notable exceptions. The evil witch-mother at the center back of the tray has been replaced by a mother-goddess as the ruling principle of the tray, bearing witness to Christina's suffering and holding the space.

In the center of the lake, the surgeons are still performing open-heart surgery on the baby, but the large mirror under the surgical procedure in place of the purple heart suggests that there is more reflection about this experience. Now she is able to put words to this horror, saying, "I feel so small and so vulnerable; I don't trust anyone, even God." She cried for the first time since our first session, ten years earlier.

The real bird's nest is in this tray, too, behind a white mother-figure on the right, which I had created out of clay. Both the empty nest and the empty-armed clay mother-figure suggest that Christina is really feeling the barren emptiness of her birthmother experience. The sword-wielding woman at the center front of the tray

suggests that when she feels this bad, she has to defend and protect herself. At the same time, diagonally opposite the empty nest and empty-armed female, a mother helps a small child to walk. I wondered if perhaps Christina was finally allowing the good mother in me back into the tray and into her life?

For the first time, Christina placed three pieces of iron pyrite into the tray. Are they frozen tears? Has her wound crystallized? Another name for iron pyrite is "fool's gold," perhaps indicating attachment problems. Every time she makes an attachment to someone, she thinks she's got the real thing, but then they wound her or leave, and she's been fooled again. When she finished the tray she said, "I especially don't trust men, or the patriarchy." I asked if she trusted me. "Yes," she said, with tears in her eyes, "I trust you. [But] I have to keep you safe and secure." I asked her if she could trust me enough to be angry with me. She laughed, saying, "I was angry with you for leaving during Christmas, when I was especially vulnerable." She was working through the negative transference. Christina's deep interiority, allowing herself to experience her smallness, vulnerability and grief with me is the essence of *albedo* consciousness.

Tray 12. Feeling Small and Vulnerable

Tray 13. Little Lost Soul

Christina's next tray came out of a poignant dream:

I'm at work. A little four-year-old girl has lost her soul. I need the help of one of the two guys in the apartment for a soul-retrieval ritual. I go into the kitchen where one of the guys is working and tell him of my need. He says, "You always want to work with these intense cases! About soul-retrieval or ritual! Something!"

Tray 13, too, holds a large central lake, of which I will say more presently. In the back-right corner of the tray sits a little girl with no face (her lost soul), but Christina's small, vulnerable little girl is now more human and embodied than the pewter Gollum she had said was "me, small and vulnerable" in Tray 3. The little girl sits in a grove of three green trees, and she has help. A Saint Bernard with a keg of brandy stands at the rescue, and there is a butterfly in the tree. In Greek, *psyche* is the word for both "butterfly" and "soul," so it is heartening to see the butterfly in the tree right over the head of the little girl whose soul has been lost.

The Day of the Dead operating table in the center of Tray 12 has been replaced by a Day of the Dead dentist in the right-front corner of this tray. Working on teeth has to do with working on basic structure, less perilous than the open-heart surgery on Christina's infant self.

Diagonally opposite the dentist, in the back-left corner is her infant self, lying face down in the sand at the feet of the white clay

Tray 13, detail. Infant Self

mother figure, now holding a mask. "The fat woman," Christina exclaimed, "so reminds me of my adoptive mother!"

It is poignant to see her infant self, lying face-down, abandoned by her adoptive mother. Her experience in the world is like this. The abandoned baby had to put on a mask to survive childhood. The mask, however, may also represent the transference at a very deep level: Christina told me once that she wanted to crawl into my womb, so this may be a chance for the baby to climb up into the womb and have a transformative experience.

In the front-left corner, a woman carries a heavy basket on her back as she walks out of the tray. Christina was still processing the

Tray 13. Little Lost Soul

possibility of leaving her marriage, but she carries the burden of grief and loss all by herself.

What is most different about Tray 13 is the content of the central lake: the Day of the Dead surgeons, operating on Christina's infant self, have been replaced by Glinda, the good witch, perhaps as a hope for something better; the iron pyrite is present in the *albedo* lake as a reminder of the *nigredo* she has suffered; and Dorothy's red shoes from the Wizard of Oz (containing the first hint of the *rubedo*) are here, too. With the help of Glinda, Dorothy's red shoes will carry her home. Christina has the ability to go home, but she just doesn't know it yet.

Later in the month, Christina bought herself a small *rubedo*-red sports car in anticipation of emancipation from her marriage. The next ten months were spent in weekly talk therapy processing the end of her marriage, but she engaged in no more sandplay. Near the end of this period, she met a man and later fell in love with him in a temple under the stars. She described that evening in ecstatic terms, saying, "Earth-energy and spiritual energy came together in my heart and it opened! It was intense! Piercing!"

Tray 14. Endings and New Beginnings

Ten months after her last sandplay, Christina began this tray saying, "Huge, new energy [the energy of the *rubedo*] is coming into my life." Estelle Weinrib warns that when creative new energies come into a client's life, one must be very careful: "If no appropriate outlet is found, there is a real danger of inflation or misuse of the energy, with potentially serious consequences."[216]

When she finished the tray, Christina said, "The left side of the tray is my dead marriage; Joe and I are getting a divorce. The right side of the tray is my sacred sexuality." The death of the old order is the realm of the *albedo*. The birth of the new order, with its "huge new energy" and sacred sexuality, is the realm of the *rubedo*, which we see, literally, in the red hues of fire, coral yarn, and pink anemone and, figuratively, in the coital couple making love near a huge phallus. In the center of the tray is a large mound.

The left and right sides of the tray, along a horizontal axis, represent Christina's physical life. On the left side of the tray, standing in front of the horse-drawn carriage is a young bridesmaid, "the part of me which bought into this culture's dream of the ideal marriage that would save me." Christina took a wedding-cake bride and groom and wound stiff wire around their necks and bodies and connected the long end of the wire to the mound. On top of the couple she placed a large stagecoach, saying, "The stagecoach is running over the marriage couple, rough-shod."

On the right side of the tray stands a huge stone phallus. The coral fluffy yarn represents "All the love this couple is feeling." Christina, humming, took a small key, threaded it onto the yarn and put the love-making couple on top of the yarn. The coral yarn and red flames are indicative of her connection to the passionate feelings of the *rubedo*.

In the center of the tray, in a direct vertical line from front to back, we see a round glass paperweight encasing a pink sea anemone. A gold bridge connects it to the mound, a bridge to the sacred. Lying atop the purple heart (of the wounded warrior) is a green snake wound

Tray 14, detail. Marriage Couple

Tray 14. Endings and New Beginnings

around a sword—symbol of Aesculapius, Greek God of Healing. Both sword and snake point toward a large goddess: "The ruling principle of my life," remarked Christina, "is bigger than I am." The vertical axis represents a new spiritual

Tray 14, detail. Day of the Dead Surgeon

attitude. And her reference to the Goddess as the ruling principle of her life confirms my speculation about figures Christina placed at the center back of the tray as the ruling principle of her trays.

During the ten months between this tray and the last, Christina had been working through her abandonment terror at the prospect of leaving her marriage, symbolized by this Day of the Dead Surgeon operating on an adult. She is still in a very painful place. After placing it in the tray, she mounded sand over it saying, "I don't mean these feelings are *buried;* it just means they're not leading; they're right here, in my body," she said, pointing to her solar plexus.

The horizontal physical axis and vertical

Tray 14. Viewing the Horizonal and Vertical Axes

spiritual axis form a cross. On the vertical spiritual axis, we have the golden bridge. Alchemical gold hints at a connection to the Self. The sword of Aesculapius has to do with healing the wounded Self. And the ancient Goddess as "The ruling principle of one's life, something bigger than we are" also points to a relationship to a larger Self. However, her growing spirituality sits atop the mound of sand covering the surgeon operating on the most painful aspect of her abandonment trauma.

On the horizontal axis—her physical life—the huge dark phallic *nigredo*-like stagecoach and phallus seem a little ominous. The disproportionate size of the lingam and the size of the fire adjacent to it suggest that her passionate side may be a little out of control, which may explain why "the carriage is running over the marriage rough-shod." The wire binding the wedding couple is connected to what is under the mound: the painful surgery she is undergoing, trying to separate from her husband.

Although Christina can feel the trauma in her body, the fact that it is buried suggests that it is going to come back and get her, that the dark thing is going to run her down.

Two months later, Christina moved out, to be closer to her lover. Four months later, after she and her husband had signed divorce papers, Christina said, "Marriage was a safe place to hide and grow and develop my career." The following month, Christina's father died. She spent the next several weeks in therapy creating several sandtrays (not shown) processing the loss of the only man in her life who had ever really loved her, albeit ineffectually. During this period she also said, "I'm not attaching to you because my primary attachment has always been onto my father and other men." And while I knew this was true for Christina, her sandplay also suggested that she did have a strong bond to me.

With her new lover, Christina became deeply involved with the kink/polyamory community, which she found fun and exciting and safe, since the element of control was something she could trust. However, given her history of sexual trauma and her inner child's need for security, I gently wondered about the long-term wisdom of polyamory and kink for her. Although she acknowledged that I had held her well and she appreciated my firm boundaries, she didn't trust that I could support her here and prepared to leave therapy for the second time.

Tray 15. Infinity as Goodbye

Just before her last session with me, Christina looked in the bathroom mirror and wondered if I was sad, then realized she was sad.

With fingers on the sand, Christina silently and reverently created a horizontal figure-eight in the sand with eight revolutions. The horizontal figure eight represents infinity—a fitting way to end this phase. According to Pratibha Eastwood, the eight revolutions to create the figure eight symbolize an auspicious Double Quadrinity: "Eight is the externalization of universal spirit in personal life . . . It is in relation to spirit that the number Eight indicates infinity."[217] This tray delves deeply into personal spirit. After the tray was dismantled, the shape also suggests two eyes with pupils, or two breasts with nipples.

Aladdin's lamp stands in the center of the left figure eight loop, with a small purple stone (the wounded soldier's Purple Heart?) inside. In the center of the right loop stands a heart-shaped box filled with sparkling jewels and a piece of iron pyrite. If the loops represent two eyes, then Aladdin's lamp and heart-shaped box, standing where the pupils would be, might represent conscious awareness, where Christina can catch a glimpse of the Self. And conjecturing on these two shapes as breasts, then perhaps the lamp and heart-shaped box as nipples might represent milk from a nurturing, good mother.

The easiest way to analyze the complexity of this tray is to follow the vertical line extending upward from the black cauldron in the

Tray 15. A larger photo appears on the next page.

Tray 15 Horizontal Figure 8 as Infinity

Tray 15, detail. Wisdom of the Heart

center front of the tray to the Madonna at the center back, and the two diagonal lines from the back corners of the tray converging into a "V" on the cauldron at the front.

Tray 15. Infinity as Goodbye

The black cauldron, sitting on a low fire and bubbling with the red yarn of the *rubedo*, suggests that the roaring fire of passion with her lover seen in Tray 14 is now more contained. An open-armed blue-and-white-robed spiritual female is tending the fire. The sword, removed from its stone, is pointing like a compass toward all the figures in the back-left corner of the tray. Moving further along the vertical axis, the seated male and female couple with prominent vulva and phallus face each other, with a white a flower between them and glittering red-and-gold jewel nearby; she called this "My sacred sexuality." Behind them, the blackened "Tree of Life" with which she started her sandplay process has sprung into full bloom, suggesting that her sexuality, wounded from such an early age, has been healed or is healing. And behind the tree in bloom stands a Madonna and child flanked by two large green trees. If the Madonna here is the ruling principle of the tray, then it appears that Christina's inner child is now being held by a loving mother.

In the back-left corner of the tray sits a tombstone and nine blue glass drops, representing the tears over her father's death. Nearby is a Sufi dancer (her lover). I wondered if the blue hand pointing his direction was a projection of her own spirituality onto him. In front of this grouping, her old pewter Warrior Woman stands guard, her sword pointing toward and defending the hunched-over black figure to the right, symbolizing her anguished, vulnerable self, grieving not only the death of her father but also perhaps the continued silence from her birthmother and maybe even the prospect of leaving me. But the close proximity of Aladdin's lamp suggests that if she makes a wish, her wounded purple heart inside the lamp will be healed. And indeed, the green snake of healing and growth is moving past the sword toward the woman tending the fire in the center front of the tray, or perhaps toward the little fairy girl to the far right of the tray.

In the back-right corner of the tray stands the castle of Tray 4 and a large green tree. Her inner child Chrissie, whom she found in the castle dungeon, is now sitting outside, surrounded by wholesome food as nurture, with a Saint Bernard standing at the ready nearby.

Moving from Chrissie toward the cauldron, we come to the heart-shaped box containing sparkling jewels and one piece of iron pyrite (removed from its box for the photo). If the iron pyrite represents the distillation of her painful *nigredo* wound, the jewels may represent the wisdom she has discovered in having faced her wounds and integrated her pain. In fact, the presence of Kwan-Yin (Goddess of Wisdom and Compassion) to the immediate left of this heart and the pewter bad mother witch to the right argues to the merit of this. She can now hold both the pain and the wisdom in her heart. To hold both the dark and the light sides of the soul simultaneously is true integration. Immediately in front of the heart-shaped container is a mysterious *rubedo*-red egg, perhaps containing something not yet born.

Behind the pewter witch stands a fairy girl and hiding behind her is a pink quartz heart. In a poignant diagonal between her father's tombstone and the fairy girl (her Father's sweet fairy-princess asking, "Do you love me?") stands the cold, hard pewter witch and her pewter Warrior Woman. These two pewter women represent some hardening, some cutting-off of feeling, which would be natural in Christina's last session with me. But both are now balanced by more embodied, more spiritual positive mothers: the open-armed woman tending the fire, the Madonna holding the child, and the archetypal goddess of Compassion, Kwan-Yin.

At the end of our session, tears welled up as Christina said, "I still miss my Dad terribly. I don't talk about it much, but I feel it all the time." And regarding our relationship, she added, "I'm leaving for now, and feeling mixed. I love you, Lynne. I'm going to miss you, but I also feel ready. You represent a container with firm boundaries. You've held me well, but now I'm going into a new place with different boundaries."

Reflections on Phase II of Christina's Sandplay Process

It was remarkable to see the huge change in Christina's sandplay during Phase II—a five-year period of deep interiority and the emergence for the first time of intense feelings of grief, anger, pain, and crushing disappointment, hallmarks of *albedo* consciousness. During this time, Christina developed and solidified a very impressive, successful career. But riding along underneath this lay profound abandonment issues, which resurfaced with painful intensity shortly after the first session of Phase II. You will recall that Christina's abandonment issues had brought her into therapy in the first place: she had been abandoned at birth; abandoned repeatedly by an adoptive mother not fit to have been a parent; abandoned again at age seven when her adoptive mother died of an overdose; and abandoned further still by a father, aunts, and uncles too blind to see or too ignorant to care that Christina was being molested, over many years, by her older male cousins. The timing of Christina's return to therapy was uncanny. The day after her first session, she received a call on her answering machine from her birthmother, saying that she would like to talk to Christina. Given Christina's lifelong depth of longing to reconnect with her, this call was the fulfillment of a lifelong dream.

How crushing, how cruelly devastating, then, that this was a call that never came.

In Christina's sandplay, the *albedo* featured most prominently in the recurring lakes of blue water in the bottom of the tray, which served as wells containing her feelings of profound abandonment. During this period, these feelings of betrayal spilled over into feelings of anger and disappointment with her marriage. The prospect of separation triggered further abandonment terror and anxiety, but her ability to work through these feelings led ultimately to a divorce and a loving attachment to another male. From fairly early on, however, even her new lover began causing disappointment, but she was not ready to go there yet. During Phase II, the first overt signs of the *rubedo* crept into Christina's sandplay in the form of Dorothy's red shoes in Tray 13, in the red fire and coral yarn as her sacred sexuality in Tray 14, and the red jewel and red contents of the cauldron and mysterious red egg of Tray 15.

After Phase II's five-year therapy, Christina took a five-year break before resuming therapy with me for the third and last time. The first sandplay of Phase III is to be found at the end of Chapter 5. The remaining sandtrays are found at the end of Chapter 6.

CHAPTER 4

Yellow—The *Citrinitas*

SINCE SULFUR IS ONE of the principal ingredients in chemistry, it is not surprising that the alchemists wrote of yellow in their alembics. Until the sixteenth century, yellow (*citrinitas,* or yellowing) was one of the four principal colors of alchemy, a transitional color between the *albedo* and the *rubedo*. Although the use of yellow as a stage gradually fell into disuse among the alchemists, the *citrinitas* does have a part to play.

In his article "The Yellowing of the Work," James Hillman lists both negative and positive cultural associations to the color yellow, but he asserts that, psychologically, yellow represents a transition in a temporal process between white and red; that is, it represents change. Johannes Fabricius, a current Danish scholar of alchemy with a medieval-sounding name, sees this change negatively, as aging, and casts the images of the *citrinitas* in a rather violent light: cutting swords, cleaving serpents, piercing rays, splitting arrows, armed eagles.[218] But Hillman makes an astute point:

It is not the yellow *per se* which is important, but the process of yellow*ing* . . . What is yellowed is the white, lunar consciousness, like milk becoming cheese. The white resists this because it feels like a regression; the white takes on body, flavor, fatness, it is hot, smelly, male, fat, oily, greasy, unctual, desire aware of itself. With a more "jaundiced" view, there may be a growing critical awareness of things.[219]

Hillman goes on to say that, in analysis, "Yellow is more than a spoiling of the white"; it is also enlivening, it turns the attention, the energy outward. "Increasingly, yellow clarification is of the world out there."[220]

In this light, the "violent" images of Fabricius take on new meaning: the cutting swords, cleaving serpents, piercing rays, splitting arrows, and armed eagles may be images for the attempts of consciousness to break through the comfortable, subjective world of the white toward a growing clarity or insight—a gradually increasing illumination.

We see the ego in the process of change in the frontispiece of this chapter. In this image from the *Splendor Solis,* the poor hero with his black body is standing knee-deep in mud, the stuff of the *nigredo.* That is, he is not yet out of the muck. His left arm has turned white and his right arm and head are turning red, but whatever is over his head and face appears embryo-like, as if he were not yet fully born. The attending angel with her yellow upper garments, representing change or transformation, holds out the red robe as the hope of attainment of the *rubedo.*

YELLOW DREAMS

Two striking *citrinitas* dreams in my dream record heralded the transition from *albedo* to *rubedo.*

August 30, 1982. *MOON PHASES. This is the first day of geology class. When the class is almost over, the instructor asks a man I know for an exhibit that he wants to show me. It is a large glossy composite photo of the phases of the moon, vibrant oranges and yellows swirling and glowing against a black sky.*

Against the backdrop of a black sky (the *nigredo*) lies the moon, premiere symbol of the *albedo.* However, in this dream of the phases of the moon, its waxing and waning have produced vibrant oranges and yellows that swirl and glow. That is, the "dead" white of the moon is beginning to stir, to come alive, the yellows and oranges moving toward the red end of the spectrum.

Five weeks later, a dream with similar colors appeared:

October 8, 1982. *BABY CRANES. On board a ship. We go in search of Mr. X and then come across a good-luck omen: a crane. When we approach, we see a baby crane, white with a patch of brilliant yellow feathers at his neck; then another crane with a patch of brilliant orange feathers, and a third, with a patch of brilliant red feathers at the neck. I see a baby boy (Asian? Eurasian?) in front of me. He reaches out for the birds and is so strong I am afraid he will hurt them, so I pull him back. He has just been suckled, and I pull him to my breast and rock him. Then he speaks; he says a certain date. I think it is his birth date. Actually, the date is a combination of the birth dates of the most important woman and the most important man in my life.*

Cranes are good omens. The three baby cranes with their pure white bodies, symbolic of the *albedo,* also contain the colors of transition, from brilliant yellow (*citrinitas*) to orange to red (*rubedo*), perhaps presaging the birth or the appearance of the magical boy in the dream. Although I appear to be in search of a man (my *animus*), what appears is the baby boy. In his unusual strength and ability to speak, the boy is similar to Hermes, Hercules, and other heroes or magical children. Also, his birth date is a combination of important female and male figures in my life, suggesting that a bringing together of inner masculine and feminine elements produces the magical child: symbol of the Self in nascent form.

The study's sample of "yellow" dreams was not large enough to be statistically significant as a stage in the process of individuation, consistent with the alchemists' gradual disuse of the *citrinitas* as one of the four principal alchemical colors. Nevertheless, both dreams, with their brilliant yellows, oranges, and reds—the colors of dawn— presaged the advent of the *rubedo*.

The *Aurora Consurgens* says, "First the word "aurora" [dawn] could be explained as "aurea hora" [the golden hour], because there is a certain good moment in this opus when one can reach one's goal; secondly, the dawn is between day and night and has two colours, namely yellow and red."[221]

Rosa Rubea

In fine exibit tibi rex suo dyademate coro
natus fulgens ut sol clarus ut carbunculo
foris effluens ut cera · prseuerabit in igne
penetrabit et retinens argentu uiuum At
color namqz rubedinis causat noldus
ex aplemento digestionis · cm sanguis
non generat in honure msi pris diligeter
coquat m opate · Sic nob cum videmg niar
de mane vrina alba · saentes parz dormi

CHAPTER 5

Red—The *Rubedo*

FOR THE ALCHEMISTS, THE *rubedo* was connected to the ancient active principle identified with the sun and the male, and associated with the dry, the light, and the fiery. As the male, the *rubedo* was often called *Vir Rubeus* (Red Man), *Servus Rubeus* (Red Slave), Red King, Red Knight, along with many other names, such as *Tinctura Rubea* (Tyrian or Purple tincture), cinnabar, red or rose-colored blood, dragon's blood, poison, blood-red earth, red lily, red rose, red coral, and so on. Zosimos called this fiery male principle sulfur, also known as red or Philosophical Sulfur.[222] Since sulfur turns fiery red when heated, it was associated with fire and with the sun, Sol. Dorn says: "The male and universal seed, the first and most potent, is the solar sulfur, the first part and most potent cause of all generation."[223] And John Pordage also says, "The sun gives spirit, color, fixation and perfection to the tincture. The color added to it by the sun is a crimson purple color, a deep pomegranate red: this being the immutable and permanent color."[224] The purple tincture mentioned by Pordage is the rare Tyrian dye designated exclusively for the vestments of the kings of Egypt, the patricians of Rome, and the priests of the Eleusinian Mysteries.[225] Since antiquity, purple, like alchemical red, has been a symbol of royalty, perfection, or ennoblement.

Like Mercurius, sulfur has a dual nature, carrying both negative and positive qualities, as described here by Jung:

> The redness (*rubedo*) of the sun's light is a reference to the red sulfur in it, the active burning principle, destructive in its effects … The sun is evidently an instrument in the physiological and psychological drama of return to the prima materia, the death that must be undergone if man is to get back to the original condition of the simple elements and attain the incorrupt nature of the pre-worldly paradise.[226]

So sulfur at the beginning is not only the corrosive, burning *prima materia* but also the glorious end-product of the opus. "Sulfur . . . when cleansed of all impurities . . . is the matter of our stone."[227] Because red was associated with the sun, it was also associated with gold, which shares *Sol's* alchemical symbol, a circle with a dot in its center. Because gold—unlike other metals including silver—is immutable and incorruptible, it was natural to associate the purified red substance with gold. For instance, in the *Turba Philosophorum* we read: "When [the composition] becomes red, it is called Flower of Gold, Ferment of Gold, Gold of Coral, Gold of the Beak"[228] When the red sulfur was cleansed of all impurities, alchemists believed the opus was complete. At this point Irenaeus Philalethes, in his *Commentary on the Fifth Gate of Ripley* declares:

> Then shall the Heavenly Fire descend and illuminate the Earth in inconceivable glory; the Crown of thy Labors shall be brought unto thee, when our Sol shall sit in the South, shining with redness incomparable. This is our true Light, our Earth glorified: rejoice now, for our King hath passed from death to Life, and possesseth the keys of both death and hell, and over him nothing now hath power.[229]

Red, with its close association to the sun and to fire, was also associated by the alchemists with blood, the body, and sexuality. For instance, Albertus Magnus says, "Increase the fire until by its force and power, the material is changed into a stone, very red, which the Philosophers call Blood, or Purple, Red Coral, Red Sulfur."[230] Zosimos refers to Adam: "the first man . . . is called . . . Adam, which is. . . virgin earth, blood-red earth, fiery or carnal earth."[231] In another place he says, "You will find the gold coloured

fiery red like blood. That is the cinnabar of the philosophers and the copper man turned to gold."[232] Because cinnabar itself is composed of white mercury and yellow sulfur,[233] unsurprisingly the alchemists thought red was the end product of white and yellow.

For the alchemists, red was associated with the sun (*Sol*), with the element fire, the humor blood, and the metal gold. In impure form, this color was associated with Adam, carnal man; with the Venusian body and sexuality; with the hot, fiery, destructive aspect of sulfur; and with the Red Lion. In purified form, red was associated with *Sol* shining in the South, the crowned king in red or purple robes, and as you shall see in the next chapter, with the Philosopher's Stone, the Elixir of Life, redemption, and resurrection.

For the symbolic or psychological meaning of the alchemical references to red, I turn to the more consciously psychological literature of the past 250 years. For the Rosicrucians, red was associated with spirit, symbolic blood, the active element *Sol*, and with procreative or producing power.[234] Hitchcock equated *Sol* with the intellect, "which becomes clarified in proportion as the affections become purified." However, he warned that "a great deal of what is called intellect—a brisk smartness and cunning and cleverness, the product of animal spirits aided by a good memory—is not the true Sol."[235] A better definition for Hitchcock's "intellect" is "understanding" or "insight." For Silberer, the sun or the gold was equated with released libido and illumination.[236] For Jung, too, the *rubedo* had to do with increasing inner consciousness:

> The growing redness (*rubedo*) ... denotes an increase of warmth and light coming from the sun, consciousness. This corresponds to the increasing participation of consciousness, which now begins to react emotionally to the contents produced by the unconscious. At first the process of integration is a "fiery" conflict, but gradually it leads over to the "melting" or synthesis of the opposites. The alchemists termed this the *rubedo*.[237]

However, Hillman warns us of a premature *rubedo*, lacking the "silvered chalice" of the *albedo* "to hold the blood": "The *rubedo* first requires a receptive soul and a comprehensive understanding, else it streams in the firmament, reddening the world with manic missionary compulsion, the *multiplicatio* and *exaltatio* as conversion, moneymaking and fame."[238] That is, the *rubedo* needs the container of the *albedo* to prevent it from spilling over.

Stephen Martin describes the *rubedo* phase in clinical terms as the transition in the opus when inner directedness gives way to ever greater involvement in life:

> In the *rubedo* the patient's transforming personality is no longer blocked, no longer cut off from the world because of archetypal interference. The insights won and instinctual energy harnessed are applied to life in a most deliberate and conscious way... Brought into closer touch with ourselves and the other... we no longer feel the outsider or the misfit. Instead, what emerges is the inspired relatedness to life all around, and a new dignity.[239]

Martin suggests that the *rubedo* is "the most individually actualized phase."[240] Of this mature *rubedo* Hillman concludes: "The work is over; we no longer work at consciousness, develop ourselves, or possess a distinct grid by means of which we recognize where we are, how we are, maybe even who we are."[241]

In psychological terms, then, the *rubedo* is associated with the active (so-called male) principle, with solar consciousness, with an intellect "clarified in proportion as the affections become purified," with the principle of spirit, procreative or producing power, released libido, harnessed instinctual energy, and relatedness to life. If we understand *rubedo* consciousness as solar rather than "male" consciousness, freed of gender identification, then it clearly belongs to both women and men.

We must remember that the red contains both negative and positive connotations. In this dream described by Jung, red is associated with chthonic Earth Woman: "In a den of snakes beneath the sea there is a divine woman, asleep ... She is wearing a blood-red garment that covers only the lower half of her body. She has a dark skin, full red lips, and seems to be of great physical strength."[242] Of this primal Earth Mother, a remnant of earlier matriarchal culture, Jung says she is "always chthonic," with "a primitive or animal expression on her face...occasionally related to the moon either through blood-sacrifice or through a child-sacrifice, or else because she is adorned with a sickle moon."[243]

Unfortunately, with the advent of Christianity, red in this carnal, embodied sexual sense took on a decidedly negative connotation. Jung reminds us that scarlet is the color of the Great Whore of Babylon and her beast[244] and that red is the color of sin ("though your sins be as scarlet, they shall be as white as snow; though they be red like crimson, they shall be as wool."[245] We see remnants of this negative association of red with sexuality in novels such as Nathaniel Hawthorne's *The Scarlet Letter*, in which the woman Hester carries the shame for the sexuality of herself, her partner, and the whole community; in the film of Chinese concubines, *Raise the Red Lantern*; and in phrases such as "paint the town red" or "red light district."

Neumann's view that the patriarchy (as represented by the Christian Church) needed to repress the earlier matriarchy (powerfully associated to the earth, the body, and sexuality) to bring about a change of collective consciousness, explains such a negative view of women and sexuality. Changing attitudes today toward the sexuality/red connection are to be found in the passion for red sports cars, in songs such as "Lady in Red," and in "Red," the name of Giorgio's perfume for both women and men.

Through its negative association to passion, red has also been associated with anger and with danger. To "see red" is the bull's view of the cape before the charge, or the burst of rage from the angered individual. To cross an enraged individual is dangerous. So red is the color of the "Stop" sign, the "Do not enter" sign, and the "Danger" sign. And many a painter's canvas splashed with red pigment is indicative of strong emotion.

But red also has positive connotations. In prehistoric times, corpses were painted red, the color of life; in ancient China red was an imperial color, used for robes, carriages, palace buildings, banners, and coffins; and red ink was reserved for important documents and magical inscriptions.[246] In present-day China, red is the color of felicitation and joy in festivals, weddings, and New Year celebrations.[247] In many cultures the color red is attached to places of importance. For example, in many Arab countries, red means the place of eminence, the "place of places"; in Grenada, Spain, *Al-Hambra* (the "red") is the palace, fortress, or "royal" house.[248]

In Hindu Tantric art and philosophy, red is "the active, the passionate attachment which creates and projects out into space and time."[249] In contrast to Western alchemy, red is associated with the feminine in the Hindu Tantric system and in the Sephiroth system of Jewish mysticism. In India, China, and most of Asia today, the bride wears the *flammeum*, a flame-red veil.[250]

In these cases, the color red brings us close to the essence of the Red Stone of the Philosophers. For instance, in Jack London's story, "The Red One," The Red One is a perfect sphere—200 feet in diameter, brighter than bright cherry red, of no metal or combination of metals ever known, cradled in black volcanic sand in the heart of a dark-skinned, cannibalistic, head-hunting jungle tribe, emitting sounds like "the trump of an archangel . . . sonorous as thunder . . . like the mighty cry of some Titan of the Elder World vexed with misery or wrath . . . thin and sweet as a thrummed taut cord of silver . . . mellow as a golden bell," for which "Walls of cities might well fall down before so vast and compelling a summons."[251] According to James Kirsch, in this encounter with The Red One, London had "come into the neighborhood of the Self . . . whose other name is TRUTH."[252]

Max Lüscher's study of the physiology of red comes remarkably close to the alchemical, psychological, and cross-cultural associations for red:

Red . . . represents an energy-expending physiological condition. It speeds up the pulse, raises blood pressure and increases the respiration rate. Red is the expression of vital force, of nervous and glandular activity, and so it has the meaning of desire and of all forms of appetite and craving.

Red is the urge to achieve results, to win success; it is hungrily to desire all those things which offer intensity of living and fullness of experience. Red is impulse, the will-to-win, and all forms of vitality and power, from sexual potency to

Figure 15. Caught in the Grips of Manic *Rubedo* Energies.
(Peter Paul Rubens, *The Fall of the Damned,* detail, 1620)

revolutionary transformation. It is the impulse towards active doing, towards sport, struggle, competition, eroticism and enterprising productivity . . . In temporal terms, red is the present.[253]

Thus, red as an archetypal image has a dual nature. In its raw, unrefined form as *prima materia*, it is manifested in obsessive thoughts, manic activity, rage, lust, concupiscence, unbridled greed and desire in all forms, including addictions, captured well in this detail of a larger painting by Peter Paul Rubens (Figure 15).

In refined form, the *rubedo* is the natural flow of ideas, creative action, anger channeled into constructive, purposeful activity, and a natural, healthy relationship to the body and its appetites, including unashamed sexuality in the service of true intimacy and love.

The *albedo* and the *rubedo* not only form two distinct stages in the alchemical opus; together they also form a complementary pair of opposites, which I consider in the next chapter.

RED DREAMS

The content of red dreams in my dream record again reveals a progression from negative to positive. Until 1981, with few exceptions, the content of red dreams was negative. However, beginning in 1981 a gradual shift toward positive content emerged.

Then in October and November 1982 a series of archetypally powerful red dreams appeared, signaling a dramatic shift toward a more positive relationship to an inner masculine energy field with its highly energetic instinctual base. Although this archetypal burst of "red" at first felt over-masculine to me, it later became integrated as positive, creative libidinal energy in the psyche.

The fact that overall there are fewer red dreams in the dream record than black or white dreams suggests that I had been living such a *rubedo*-saturated lifestyle that my unconscious needed little more than to usher in a positive relationship to my inner masculine. Its flowering into the true *rubedo* in my outer life was yet to come.

The following dream is the initial red dream in my record.

November 26, 1974. *BLOODY SCRATCH. Men and women are in a room together, dancing. An announcement is made that one woman or one couple will be chosen. The woman who is chosen has been severely scratched by her partner's beard and has blood all over the lower part of her face, where a man's beard would be. She is embarrassed by the blood and stands in deep shadow in a doorway, so as not to be seen by the crowd as she talks to them and answers questions.*

The red in this dream is blood, a primal *rubedo* substance. The dream says that the woman (a part of me with which I have not yet identified or internalized) has been wounded in the area of my own masculinity by my male dance partner. Thus, the red clearly establishes an association of wounded- and woundingness between outer and inner masculine. The painful imagery of the dream speaks to the pre-*rubedo* sulfur in need of purification. *The Red Shoes*, a 1948 British film about ballet—based on Hans Christian Anderson's fairy tale of the same name—is a cautionary tale reminding us that if we get caught up in animus-driven workaholism or addictions of any kind, it can kill us.

June 1, 1977. *WOMAN IN RED WEARING ANTLERS. A woman in a long red gown has a huge set of antlers on her head. The antlers are almost as tall again as she is and are twice as large as the ones she normally wears.*

I puzzled over this dream for years, uncomfortably aware that the woman in red was a part of me and that antlers, found only on male Cervids (deer, elk, moose, caribou, and reindeer) had something to do with my inner masculine self.

Since she is wearing red, she is an aspect of my inner masculine spirit. But the fact that her antlers are so disproportionately huge suggests that my *animus* is way out of balance, an overweening, overzealous male spirit defending against low self-esteem and lack of relationship to a genuinely healthy inner animus. Neither of my parents had been able to provide models for a healthy *anima* or *animus*. I had to discover these on my own.

During the writing of this book I was heartened to learn that antlers also carry positive connotations. "From ancient times, deer ... represent ... the capacity to communicate with the spirit world. The stag's antlers, which are lost and renewed annually, are symbols of death and rebirth. Their branching pattern or growth evokes the growth of plants—and when worn by a human represents the growth of consciousness."[254]

Four years later, the following two strikingly red "Annunciation" dreams herald the arrival or birth of something important, the true *rubedo*.

June 1, 1981. *RED CHRYSALIS ON A RED WALL. Just inches from my view is a large chrysalis, red in color, hanging attached to a red wall. There are two antennae coming out of the chrysalis. I watch them move, so I know the butterfly inside is alive.*

Like a womb or the therapeutic *temenos*, a chrysalis contains what is being transformed; it is thus a symbol of metamorphosis. Here, a caterpillar still in the hard, deathlike pupal (*albedo*) stage inside the chrysalis is being transformed into a butterfly. Symbolically, the butterfly is a symbol of rebirth. Thus, the chrysalis, like the therapeutic *temenos*, may be understood as a vehicle of rebirth, or soul-making. The Greek word *psyche* meant both butterfly and soul. The moving antennae signal that what is inside is alive. Similar to the dazzling sequence of white objects that presaged the emergence of the *albedo*, the saturated, brilliant red of the chrysalis and the red wall on which it hangs is also unusual and striking. In both color (red) and content (chrysalis), this dream portends an emergence, a birth, indicative of the *rubedo* stage.

July 17, 1982. *RED CHINESE CHARACTERS. Men and women engaged in a chase. The men, out of breath, end up on a platform on one side of a room, and the women, all out of breath and excited, on a platform on the other side of the room. Then suddenly from the roof a string of red Chinese characters drops down like a clothesline between the two groups; I wonder what it means but have a feeling it is felicitous.*

In this dream, inner male and female energies have been "rounded up" and separated on opposite sides of a room, ready to be brought together. The red Chinese characters appearing suddenly out of nowhere, in a line connecting the two groups—masculine and feminine—are a portent of something felicitous.

A month later, the two yellow dreams discussed in the previous chapter on the *citrinitas* appeared: "Moon Phases" with its vibrant yellows and oranges enlivening the "dead" white of the moon against the backdrop of the *nigredo*-black sky; and the dream of the "Baby Cranes" with their brilliant yellow, orange, and red feathers at the neck, "announcing" the transition from white to red. In the "Baby Cranes" dream, although the woman is in search of a man, what appears is the hero-like baby boy or magical child, whose birth date, a combination of important female and male figures in my life, suggest a bringing together of masculine and feminine elements. The following month, within a space of thirteen days, four remarkable "red" dreams appeared:

November 12, 1982. *THE RED-HEADED BOY. We are in a foreign country and I see a group of children. As I look more closely at the children, I notice that their faces are all slightly "off," perhaps the result of inbreeding? It gives us all a slightly uneasy feeling. But then in the midst of these children I see a robust red-headed boy, energetic and happy. He is obviously an American, and when we say something to him, he says "Hi!" and runs off. What a pleasant surprise to see him! For some reason, I feel a sense of belonging, just knowing he is around.*

November 14, 1982. red *GYMNAST FIGURINE. I am walking along and come to an auditorium filled with people waiting for a movie or lecture. I see something on the floor—a very small figurine—and pick it up. When it was on the floor, it appeared to be only an inch or two long, but as I hold it in my hands, it is six or eight inches long. At first, I think it looks a bit like Kwan-Yin, God/Goddess of Compassion, but then as I look, it seems more like a group of gymnasts or acrobats. The man in the center, holding everyone together, seems to come alive as I look at him. He is red in color and looks piercingly alive. I hear a voice saying, "They say he is as old as the stars." As I look at him, he seems so vitally youthful and strong I think to myself that he must be a manifestation of God. I am fascinated by him.*

November 21, 1982. *RED STRONGBOX. I have moved into a new house. As I go through the rooms, I open a lower cupboard I had not noticed before. The doors do not open all the way, but as I peer through the slats, I see a red strongbox inside. I pry the lid up with a stick, and underneath see a gold necklace lying in the corner of the box.*

November 25, 1982. *THE RED-HEADED MAN. I am in a room crowded with people. I see a red-headed man across the room holding a baby. I am attracted to him.*

Three of these dreams unmistakably connect me with positive inner "male" aspects: the healthy, happy, energetic young boy; the nurturing adult male; and in the dream of the red figurine, archetypal phallic energy. The threatening and murderous male energy of the *nigredo* phase, the tormented and tormenting male energy at the beginning of the *albedo* phase, and early negative male *rubedo* energies have been transformed into the robust, vital, and piercingly alive "male" energy of the mature *rubedo* phase. Similar to the *albedo* dream of the piano found in the junkyard, or the Philosopher's Stone found in the streets or on the dung heap, the red figurine is found under the shuffle of feet on an auditorium floor, unseen by anyone but me. At first I associate the figure to Kwan-Yin, the androgynous God/Goddess of Compassion. However, as I hold it, it grows in size like a phallus and becomes "piercingly alive." A voice says the figure is "as old as the stars." Indigenous peoples from the earliest times believed that stars were bits of life that incarnated as souls on earth and returned to the heavens as stars after death. The red gymnast may thus be a piece of my previously split-off negative masculine spirit, which, in positive "solar" form, can now become embodied in consciousness. This figure is a center of energy that holds "the others" together. As an aspect of the Self, it is the "center that holds." This center is also symbolized in the dream of the red strongbox that holds the gold. For the alchemists, the strong inner center, the Self, was the alchemical "gold" they were unconsciously seeking.

January 23, 1983. *MAN'S HAIRCUT. I am with a group of women. Our photos will be taken with our children. I see others being positioned for their photos in the afternoon sun. I glance in a mirror and to my surprise see that my hair is short-cropped and red, almost like a man's haircut. I dislike it and wish it were long. I also have no makeup on. I go into the restroom to put on some lipstick and see what I can do with my hair before the photo. Men and women are in this dressing-room together. I go into one cubicle and a man is hanging around in there; he seems to be hiding from someone, a woman, I think. In the next cubicle, unoccupied, I go in and pick up a white hand towel decorated with red valentine hearts.*

The powerful archetypal solar energy flooding into my psyche two months earlier made me feel too "male" (my hair is short-cropped; it's red, like the men's hair in the previous dreams; and I wear no makeup). I try to make myself more "female" by putting on lipstick and fussing with my short red hair. The fact that in this dressing or "changing" room men and women are mingling together suggests that there is a coming together of male and female energies. However, the male hanging around hiding from a woman is my own strong inner male energy, which is so initially uncomfortable to me that I try to hide it by making myself appear more feminine. However, the hand towel with red valentine hearts on a white ground again suggests a loving or heartfelt coming together of white and red, female and male.

March 7, 1983. *TOMATOES. I am growing tomatoes in a little square plot, ringed on all sides by a tall fence. Now the tomatoes are beginning to grow red, ripe, and juicy. I pick a couple of large ones and hold them in my hands, marveling at them. I see many others beginning to ripen too.*

In American slang, a "tomato" is often associated with a physically attractive woman.[255] Tomatoes are also associated with eros and feelings. In this dream, the protected tomatoes growing to full ripeness and maturity may be a symbol of loving, libidinal, or erotic energies coming into their own, in a way that feels more comfortable to my natural feminine self.

November 22, 1984. *JOURNEY TO THE CITADEL. I live in a place that is below ground level. This day, it is all I can do to get out. I walk to a town that seems to be in the middle of nowhere—almost deserted. But I run into Joy; she lives here. She is expecting someone, so we go out looking for her. Sure enough, her woman-friend happens along! After we get to Joy's we set off to see some dear mutual friends. The journey there reminds me of traveling to a Citadel—a King's palace in the center of the kingdom—although there is nothing fortified or defended about it. Quite the contrary: it's a small cottage in the middle of the forest, close to the earth and to nature—a Citadel only in respect to its position of centrality or importance. To get into this forest I have to cross a raging torrent that flows all the way around the forest. This torrent is too wide to step—or even jump—across, so I must make a "leap of faith"—a great leap, with the hope of catching/holding something on the other side. This I do, to my immense relief. I travel along for a long time, through what seems like a dark forest. I must overcome many obstacles: rivers or bridges that I am not at all sure will sustain me. But finally, with one final great leap over another raging torrent, I make it to the house of our friends. Joy and her friend are already here. Apparently they went on ahead, via a more direct route. Two men are here; it seems I have known them (or at least one of them) for a long time. Now that I am here, I am feeling energized. One of the men gives me a mischievous smile and I smile back. This man is somehow my "intended," but then before my eyes I see a last river to cross. It is the largest river and the deepest canyon yet, and I cannot cross it directly. If I do not, the alternative is to walk "halfway around the world." I know I will be doing the latter and must do it if I am to have this man, but in the meantime, he gives me a "taste" of what it would be like to be with him. He kisses me. But these are like no kisses I have ever had; they feel more like he is covering me—my lips, my face, my neck, my breasts—with pools of wetness—long, slow, deliberate kisses that I experience as the most deeply sensual, deeply sexual, deeply erotic kisses I have ever experienced. They are not even kisses, as much as "being made love to" in the truest sense of the word. Then a chubby little boy, about age three, with blue eyes, curly red hair, and pink chubby cheeks, toddles over and sees me lying thus and starts to kiss me too. With his wet little lips, he not only kisses me, but "tastes" me as well. He has a piece of reddish fruit (is it papaya?) in his mouth, and in his interest in tasting me, he spits out the papaya, which is then in my mouth, sweet and juicy and succulent. The man watching him later puts an orange section in the boy's mouth, but the boy comes back, and in tasting me some more, spits out the orange, which also enters my mouth. Then he says, in his baby-like voice, "She's covered with seeds!" I smile in deep satisfaction.*

This dream may be seen as a metaphor of my long and difficult inner journey to the "Citadel," the center, the Self. But the journey is not over. Through the sensual kisses and the delicious fruits, I am given a "taste" of what is to come: the possibility of a fully satisfying integration of healthy inner male *animus* energies with healthy inner female *anima* energies, for a *joy*-ful *coniunctio* in consciousness. As joyful and hopeful as this dream is, the dream's message that the journey is not yet over was disconcerting. What did it mean, that the last obstacle (the widest river and the deepest canyon yet) could not be crossed directly? That I still needed to walk "halfway around the world"? The answer to that question was not clear until I was writing this book; I discuss it in Chapter 5.

Reflections on the Red Dreams

The color red is related to the sun and to fire, to blood as the color of life, to the masculine archetype as *animus* (spirit), vitality, power, sexuality, sensuality, procreative action, felicitation, and joy. The content of all of the selected red dreams is remarkably similar to this *rubedo* imagery.

The year 1982 was a period of intense rubedo activity in the dream record, presaged by two "annunciation" dreams: "Red Chrysalis on a Red Wall," in mid-1981, and the felicitous "Red Chinese Characters" in early 1982. The burst of three "red" dreams over a two-week period in late 1982 (of the energetic red-headed boy, the phallus-like powerful vitality of the male gymnast, and the nurturing red-headed man holding the baby) marked a truly powerful, unmistakably "masculine" or solar energy entering my psyche. My dream of the "Man's Haircut" suggested that this masculine energy was at first overpowering. I needed to integrate it into my own female psyche in a way that would serve me and others: as "Tomatoes" (1983) and in the next chapter, as "Berry Pie" (1984) and "Shrimp Feast" (1985). The dream in "Journey to the Citadel" (1984) summarizes my long inner journey through the unconscious, bringing the promise of joyful union to the conscious plane where it can now be actualized, as I describe in the three dreams near the end of the dream section in the next chapter.

CHRISTINA'S SANDPLAY—PHASE III: THE RUBEDO

During Phase III, Christina continued therapy with me for another three years. She created twenty-two trays, of which I present nine. I discuss the first of the nine sand trays (Tray 16) here; the following eight trays will be found in Chapter 6.

During the five-year period she had been away, Christina had lost her lover's baby, whom she had hoped to name Ruby (a synchronistic derivative of the Latin word *rubedo*); she had broken up with her lover, less psychologically developed than she; and through the kink community she had met and fallen in love with a new man, a farmer named "Jack." Jack was gentle like her father, a great lover, and he loved to cook, so he was the good father and mother in one. But Jack had Asperger's and was unable to provide the empathy and mirroring her little girl needed. With Jack she had started smoking pot (an *albedo* potion), which she said was opening her up to more hurt, tears, and grief. She was returning to therapy for three reasons: Jack had fallen in love with a twenty-four-year-old woman with the dream (which Christina thought unrealistic) of having three children with her; the place where she was working was losing its female CEO, a kind of mother-figure for Christina; and two and a half years earlier, Christina had found her birthmother and older sister online, had never contacted them, but was now considering it.

Tray 16: Troubles Brewing Amid Success in a *Rubedo* Life

During our first session, Christina reported that she was about to travel to the state where her birthmother lived. She casually handed me a letter she had written her birthmother, but said she was not going to mail it: "Because it brings up too much grief." I encouraged her to send the letter anyway, but she insisted that I hold onto it, which I did.

All the red objects in this first tray of Phase III suggest that in the five years since she left therapy, Christina had been living a full *rubedo* life out in the world. And it was true. The little boat laden with bounty on the left side of the tray attests to the fact that her career had become extremely successful: she was earning lots of money; she had bought herself a house; and she owned three vehicles, including her red sports car. However, it is curious that the five bright red objects in the tray form the shape of the letter "Y," begging the larger question of "Why" she was returning to therapy.

The psychological pain she was experiencing at this point in her life appears in the back-left corner of the tray. In front of a black, blasted tree with a black heart at its base, a red mask lies half-buried. In front of these stands

Tray 16. Troubles Brewing Amid Success in a *Rubedo* Life

a red "Stop" sign.[256] She wants the pain in her heart and in her head to stop.

At the center back of the tray, a baby stands next to a large pink heart, surrounded by three positive mother-figures, and behind them, a more ape-like parental couple holding a child. The baby is also looking at itself in a mirror, suggesting that, while seeking mirroring from others, Christina is also self-reflective, able to look into her own depths.

In the back-right corner of the tray, a mermaid, able to live on the surface and dive into the depths, is moving toward the two red hearts in the center of the tray. Christina concluded the session by saying, "I'm deep into my abandonment, but I only want once-a-month therapy." However, a series of personal disasters in the following three months ripped her wide open.

Christina's Phase III continues in the next chapter.

Particularia

Lac Virginum

Via Vniuersalis particularibus Inclusis.

CHAPTER 6

The Sacred Marriage, or *Coniunctio* of White and Red

THE ALCHEMICAL LITERATURE with few exceptions declared that the *rubedo* was the final stage of the opus. But it's not. We cannot have the red without the white. The fully separated and purified opposites of the *albedo* and the *rubedo* together form a complementary whole, and this is the glorious end-product of the opus, the matter of "our Stone," symbolized by incorruptible gold.[257] But it takes work to get there.

At the beginning of the opus, the white and red pair either exists as a static and unconscious unity (the two-headed Rebis in Figure 18) or is brought together in a fiery, destructive union of opposites, as in the image of two lions fighting (see Figure 6, page 32). This pair, locked in an unconscious merger known as a lesser *coniunctio*, must be fully separated and differentiated into their unique essences as *albedo* and *rubedo* before they can be brought together in a true conscious union known as the greater *coniunctio*. The coming together of this pair is commonly referred to in the alchemical literature as a *coniunctio* (Latin for "joining" or "bringing together"), *heiros gamos* (Greek for "sacred marriage"), Chymical Wedding,[258] the marriage of the "faire White Woman" to the "Ruddy Man,"[259] and so on.

Figure 16, my distillation of Jung's *Mysterium Coniunctionis*, illustrates this movement of the pair of opposites as salt (white) and sulfur (red)—with Mercury as the god of the beginning as well as the end—from unconscious conjunction (black) to the separation of white and red, to the conscious conjunction of white and red (the alchemical gold).[260]

In the alchemical literature this coniunctio is pictured as a red and a white lily, a red and a white rose, a red lion and a white eagle, red blood and white bones, red and white garments, a red man and a white woman. In the literature we find references to the bringing together of sulfur and salt, gold and silver, Sol and Luna, and so forth. For instance, the Greek poem of Archelaos, "Upon the Sacred Art" says, "Take from the four elements . . . the white and the red, the female and the male in equal balance, in order that they may be joined to one another."[261]

What is being conjoined?

The words *coniunctio oppositorum* suggest a bringing together of opposites, a duality. Figure 17 shows pairs of opposites and quaternities. In *Mysterium Coniunctionis*, Jung lists images of opposites found in the alchemical texts: moist/ dry; cold/warm; upper/lower; spiritus-anima, or spirit (soul)/corpus (body); heaven/earth; fire/water; bright/dark; active/passive; volatile,

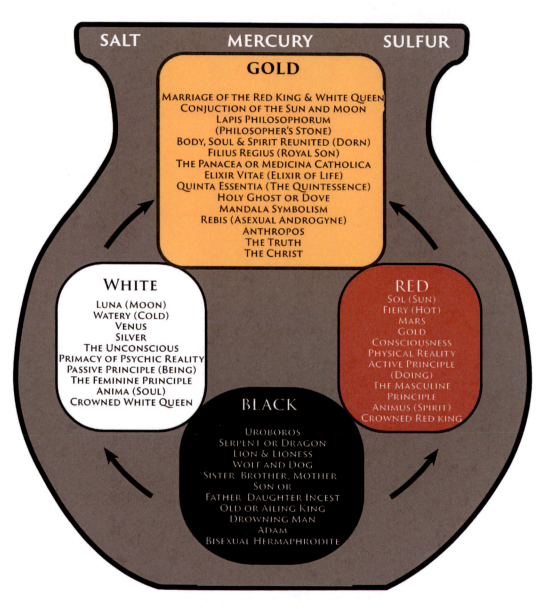

Figure 16. The Alchemical Black, White, and Red: Stages of Transformation
(L. Ehlers)

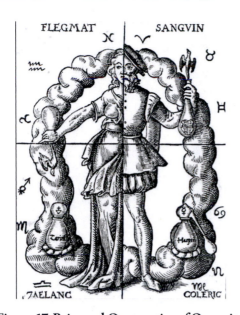

Figure 17. Pairs and Quaternties of Opposites
(Leonhart Thurneisser zum Thurn, *Quinta Essentia*, 1574)

Figure 18. Two-headed Rebis
(Herbrandt Jamsthaler, *Viatorium Spagyricum*)

or gaseous/solid; precious, or costly/cheap, or common; good/evil; open/occult, or hidden; East/West; living/dead, or inert; masculine/feminine; Sol/Luna.[262]

In the alchemical literature favorite theriomorphic images of the opposites are an eagle flying in the air attached by a chain to a toad on the ground, or two birds or dragons, one winged, the other wingless. In the *Book of Lambspring* are images of two fish swimming in opposite directions,[263] quarreling wolves(Figure 19),[264] a stag and a unicorn standing together in a forest (Figure 24),[265] or in *Philosophia Reformata,* a lion and lioness (Figure 6).[266] All symbolize a polarity, which for Jung "constitutes the phenomenology of the paradoxical self, man's totality."[267]

If the red and white opposites are present from the beginning as the *prima materia*, they

are pictured by the alchemists as the *uroboros,* the snake with its tail in its mouth; as a serpent or dragon; as sister/brother, father/daughter, or mother/son incest, and so on. In creation myths, such as the Egyptian myth of Nut and Geb, the pair are the World Parents united in eternal sexual embrace who must be forcibly separated so the world can be created. This unconscious union of opposites is often pictured in the alchemical literature as a Rebis (Figure 18). The *Rebis* (Latin for *res bina,* "double thing") was a symbol of Mercurius, god of the beginning (for Poncé, as hermaphrodite (see Figure 5) and the end of the opus (as androgyne).[268]

As the *prima materia* or *masa confusa,* these images represent the original unconscious, the static union of opposites. Psychologically, this represents an unconscious state of being in an individual, like the unconscious merger of

Figure 19. Quarreling Male and Female Wolves
(*Musaeum Hermeticum*, 1678)

Figure 20. Crowned Couple Lying in a Coffin
(Mylius, *Philosophia Reformata*, 1622)

infant with mother, akin to the paranoid/schizoid position, an inner psychological state with little perspective outside of oneself.[269]

If the opposites are brought together before the substances have been properly separated or differentiated, they are caustic or poisonous to one another. As noted earlier, the dark (white) moon is dangerous; salt can be corrosive, biting; and untreated (red) sulfur can be caustic, burning, and destructive. Jung says at first the process of integration is a "fiery conflict . . . The intensity of the conflict is expressed in symbols like fire and water, height and depth, life and death."[270]

The result of a premature *coniunctio* is a *mortificatio*, as seen in the chapter on the *nigredo*, or a "Dysfunctional *Coniunctio*." At this stage, the alchemical literature contains images of fighting, dismemberment and death (see Figure 16, lower section).

At this stage, male and female wolves (Figure 19) or lion and lioness (Figure 6), fight or consume each other and are destroyed.[271] *Sol* disappears into the well of *Luna*; the paws are cut off the Lion; the wings of the Eagle are clipped; the King is killed or drowned; a body is dismembered (Figure 11); or a couple lie in a coffin (Figure 20).

The conflict is also expressed in this alchemical passage from *Consilium coniugii*. The warring opposites as *prima materia* mate, kill each other, and die:

> This is the red Sulfur … of the Philosophers, and it is also called the poisonous serpent, because, like this, it bites off the head of the male in the lustful heat of conception and giving birth it dies and is divided through the midst. So also, the moisture of the moon, when she receives his light, slays the sun, and at the birth of the child of the Philosophers she dies likewise, and at death the two parents yield up their souls to the son, and die and pass away. And the parents are the food of the son.[272]

This passage is an example of the premature *coniunctio* as a death-marriage, as seen in my *albedo* dream of the "Death Marriage." We also see it in this woodcut of the King and Queen in a coffin (Figure 20), with Saturn and Death flanking the mortified couple. The coffin is not unlike Sleeping Beauty's. Inside, the King and Queen (an actual couple, or a woman and her *animus,* or a man and his *anima*) are in a death-like stillness or torpor.

What do these images of fighting, dismemberment, or death mean? In analysis, it means that an uprising of unconscious contents is often accompanied by a corresponding lessening of ego-consciousness (that is, the ruling dominant represented by the red lion, the king, or *Sol*) so that the encounter feels like a death, a mortification, a putrefaction— the stuff of the *nigredo*. Furthermore, authors such as Grinnell posit that it is our negative, destructive shadow qualities that need purifying before they can be brought together in a true *coniunctio*.[273]

Before the unrefined *prima materia* of the red and white, sulfur and salt, *Sol* and *Luna* can be happily joined, what is needed first is a separation or differentiation of the opposites into their separate archetypal poles (see Figure 16, middle section). The alchemist Ripley says, "The *coniunctio* is the uniting of *separated* qualities, or an equalizing of principles."[274] Hillman carries the point further: "Alchemy warns that only separated things can join. Before any two things such as moon and sun can be conjunct or experienced as conjunct, they must be distinguished … Their union requires that each must be stubbornly different."[275]

But what is it that must be separated? In the alchemist Dorn's view, it is the little figures of Spirit (*animus*) and Soul (*anima*) that must separate from the body (Figure 9) before they can reunite with it. Von Franz says this separation is what the Christian mystics understood as the separation from the body and the surrendering of instinctual desires to the spiritual part of the soul.[276]

The necessary separation or splitting of the original unity always feels like a death, a *mortificatio*. However, Charles Poncé says, "In

Figure 21. The Peacock
(*Splendor Solis*, folio 28)

every instance the splitting of the hermaphrodite leads to the birth of consciousness."[277] The painful separation, which in analysis may take time and a great deal of effort, leads to a more sharply defined, clearly delineated pair of opposites, the *albedo* and *rubedo*.

As Hillman has said, before the opposites can be conjunct, they must be firmly separated, stubbornly different. As Chapters 3 and 5 on the *albedo* and *rubedo,* respectively, have demonstrated, the cool, watery, silver-white *Luna* complements the hot, fiery, gold-red *Sol*. And lunar consciousness, a yielding, receptive, interior world of images and dreams embodying

22. Marriage of the King and Queen
(Mylius, *Philosophia Reformata*, 1622)

the primacy of psychic reality contrasts sharply with the active, strong, energetic, vital force embedded in physical reality that is solar consciousness. When—and only when—the impurities present in the white and the red themselves have been cleansed (washed) and calcined (burned away) are the two ready to be joined in a true "greater" *coniunctio*.

As is true of all archetypal images, the *coniunctio* was pictured by the alchemists in many different ways. In Figure 21, The Peacock, we see the first hints of this coming together of masculine and feminine in the many figures of happy couples dressed in red and white garments, enjoying themselves with food, drink, music, poetry, dance, and lovemaking. The Peacock, spreading its shimmering fan, heralds the *dawn* of the new day, but it is not

the new day.[278] It is an awakening to an entirely new basis for life and for true relatedness—yet much work remains for it to manifest in life.[279] My 1984 Citadel dream was an example of the dawn of the new day, but it took another four decades for it to become fully realized.

The *coniunctio* was also pictured as a marriage of bridegroom and bride or King and Queen, as in the alchemical engraving shown in Figure 22. Here, King and Queen, right hands joined, standing triumphant on the backs of a united lion/lioness, have finally been brought into a united harmony with one another. From the jaw of the united lion/lioness the waters of life now flow freely. Jung says this is an image "in which the marriage of the red man and the white woman, Sol and Luna, is consummated."[280]

Neumann describes this union of the white and the red in terms of matriarchal and patriarchal principles:

> Then, patriarchal sun-consciousness reunites with the earlier, more fundamental phase, and matriarchal consciousness, with its central symbol, the moon, arises from the deep, imbued with the regenerating power of its primal waters, to celebrate the old *heiros gamos* of moon and sun on a new and higher plane, the plane of the human psyche.
>
> For the masculine as for the feminine, wholeness is attainable only when in a union of opposites, the day and the night, the upper and the lower, the patriarchal consciousness and the matriarchal, come to their own kind of productivity and mutually supplement and fructify one another.[281]

However, I must stress that the Red King and the White Queen are not *two individuals*, but two archetypal principles found within *one individual*, which Jung termed *anima* and *animus*: "As numina, the *anima* and *animus* represent a supreme pair of opposites . . . giving the promise of union.[282] For many alchemists the union of the male and female, or marriage of King and Queen, was the ultimate goal of the opus. For others, the *coniunctio* resulted in the

Figure 23. The Royal Son
(Mylius, *Philosophia Reformata,* 1622)

birth of a "third thing," a royal son (Figure 23).

The alchemists called this child *infans* (baby), *puer* (boy), *filius regius* (royal son), *filius philosophorum* (Philosopher's Son), and so on. Consider the description of the royal son from *Artis auriferae* II:

> I am crowned and adorned with a diadem and clothed with kingly garments; for I cause joy to enter into bodies . . . Come hither, ye sons of wisdom, let us be glad and rejoice, for the dominion of death is over and the son reigns; he is clothed with the red garment, and the purple is put on. Our son of royal birth takes his tincture from the fire, and death, darkness and the waters flee . . . The hidden treasures will be laid open, and our son, already vivified, is become a warrior of the fire and surpasses the tincture.[283]

The glorious end-product of the opus was

referred to by the alchemists in many ways, listed in the upper section of Figure 16: The Marriage of the Red King & White Queen; Conjunction of the Sun and Moon; Body, Soul, and Spirit Reunited; the Philosopher's Stone; the Philosopher's Son; the Elixir of Life; the Panacea; the Quintessence; the Mandala; the Rebis or asexual androgyne; the Anthropos or universal human, to mention only a few. These are all alchemical terms or images for the Self, the alchemical "gold" that the alchemists were seeking.

Jung says, "Psychologically, the self is a union of consciousness and unconsciousness. It stands for the psychic totality"[284] and "represents a state of interior oneness which today we call individuation."[285]

The alchemist Dorn conceived of it as "a psychic equilibration of opposites . . . a state of equanimity transcending the body's affectivity and instinctuality."[286] For Jung, "In our psychological language today we express [this as] becoming conscious of the good and the bad qualities in our character . . . maximum consciousness, which amounts to maximal freedom of the will."[287] For von Franz, the *coniunctio* is a bringing together of spirit and body; in the process, the "white" is "reddened" and the "red" is "whitened." In psychological terms, she explains that:

> The body, the material thing, becomes spiritualized and the spirit in turn becomes concrete . . . In practice . . . that means if you recognize something as right and put it into action then it becomes real . . . And to understand a concrete situation symbolically . . . is to take myself out of it and see its symbolic aspect . . . that would be spiritualizing the physical.[288]

Other ways of expressing the *coniunctio* as the bringing together of the white and the red are found in the words of two Jungian analysts: Steven Joseph terms the white as "image," the

Figure 24. Stag and Unicorn in the Wood
(Basilius Valentinus, *Philaletha*)

red as "affect"; or the white as "psyche" and the red as "soma." The goal of the work is the "healing of the psychosomatic split."[289] In slightly different terms, James Hillman conceives of the "whitened" or "silvered" contents of the unconscious as "psyche," and the "reddened" contents as "life." In his words, "Psyche is life, life psyche"; they unite.[290] I would add white as "being," red as "doing," and their conjunction as a balanced, harmonious blending of life's "being" and "doing."

The text below Lambspring's image of the stag (red deer) and unicorn in the wood (Figure 24) says, "Soul and Spirit are in the Body." We met the stag in my 1977 pre-*rubedo* dream of the woman in red with huge antlers on her head. At that point in my work, the too-big antlers were part of my distorted inner masculine (*animus*), as my true inner masculine spirit was not yet embodied in consciousness.

It would be three more years of intense and painful work before my 1980 *albedo* dream of the unicorn, heralded a more balanced inner feminine soul (*anima*). Only after the *rubedo* period of 1982 ushered in a healthier *animus* in my psyche were the two ready to be brought together as more fully developed and balanced aspects of my inner feminine and inner masculine nature.

The idea of the totality of the Self is not original to Jung, however. Over 130 years ago Hitchcock intuited this center of the personality when he wrote the following:

How can anyone one fail to see that . . . the centre of the universe is in himself... ? This is that centre which is said to be everywhere, but whose circumference is said to be nowhere . . . This so-called centre has never been named by any word conveying an idea of it . . . It has been treated of in figures and symbols in infinite ways. Probably no single building in the world would contain the books that have been written about it. It has been called the one, the middle, the equilibrium, the eternal, the unchangeable, the immutable, the self-sufficient, the self-existent, &c., and yet not any of these words serve to make it known; and the moment any name is acknowledged for it, the word becomes "ill-assorted," and its sense passes out of view; and yet this centre remains the sole foundation of philosophy, without which or out of which no man can feel any assured and continued conviction that he has the truth.[291]

And in the Dead Sea Scrolls, we find this in the "Gospel According to St. Thomas":

Shall we, being children, enter the kingdom? And Jesus answered them: "When you make the two one, and when you make the inner as the outer, and the outer as the inner, and the above as the below, and when you make the male and the female into a single one so that the male will be not only male and the female not be only female, then shall you enter the kingdom."[292]

Totality in this sense is beyond difference. Hillman makes the same point: "It is not the recognition of two differences, but the

Figure 25. The White Queen and the Red King
(*Splendor Solis*, folio 10)

realization that differences are each images which do not deny each other, oppose each other, or even require each other. In fact, as differences, they have gone away."[293] This "single one" whose differences "have gone away" is, for Poncé, symbolized by Christ: "In religious traditions this figure is always thought of as an intensification and broadening of our humanity, a time of unequivocal freedom symbolized as the result of a marriage."[294]

Thus, the initial or lesser *coniunctio*, eventual separation, and final or greater *coniunctio* of the opposites can be understood as an archetypal death, rebirth, and transformation mystery. What began as a fighting lion, snarling dog, sick old man, or ailing King is transformed into the robust, red-robed King; and the lioness, bitch, or dragon into the regal white-robed Queen (Figure 25).

If the archetypal feminine principle (*albedo*) and the archetypal masculine principle (*rubedo*) have each been fully realized, then the alchemical *coniunctio* (marriage) of the White Queen and the Red King can take place: fully separated and purified opposites brought together in a union of moon and sun; the four elements (Earth and Water as the feminine elements upon which the Queen stands, Air and Fire as the masculine elements upon which the King stands); the unconscious and conscious; soul and body; matter and spirit; the cool, watery, passive silvery-white lunar principle with the hot, fiery, active gold-red solar principle. The white, as Yin, or lunar consciousness, is a yielding, receptive, interior world of images and dreams embodying the primacy of psychic reality. This contrasts sharply but does not oppose the red as Yang: the active, energetic vital force of physical reality that is solar consciousness. Together, they form a complementary whole—a healthy balance of masculine and feminine energies. To be whole, one must have both.

So why did the early alchemists claim that the achievement of the *rubedo* alone was the culmination of the opus? From our modern perspective this question is troublesome. But if looked at from a broader perspective, it makes sense. When alchemy flourished, from at least the sixth century BCE through the Middle Ages, the world was basically an *albedo* world steeped in lunar consciousness and connected to the rhythms of nature—day and night and the round of the seasons—and therefore to a deep connection to the timeless cyclical qualities of Mother Earth. Thus, to the alchemists of antiquity and the Middle Ages, a more active, masculine-centered *rubedo* consciousness anchored in time would, of course, have been the climax of the Great Work.

From today's perspective, through the suppression of the archetypal feminine and the gradual rise of solar masculine consciousness (aided by the advent of the Industrial Revolution), Western civilization has evolved into a heavily lopsided *rubedo* world, with little room, patience, understanding, or respect for *albedo* consciousness. Our work today is to reclaim the lost feminine and put her on equal footing with the masculine: an archetypal pair working in complementary harmony. (Concrete ideas of how to achieve this balance are presented in Appendix D, "Balancing White and Red: Pearls of Wisdom for the Journey Ahead.")

The fact that the *albedo* and *rubedo* belong together as parts of a greater whole is corroborated in many cross-cultural symbol systems: in the ancient Chinese concept of Yin and Yang; in the Indian system of Tantric Yoga; in cross-cultural rites and customs; and surprisingly, in the physiology of the human body, as explored in the following section.

WHITE AND RED IN CROSS-CULTURAL MOTIFS AND SYMBOLISM

As archetypes, the white and the red as a pair are universal. Thus, we find correspondence to the alchemical motifs and symbolism of the white and the red in many cultures across time. I mention two of these motifs, found in Chinese Taoism and Indian Kundalini Yoga color symbolism, briefly.

Yin and Yang in the *I Ching*, or *Book of Changes*

Perhaps the first and most well-known differentiation of these two principles or polarities is to be found in an ancient Chinese system, the *I Ching*, or *Book of Changes.* The earliest collections of hexagrams come from the second and first millennia BCE.

The philosophy underlying the *I Ching* is to be found in the idea of change, the law of the "tao" by Lao-Tsu in the sixth century BCE. In his philosophy, the great primal beginning of all that exists, *t'ai chi*, is represented by a circle divided into opposites, light and dark, Yang and Yin.[295] In the *I Ching* these two principles are *Ch'ien*—the creative, active, light, spirit principle known as Yang, and *K'un*—the receptive, dark, earth principle known as Yin. In the Richard Wilhelm and Cary Baynes' translation of the *I Ching* these two principles are described as follows:

Ch'ien, The Creative: The first hexagram is made up of six unbroken lines. These unbroken lines stand for the primal power, which is light-giving, active, strong, and of the spirit. The hexagram is consistently strong in character, and since it is without weakness, its essence is power or energy. Its image is heaven. Its energy is represented as unrestricted by any fixed conditions in space and is therefore conceived of as motion. Time is regarded as the basis of this motion. Thus, the hexagram includes also the power of time and the power of persisting in time, that is, duration.[296]

Ch'ien, the solar principle, is similar to the alchemical *rubedo*. *K'un* is its female complement:

K'un, The Receptive: This hexagram is made up of broken lines only. The broken line represents the dark, yielding, receptive primal power of yin. The attribute of the hexagram is devotion; its image is the earth. It is the perfect complement of The Creative—the complement, not the opposite, for the Receptive does not combat the creative but completes it. It represents nature in contrast to spirit, earth in contrast to heaven, space as against time, the female-maternal as against the male-paternal. However, as applied to human affairs, the principle of this complementary relationship is found not only in the relation between man and woman, but also in that between prince and minister and between father and son. Indeed, even in the individual this duality appears in the coexistence of the spiritual world of the senses.[297]

K'un is similar to the alchemical image of the *albedo*. *Ch'ien* and *K'un* are not opposites, but complementary halves of the same whole. As the *I Ching* says, "The Receptive . . . is the perfect complement of The Creative—the complement, not the opposite, for the Receptive does not combat the creative but completes it."[298] This poem by an early Chinese alchemist, Pai-Chu-I, expresses this complementarity:

> The Yin and Yang ingredients were in
>   conjunction
> Manifesting an aspect I had not foreseen,
> Locked together in the posture of man
>   and wife
> Entwined like dragons coil upon coil.[299]

In China as in the West, alchemists created numerous phrases to describe the union of Yin and Yang. In 1284 CE, Yu Yen collected a list of these, which sound strikingly similar to Western alchemical expressions for the union of salt and sulfur or *Sol* and *Luna*:

> entwining of the tortoise and the serpent
> union of the red and white
> intermixture of heaven and earth
> the male and the female following one
>   another
> reunion of the Herd-boy and the Weaving
>   girl

> conjugal felicity
> the moon and the sun in the same
>   palace[300]

This is the idea behind the alchemical synthesis or conjunction of opposites: spirit and body, psyche and soma, being and doing. Female and male energies are no longer warring but living in harmonious complementarity.

Indian Kundalini Yoga Color Symbolism

A striking corollary to the female-male symbolism of white and red and their conjunction in alchemy is also found in the Indian Kundalini Yoga chakra system. According to Kundalini Yoga philosophy, within the human body along the spinal axis, there are centers of energy called *chakras*. Connecting the chakras are three *nadis*, known as nerve centers or channels. The *sushumna nadi* rises straight up the center of the spine, from its base to the top of the head, locus of "the lotus of the 1,000 petals."[301] The *ida nadi* originates at the base of the spine to the left of the first chakra and culminates in the left nostril; it is known as the moon nadi: its color is white, and its function is cooling. The *pingala nadi* originates to the right of the first chakra and culminates in the right nostril; it is known as the sun nadi: its color is red, and its function is heating. The breath from the left nostril is known as the moon breath; the breath from the right nostril is known as the sun breath. Through breathing exercises, the individual learns to equalize the flow of breath from both nostrils in order to come into harmony with the body's energy centers.[302]

At the level of the first (lowest) chakra, *Kundalini* (divine female energy known as Shakti, the "Inner Woman") in the form of a serpent lies dormant, coiled three times around the divine *Lingam*, or male phallus.[303] The Lingam rests within a yellow triangle identified as the *Yoni* or female genitals.

Through the practice of yoga involving special body positions (*asanas*) and breathing exercises (*pranayama*), the individual awakens Kundalini, which cannot rise until both breaths are equal. When sun and moon breaths are equal, Kundalini (divine female energy) rises through the *sushumna* to unite with Shiva (divine male energy), sitting in the last chakra. The union of Shiva and Shakti, divine male and female energies, is a transcendent experience, an experience of personal wholeness. This union finds its corollary in the sacred marriage of alchemy, which Mookerjee compares to the "*mysterium coniunctionis*" described by Jung.[304] He says, "By yoking together the opposites within himself, the individual harmonizes all experience, thereby abolishing duality and transcending the phenomenal world."[305]

Curiously, in the symbolism of Indian Kundalini Yoga and in Tantric art and philosophy, the colors of the male and female principles are reversed: Shiva, the white (male) principle, or pure consciousness, represents the inactive static aspect of the ultimate. And Shakti, the red (female) principle, represents the world force, the kinetic energy of the concrete universe, the power to respond and to evolve.[306] In this system, visible in Tantric painting, the inactive male essence—"form"—is white, and the active female essence—"energy"—is red. In Jewish mysticism too, red corresponds with the feminine and white with the masculine side of the Sefiroth system; the two together constitute the perfect human.[307]

The correspondence of the red and white with alchemy in these systems lies in their essence as "active" and "passive" principles, but the assignment of "male" and "female" to their colors is reversed. Why? One can only wonder if, when these systems evolved, the more ancient civilizations of the East, still rooted in matriarchal consciousness, would have conceived of the birth-giving feminine as the active principle, whereas in the more swiftly developing patriarchal world of the West, the "active" principle would be appropriated by the masculine.

Physiological Corollaries to White & Red: Cross-Cultural and Split-Brain Research

Cross-Cultural Research. William Domhoff's thoughtful exploration of the myth and symbolism of left and right recognizes the male-female duality in human consciousness in other cultures. For instance, Australian Aborigines hold the "male" stick in the right hand and the "female" stick in the left hand. The Mojave Indians believe the left hand is the passive, maternal side of the person;

the right hand is the active father. Bedouin Arabs believe women are bad and live on the left side of the tent; men are good and live on the right side of the tent. For the Maori of New Zealand, left is associated with bad, dark, profane, feminine, night, homosexuality, and death; the opposites of these are associated with the right.[308] Domhoff concludes that the left is often the area of the taboo, the sacred, the unconscious, the feminine, the intuitive, the dreamer; the right is the opposite.

Domhoff also describes a study of left and right by Osgood et al., using a technique called the *semantic differential*.[309] Left is described as bad, dark, profane, female, unclean, night, west, curved, limp, weak, mysterious, low, ugly, black, incorrect, and death. Right is the opposite: good, light, sacred, male, clean, day, east, straight, erect, strong, commonplace, high, beautiful, white, correct, and life.[310]

Expanding on this male/female dichotomy between left and right, I assumed that in cultures with shamanic traditions, it would be the inward-looking left eye that is clouded or closed while the right eye, focused on outer reality, would be open or clear. But in doing further research, I discovered that the crossover of optic nerves at the optic chiasm from each eye extend to both sides of the brain. So it is no surprise that although most of visionary artist

Figure 26. *Palimpsest*

Susan Seddon-Bouilet's numerous paintings of shamanic figures show one eye clouded or closed and the other eye open and clear, there is a fairly even split between those with the left eye clouded or closed, as in her painting Palimpsest (Figure 26), and those with the right eye closed, as seen in this Inuit whalebone carving (Figure 27) with its left eye open and right eye closed.[311]

Considered either way, "with one eye closed, focused on the inner world of dreams and the mytho-poetic images of the imagination, and one eye open, focused outwardly on the harder edges of material reality,"[312] Donald Kalsched might as well be describing the *albedo* with its clouded or closed "eye" turned toward

Figure 27. *The Storyteller*
Alaskan Inuit whalebone carving. Artist unknown.
(Courtesy of Donald Kalsched)

the inner world and the *rubedo* with its clearly focused "eye" on the outer world: "the two worlds that must be kept in view if a genuine and compelling human story . . . is to be told."[313]

Thus, the Chinese Taoist system of Yin and Yang, the Indian Kundalini Yoga concept of Ida and Pingala or Shakti and Shiva, anthropological research on left and right, shamanic traditions, and the alchemical colors white and red are all embodiments of the archetypal principles of female and male. In addition, the concept of Yin and Yang, or Shiva and Shakti, as complementary halves of the same whole find their corollary in the alchemical *coniunctio* of white and red as the balance of energies

necessary for the inner unity or wholeness of the individual. Thus, the two principles left and right, masculine and feminine, are found not only across cultures and time, but also in the physiology of the human brain as well.

Split-Brain Research. In a fascinating study of the two sides of the brain called *split-brain research*, Robert Ornstein notes differences between the right and left cerebral hemispheres:

Although each hemisphere shares the potential for many functions, and both sides participate in most activities, in the normal person the two hemispheres tend to specialize. The left hemisphere (connected to the right side of the body) is predominantly involved with analytic, logical thinking, especially in verbal and mathematical functions. Its mode of operation is primarily linear. This hemisphere seems to process information sequentially. This mode of operation of necessity must underlie logical thought, since logic depends on sequence and order. Language and mathematics, both left-hemisphere activities, also depend predominantly on linear time.

If the left hemisphere is specialized for analysis, the right hemisphere (connected to the left side of the body) seems specialized for holistic mentation. Its language ability is quite limited. This hemisphere is primarily responsible for our orientation in space, artistic endeavor, crafts, body image, recognition of faces. It processes information more diffusely than does the left hemisphere, and its responsibilities demand a ready integration of many inputs

	LEFT HEMISPHERE	RIGHT HEMISPHERE	SOURCE
ORNSTEIN	RIGHT (SIDE OF BODY)	LEFT (SIDE OF BODY)	Domhoff
	DAY	NIGHT	Many sources
	VERBAL	SPATIAL	Many scources
	INTELLECTUAL	SENSUOUS	Blackburn
	TIME, HISTORY	ETERNITY, TIMELESSNESS	Oppenheimer
	ACTIVE	RECEPTIVE	Deikman
	EXPLICIT	TACIT	Polanyi
	ANALYTIC	GESTALT	Levy, Sperry
	PROPOSITIONAL	APPOSITIONAL	Bogen
	LINEAL	NON-LINEAL	Lee
	SEQUENTIAL	SIMULTANEOUS	Luria
	YANG	YIN	*I Ching*
	THE CREATIVE: HEAVEN, MASCULINE, LIGHT	THE RECEPTIVE: EARTH, FEMININE, DARK	*I Ching*
	TIME	SPACE	*I Ching*
	INTELLECTUAL	INTUITIVE	Many sources
	BUDDHI	MANAS	Vedanta
	CAUSAL	ACAUSAL	Jung
	ARGUMENT	EXPERIENCE	Bacon
TAYLOR	HEAD	HEART	Taylor
	DOING	BEING	Taylor
	THINKING	FEELING	Taylor
	CONSCIOUSNESS	BODY'S INSTINCTIVE CONSCIOUSNESS	Taylor
	YANG	YIN	*I Ching*
	WORK MIND	VACATION MIND	Taylor
	RESEARCHER MIND	DIPLOMATIC MIND	Taylor
	MASCULINE MIND	FEMININE MIND	Taylor
	HARDER EDGES	SOFTER BOUNDARIES	Taylor
	CONCERNED WITH PARTICULARS	FOCUS ON THE BIGGER PICTURE OF HOW THINGS RELATE TO ONE ANOTHER	Taylor
	SENSING MIND	INTUITIVE MIND	Jung
	JUDGING MIND	PERCEIVING MIND	Jung
	SMALL-S SELF	OUR INNER AUTHENTIC SELF (SIMILAR TO CAPITAL-S SELF)	Taylor

Table 4. Dichotomies between Left and Right Hemispheres of the Brain: Ornstein[315] compared to Taylor[317]

at once. If the left hemisphere can be termed predominantly analytic and sequential in its operation, then the right hemisphere is more holistic and relational, and more simultaneous in its mode of operation.[314]

Ornstein says recognizing that these two cerebral hemispheres are specialized to operate in different ways allows us to understand much about the fundamental duality in our consciousness. This duality is reflected in literature as between "reason and passion," "mind and intuition," "conscious and unconscious." Ornstein says, "The workings of the 'conscious' mind are held to be accessible to language and to rational discourse and alteration; the 'unconscious' is much less accessible to reason or to verbal analysis. Some aspects of 'unconscious' communication are gestures, facial and body movements, and tone of voice."[315]

Ornstein believes these two modes of consciousness are manifest on several levels simultaneously: within each person, between people, within different disciplines (especially psychology), and in the organization of cultures. He clarifies the concept by presenting (see Table 4) a set of dichotomies between the two modes of consciousness.

In this list we recognize fundamental differences similar to those found in the dichotomy between white and red, lunar and solar, feminine and masculine. But Ornstein does not stop there: "A complete human consciousness involves the polarity and integration of the two modes, as a complete day includes the daylight and the darkness."[316]

Jill Bolte Taylor's book *My Stroke of Insight: A Brain Scientist's Personal Journey* corroborates—from her lived and very personal perspective—Ornstein's theoretical/scientific research into the two hemispheres of the human brain.[317] After a stroke that rendered her dominant left brain incapacitated and her eight-year effort to fully recover, Dr. Taylor, a Harvard brain scientist, drew similar distinctions between the brain's two hemispheres (Table 4).

While Taylor's descriptions contain a great deal of overlap with Ornstein's model, Taylor differs with Ornstein in two key respects. Where Ornstein labels the left brain as "Conscious" and the right brain as "Unconscious," Taylor disagrees:

In the case of the Dr. Jekyll and Mr. Hyde analogy, our right hemisphere personality is depicted as an uncontrollable, potentially violent, moronic, rather despicable ignoramus, which is not even conscious, and without whom we would probably be better off! In vast contrast, our left mind has routinely been touted as linguistic, sequential, methodical, rational, smart, and the seat of our consciousness.[318]

From her experience, however, the right brain, focused on the "right here, right now" is highly conscious. She labels it "our body's instinctive consciousness."[319] This side of the brain "accurately decodes emotion and is sensitive to nonverbal communication."[320] The body's instinctual consciousness includes "awareness of the richness of this present moment . . . [in which] everything exists on a continuum of relativity, heedless of territories or artificial boundaries like race or religion, in which we are all equal members of the human family."[321] In this vein, Taylor's experience moves us beyond Ornstein's scientific/theoretical model into the metaphysical realm. Immediately after her stroke, with her left hemisphere incapacitated and its language center silenced, but with her right brain's functioning fully intact,

> All I could perceive was right here, right now, and it was beautiful."[322] . . . An unforgettable sense of peace pervaded my entire being and I felt calm.[323] . . . I was completely entranced by the feelings of tranquility, safety, blessedness, euphoria, and omniscience.[324] . . . Heaven existed in a consciousness that soared in eternal bliss.[325] . . . I was a being of light radiating life into the world.[326] . . . My left hemisphere had been trained to perceive itself as a solid, separate from others. Now, released from that restrictive circuitry, my right hemisphere relished in its attachment to the eternal flow. I was no longer isolated and alone. My soul was as big as the universe and frolicked with glee in a boundless sea.[327] . . . I felt like a genie liberated from its bottle. The energy of my spirit seemed to flow like a great whale gliding through a sea of silent euphoria.[328]

She describes this side of her being as content, compassionate, empathic, nurturing, and eternally optimistic; here she experiences innocence and inner joy and feels free to explore the world again with childlike curiosity: "open to the eternal flow whereby I exist as one with the universe. It is the seat of my Divine Mind, the Knower, the Wise Woman and the Observer, my Intuition and higher consciousness."[329]

However, in line with Ornstein, Taylor concludes, "Whatever language you use to describe your two parts, based on my experience, I believe they stem anatomically from the two very distinct hemispheres inside your head."[330] Thus, what I have been exploring throughout this book is a fundamental bipolar archetype, manifested intuitively at the cultural, religious, psychological, and philosophical levels, two thousand years before its discovery at the physiological level. This argues for the fact that the *albedo* and *rubedo* as lunar and solar essences are not random, but based on profound human intuitive "knowing," beyond modern "scientific" knowing.

During the eight-year process of her recovery Dr. Taylor says, "My goal has been to find a healthy balance between the functional abilities of my two hemispheres."[331] This balancing of the two hemispheres, or, in alchemical terms, the balancing of the red and the white—the *albedo* and the *rubedo*—is a theme explored in the Epilogue.

DREAMS OF WHITE AND RED TOGETHER

After the healing of the wounded feminine and the development of a stronger, more confident *anima* during the *albedo* phase of my work, and after the arrival of a healthy inner masculine *animus* during the *rubedo* phase and the dream of the Citadel as my true center, or the Self, the union of the white and the red, *albedo* and *rubedo*, female and male, *anima* and *animus*, is now possible. Three dreams confirm this.

June 4, 1983. *BERRY PIE. I am carrying a pie shell (just the crust) and step barefooted into an earthen or sod hut with a thick old wooden door. Inside, I am to exchange my empty pie shell for a filled pie shell. The filled pies are embedded in the earthen floor, on a level with the floor. We must watch where we are stepping so as not to step on a ready-made pie. I look around and choose what I think is an apple pie and begin to unearth it. The pie is just for me. The pie crust I came in with was about eight inches in diameter, and I am about to replace it with one of comparable size. However, as I unearth it, it seems to grow in size until I stand with an enormous pie in my arms, approximately eighteen inches in diameter, enough to serve eighteen people! I vaguely remember a man standing in front of me telling me this one is too large for me alone, but now that I have unearthed it, it is mine. I'm surprised to see it is a berry pie and marvel at its deep berry-red color.*

The setting is an old earthen hut, suggesting a womb-like feminine *temenos*. My pie shell, a symbolically feminine container, has been baked (an *albedo* activity) and is now ready to be filled. I enter a low earthen hut, and from the earth itself dig up a finished pie. That is, from the ground of my own feminine being, I unearth something with which I can now serve others. Although I think I want apple pie—something belonging to the collective American psyche—what I unearth is something more unique to me: a berry pie, the color of the *rubedo*, a masculine *rubedo* consciousness contained within the fully baked white pie shell of feminine *albedo* consciousness. Once it is dug out of my unconscious and is in my hands (brought up into consciousness), it grows to a surprising size, suggesting that in the course of my analysis I have grown, and further, that if I work with the *rubedo* energies this pie represents, further growth and expansion is possible—more than I ever imagined. Although I hear a male voice telling me this pie is too much for me alone, now that it is in my hands, it is mine. Is this the voice of the collective male, fearful of women's power and authority? Or my own voice, fearful of my own power and authority? Or is this voice simply positing a truth: that this numinous pie that expands when unearthed is not meant for me alone; it is a gift that must be shared. Gertrude Jobes's definition of "pie" as a round sacrificial cake would confirm the last interpretation—that I offer myself in service to others.[332] Jobes defines "berry," with its many seeds, as the fruit of marriage.[333] From the inner marriage, or *coniunctio* of white and red or lunar and solar energies within, I am given the fruit of that marriage, a berry pie, with which I can now serve many people—more, even, than I had ever dreamed.

January 9, 1985. *SHRIMP FEAST. I go to visit a woman. She flies me around her land. We stop in the center of her land and enter an old abandoned building (a school?). We sit down on the floor, spread out newspapers and have a feast of shrimp and langoustines. Then I am planting the shrimp in the center of something else, so they will multiply. Now there are more langoustines.*

The colors of red and white in this dream are more implicit than explicit: red shrimp spread on a white-and-black newspaper. The image of centrality appears twice: I'm in the center of the land, and I plant shrimp in the center of something and they multiply. The shrimp feast, too, may be a symbol of *albedo-rubedo* energy, which when firmly planted in one's psychic center, can multiply. This theme of making use of or giving back what has been given has been seen repeatedly in the dream record: the black oil, the white ash, the berry pie, and now the shrimp or langoustines. This theme of *multiplicatio* appears again in the final dream:

May 7, 1985. *IMMERSION. I have been selected by the whole village to be the Spring Maiden or the Harvest Queen. I am to be immersed in the village water supply. I must disrobe, carefully wrap my whole body with sterile white gauze, and then immerse myself in the water, which serves the whole village. It will then turn red. Since all the separate sheds and tubs holding the water are connected to each other,* all of the separate supplies will turn red.

A ritual is being enacted. To be selected as the Spring Maiden or the Harvest Queen is ambiguous. Similar to the ambiguity of the white-robed women as mourners or midwives, their presence as paradoxical opposites—*both* mourners *and* midwives, Spring Maiden *and* Harvest Queen—seems apropos. Spring, representing the early years of one's life, necessarily precedes the ripe maturity of Harvest time.

Wrapped like a mummy in sterile white gauze, I am in the unborn, disembodied pupa-like stage of *albedo* consciousness—a Spring Maiden not yet fully born into life. The purity, naïveté, and innocence of the Spring Maiden must be sacrificed. The body wrapped in white gauze and lowered into the water is associated not only with death and mummification, but also with baptism and rebirth. Inside the mummy-like cocoon (the therapeutic *temenos*), the process of becoming grounded in the physical reality of the body, its instincts and passions, turns the water red, the color of the *rubedo*, and what emerges is a magnificent butterfly, the ensoul'd Harvest Queen. Like Persephone—the innocent, unconscious maiden abducted into the underworld, initiated by Hades into her womanhood, and brought back as Queen of the Underworld—the Spring Maiden, after a long period of underworld or "inner-world" suffering, has been alchemically transformed into the "Harvest" Queen. The implication is that what was planted in the Spring can now, ripened and mature at the end

Figure 28. Twin Fountains (*La Toyson d'Or*)

of a long growing season, be harvested. This dream of my immersion as the white Spring Maiden and emergence from the reddened waters as the Harvest Queen is truly a dream of death, rebirth, and transformation—symbolic of the whole alchemical opus.

The alchemical image of the Twin Fountains (Figure 28), of which I had no knowledge at the time, is astonishingly similar to my "Immersion" dream.

In Figure 28, a knight with the alchemical colors black, white, yellow, and red on his breastplate stands astride two fountains connected by a conduit. In his right hand he holds a sword—the sword of discrimination, forged in the fires of suffering; in his left hand, a red shield is inscribed in gold letters in Latin. His head is surrounded by a halo of seven stars, representing the seven known planets, each connected to a metal used in the alchemical opus. His left foot stands on a fountain containing white liquid; his right foot rests astride the adjoining fountain whose liquid has turned red. The red water pours out of the twin fountain and flows through the fields toward a village in the distance. A translation of the Latin inscription on the shield reads: "From two waters make one, &c. [whereby seek to make the sun and moon . . . and multiply the stone]."[334] That is, from the uniting of the white water with the red water, or from the marriage of the sun and the moon into a true union of opposites, the "stone" of the Philosophers is multiplied.

The alchemists often wrote of a *multiplicatio*—the ability of the Philosopher's Stone to transform base matter into gold. Edinger relates the *multiplicatio* to psychotherapy:

> The psychological implications of *multiplicatio* . . . suggest that transformative effects emanate from the activated Self—the inner center—in the process of conscious realization. Also, *multiplicatio* gives us a hint as to how psychotherapy may work. To some extent, the consciousness of an individual who is related to the Self seems to be contagious and tends to multiply itself in others.[335]

So the life-giving waters, forged from the *coniunctio* of the *albedo* and the *rubedo,* will serve the whole community. In this sense, the red and white dreams are teleological, pointing my soul in the direction it needed to go: out into the world in the service of others.

The inscription on the banner sums up the entire individuation process. After my long dark night of the soul during the *nigredo* phase, followed by the gradual transformation of the *albedo* from too-naïve, too-white attitudes to a more grounded, realistic *anima,* and from the transformation of my wounded and wounding inner masculine into a more confident, assertive, energetic *animus,* I am heartened to see their conjunction at last at the Citadel, where the lunar white of *albedo* consciousness and the solar red of *rubedo* consciousness become unified into a complementary pair. Truly an alchemical opus of healing and transformation. With the resolution of my depression and anxiety, I became a therapist, a teacher, and a mentor to many—the *multiplicatio* realized.

CHRISTINA'S SANDPLAY—PHASE III: FROM TRAUMA TO *ALBEDO-RUBEDO* CONSCIOUSNESS

After Christina's return to therapy, a series of traumatic events early during Phase III changed Christina's life and paradoxically brought about a profound inner transformation. Toward the end of Phase III, when another catastrophic event occurred, Christina was able to cope with it in a remarkably centered way.

The month after Christina's *rubedo* Tray 16 (discussed in Chapter 5), she came in, reporting that the place where she worked had asked her to be its new CEO, but when she was gone on her vacation (which she reported as "the trip from Hell"), they had given the position to someone else. Feeling deeply betrayed, she wept openly with me.

The following month, still feeling betrayed at her work and by Jack, she now openly allowed her vulnerability, heartbreak, and tears to pour out. She no longer held back.

The month after that, disaster struck. Her beloved dog, who had seen her through her marriage and divorce and for years had snuggled right next to her on the bed at night, was viciously attacked and mortally wounded in front of her by two killer dogs. Despite attempts by her veterinarian to save his life, he was too badly wounded, and she had to put him down. As she told me this, Christina sobbed, saying, "He was my baby, my son, my companion, my love, my protector. My heart's been ripped open and I have no defenses left."

Tray 17. *Nigredo, Albedo, Rubedo,* and the Broken-Open Heart

Christina began by clearing out a large lake, then scattered clear glass beads around the tray, saying, "These are my tears over abandonment and loss and my heart broken open." In the *albedo* pool of deep feelings, things are coming together. The two tall women in the pool are "both the dark and light sides of my soul." The dark side is seen in the black African woman. Behind her and to her left, we see meat being roasted on a spit. Christina explained, "This is my most raw, open, wounded self. Viscerally I can 'feel' being roasted on a skewer." When I saw it, I gasped. Dismemberment and flaying are at the core of the *nigredo.* Many shamans report experiences of dismemberment as part of their initiatory ordeal. The ones who cannot survive the ordeal are the sick ones; those who survive the ordeal become the shamans and healers. The light side of Christina's soul is the tall woman in prayer; on her robe we see seven red circles, perhaps the seven chakras representing the *rubedo* life force. The goddess stands on this stone, which Christina explained was "her base." She continued, "I don't know what this is, but my heart thought it was ancient." I was stunned. This is a Native American fire starter, given to me as a parting gift by "Rose"—the only other woman besides Christina ever to put Kali into a tray. Both of their stories were presented in my article on Kali.[336] Perhaps this "base" would help Christina find her own true inner fire.

The woman on the bench is "my pot-smoking addict-self." Christina half-buried two pewter figures connected to a piece of red yarn: the open-armed woman and the kneeling woman embracing the small child. Next to the head of each woman she placed a piece of iron pyrite, saying, "These are my old pewter selves, melted and transformed," showing Christina's conscious awareness now of the hard, cold unfeeling pewter.

But she has support: just behind the tall praying woman we see her Warrior Woman with a sword: "She's got my back." In front we see Mary in a blue cape with arms outstretched, "my 'open' self." She's more human and embodied than the open-armed pewter woman. The snake with head raised "is protecting me." The apple tree is "my bountiful, giving self," the seated nude couple, "my sacred sexuality," and the jeweled red heart-shaped box into which she placed a red huayruro seed (looking for the perfect red) is "my heart's treasure." All but her Warrior Woman are pure *rubedo.*

Around the edges of the pool are five large green trees, owl and vulture

Tray 17, detail. Fire Stone

Tray 17. *Nigredo, Albedo, Rubedo,* **and the Broken-Open Heart**

totems—"Spirit-animals that came to me in a vision"—and a green "healing" snake. The red heart is "love"; the red yarn "connects my old selves with the heart"; and the blue hand with the golden heart in the palm is "soul."

If we follow a vertical *rubedo* line from the red heart in the front of the tray to the open heart box to the red circles on the gown of the tall praying goddess to the blue hand at the back of the tray, we see a deeper connection to her own true Self, now held, not in defensiveness, but in love, understanding, and compassion, symbolized by the blue hand with the golden heart in its palm as the ruling principle of this tray.

Christina was tearful the whole session about her betrayal at work, about Jack, and about a rift with AA friends over her return to pot-smoking. She said, "Now my tears are there and they're flocking to me like moths to a flame."

"Your broken-open heart has allowed your truly authentic Self to shine forth," I replied.

Christina was ready for once-a-week therapy.

Tray 18. The Self Tray

The following week Christina came in, smoothed away the sand into a perfect heart shape, and carefully brushed it clean. The Day-of-the-Dead open-heart surgery of previous trays has been transformed in the sand as a differentiation of feelings.

Then she created Tray 18.

This is one of those trays that took my breath away. I stared in awe. To speak seems sacrilege, but there is much to say.

At the top of the tray, flanked by five large green trees, the tall praying goddess with the seven red chakras stands on her fire-starter stone base. Christina said, "She holds my heart and my love." The dark goddess to her right "holds my dark pot-smoking girl." The archetype of the Self, as with all archetypes, holds both sides, the light and the dark, and both are here, side by side, as the ruling principle of the tray.

In the back-left corner is the black snake with mammalian head raised. "I don't know what this is," Christina said, but given her rootedness in her body, it seemed likely that it was her feminine Earth- or body-based wisdom.

In the center of this *albedo* lake we find something different: The Holy Family—Mary with child and an old man led by a young girl— "all parts of me," Christina indicated. They form a quaternity: man and woman, boy and girl. In front of them is an angel in an eggshell "cloud." She said, "There are three angels inside me. Grandmother: she's old, wizened, wrapped in a blanket with long gray hair and doesn't speak. Little Baby Angel Spirit: the baby I lost, still inside me. And Little Doggie-Spirit Angel: his spirit's still inside me." I felt a lump in my throat.

Christina then pulled the sword Excalibur out of the Stone and carefully placed it in the hands of the androgynous young girl/boy, gentle but strong. According to Arthurian Legend, Excalibur was the sword of Uther Pendragon, the most powerful sword ever made. In battle the glint of the sun on its blade was strong enough to blind enemies. Nearing his death, Pendragon thrust the sword into a rock and placed it under a spell that could be broken only by the next "true" King, Arthur. When she had finished, Christina asked, "What did it take in me to pull it out?" It had taken unbelievable courage to face her deepest wounds and fears, but let us look back at the whole tray to see what's happened!

The three pieces of gray stone fencing ("my old triangle fence holding my inner baby," she recalled) have split open. The defended infantile ego has been transformed into a blue stone slab (a spiritual color), with the mysterious *rubedo* egg of Tray 15 on top of it and three white blossoms nearby. Around the outside of this powerful blue heart with all of its *albedo* feelings, Christina added fifteen red blossoms, announcing the full arrival of the *rubedo*. So here we have the *coniunctio*—the sacred marriage of the white and the red, the

Tray 18. The Self Tray

albedo and the *rubedo*. When viewing other sandplay cases at conferences, I have noticed that the tray illustrating the constellation of the Self very often has this striking combination of red and white.

Joseph Henderson says, "Whenever the Self appears, the Shadow is right there."[337] Given the severity of Christina's most recent traumas, at the tip of the heart-shaped lake lies a rattlesnake in "strike" position. In later trays, Christina said this figure was Jack, "He's my poison." During a much later session, however, Christina recounted a rattlesnake dream, associating the rattlesnake to her "own wounded

self." Christina's pewter Warrior Woman is still here, protecting this new Holy Family and the young girl. Also, in the lake are "my old

Tray 18, detail. Perfect Heart

**Tray 18, detail. She
Released the Spell**

allowing space for something new and profoundly healing to enter.

The Self carries both the dark and the light sides of the soul. So the constellation of the Self can be paradoxical: the newly freed-up energies of the Self, contained in the mysterious red egg, brought new highs and new lows. In the next month, Christina had a vision of herself as a "fierce-hearted Medicine Warrior with a red office, doing Shamanic Healing." At work, she asked for—and received—more responsibility and an increase in pay. And over the next several months she decorated her office with the red she had envisioned, doubled her clientele, and began paying off debts incurred from having to cut back work during her breakdown. She also shared a collage Book of Transformation she had created, from the blackness of last year's breakdown to a garden with new life springing up. By the same token, the constellation of the Self in this last tray had given Christina the strength needed to feel her core wound to its roots. For the next several months, even as her outer world was expanding, Christina allowed herself to be depressed and to grieve openly, both in talk therapy and in her sandplay. In fact, in the very next session, Christina came in saying she had left her persona in the wastebasket out in the waiting room and over many weeks and months began revisiting the darkest parts of her childhood.

pewter selves, melted and transformed" into three pieces of iron pyrite. And just outside the lake we see two green snakes (the benign Aesculapian snake and a small green cobra) leaving the lake, their healing work done. The energies of the Self, tied up inside the lake, can now move out into the world to do their healing work—the *multiplicatio* at work in the sand.

Tray 18 is a Self-tray. The *nigredo*, *albedo*, and *rubedo* are all here. The sacred marriage of the masculine and the feminine, the *coniunctio*, was made possible because the hard, unfeeling defenses Christina had put up to protect her deeply wounded feminine have fallen apart,

Tray 19. Suffering

Tray 19. Suffering

Three months later, having connected to the Self in the last tray, Christina now had the strength to dive into the very depths of the *nigredo* and consciously face what Winnicott has described as "primitive agonies"[338] and what Kohut called "disintegration anxiety," an unnamable dread associated with the threatened dissolution of a coherent self.[339] She was tapping into feelings she had as a baby that she had warded off all her life because this was how *bad* it felt.

The four corners of the tray are anchored by black figures: clockwise from the back left, we have the black African goddess; the large blasted tree; and a polished black stone with the image of a hand etched into its surface, accompanied by a Native American woman on horseback with her travois leaving the tray, recalling her sponsor's words, "When I hurt, I leave."

New to her sandplay is a black Mayan pyramid and next to it, a Native American man on a black horse, also leaving the tray. The Native American man and woman, on their black and white horses, appear to be a pair—the male perhaps, a new, more human *animus*—also feeling the hurt enough that he is leaving the tray with her.

Inside the very large blue pool of her grief in the center of the tray are three scattered pieces of fence. Her *defenses* have been blasted open. Inside this looser triangular space is a white seashell cradling a black stone and two babies, one black (encased in fur) and one white. Are these the inner children of the Native American couple? Behind them, the black hunched-over "despair" figure sits atop a mirror, facing the shell and its tiny contents. Her pewter Warrior Woman, no longer able to protect her, has been reduced to the hunched-over figure in despair. She is now openly grieving the wounded little children inside her.

Other figures around the edges of the lake include a blue geode slab with a rattlesnake on top. After she finished the tray, Christina pointed to the rattlesnake saying, "Jack is my poison." Jack was, on the one hand, the good father/mother for her with his good cooking and tender love-making; she loved staying on his farm, close to the Earth, but she was tearful about Jack's Asperger's, saying, "He's no mirror, he's like cardboard, he can't give back." She continued, saying, "Every morning at four a.m. I awaken with a startle! Feeling huge fear!" This was her core wound, the primal terror of annihilation.

I asked, "What can hold you in comfort and security?" She closed her eyes and after a time said, "I visualized a huge black eagle swoop in. I was riding it, my arms wrapped around its neck." Symbolically, the eagle conveys the powers and messages of the spirit; it is her connection to the divine. In light of her visualization, it is interesting that Christina had put Garuda (half Eagle, half human) into the tray next to the Black Goddess. As the Hindu god Vishnu's mount, Garuda is a psychopomp, carrying the God between the upper and lower worlds. Just in front of Garuda sits a girl on a bench. Outside the lake of grief, her child-self appears more at peace, with doves around her, so something has been healed. And a green snake as healing energy moves from the girl into the blue lake, to heal the inner children of her wounded feminine and her wounded masculine. At the center back of the tray is a tepee, a portable home she can take with her. In light of her Self tray, I wonder if she is now beginning to internalize "home" as the spiritual home within.

The *nigredo* in this tray is found in the four black figures anchoring the four corners of the tray. The diagonal lines from these figures form a cross at whose center sits the black figure of her despair, grieving and in pain. The *albedo* is found literally in the white shell and figuratively in the deep interiority of the lake and all the figures in it, including the death of her defended pewter Warrior Woman persona. The faintest blush of *rubedo* is seen around the edges of Garuda, who will carry her between the upper world of spirit to the lower world of physical reality, where she can take her tepee with her.

During this period of grieving Christina made many trays with broken-heart lakes. She had lost her appetite, couldn't eat, and started losing weight, enough to cause me concern.

Tray 20. Down to the Bare Bones

One of the processes of alchemy is "distillation." The colors and contents of Trays 20 and 21 are quintessential distillations of her entire alchemical process. Christina's inner journey has been distilled to its essence, the bare bones. This tray was created five months after her Self tray and two months after Tray 19.

The alchemical black, white, and red are clearly evident in this tray. The defensive pewter figures of the *nigredo* have been melted and transformed into three pieces of iron pyrite. The interior world of the *albedo* lake with its central pure *albedo*-white flower is now strong enough to hold the pyrite *nigredo* with love inside her wounded heart. All around the outside of the lake we see the *rubedo* in the red flowers. The softness of the red petals symbolizes a softening of her previously hard, defended, and occasionally manic *animus*. If the *albedo* of the lake and its contents represents Christina's inner world, the *rubedo* represents the outer world. Elemental seaweed and driftwood, worn by ocean tides, bracket this elemental tray. She identified herself with the seaweed, while she associated the more solid driftwood with Jack. The blue agate slice on "his" side suggests that he carries her spiritual side. Its placement in the tray bordering water and land makes it the connector uniting the inner world of the *albedo* with the outer world of the *rubedo*.

Tray 21. Alchemical Transformation

Three weeks later, Christina smoothed out the sand into another loosely shaped heart. It is love that melts defenses.

In both color and content, we see the *nigredo* in the black raven and the black panther. The *albedo* is found as an oyster shell in the center of her blue pool of pain. Inside the shell, like a grain of sand, her suffering has produced a precious pearl—symbol of the Self. Also, in the center of the lake stands a white fox, as a healthy connection to her embodied instinctual self.

The three pieces of gray fencing, as part of her early defensive structure, are now on dry land, bleached white. We see the *rubedo* in its earlier negative aspects as the fiery volcano of hot emotions and earlier manic persona-as-defense and in the somewhat out-of-control fires of passion. But the heat of these fires appears to have melted and transformed the hard, cold unfeeling pewter into the three pieces of iron pyrite lying nearby. And the *rubedo* itself has been transformed from the earlier corrosive fiery elements into the softer five red flowers. Five is a number of embodiment as well as quintessence, awakening, and regeneration.[340] The tepee of Tray 19 has been transformed into a safe nest with two eggs inside. In the back-right corner, in the figure of the breast-feeding "caveman/woman" (Jack?), the baby is being fed. And the three blue butterflies (the ancient Greek word for "soul") hold her connection to the spiritual.

Since her triple trauma ten months earlier, Christina had lost thirty to forty-five pounds and looked anorexic. In questioning her about this, as I had often done, her angry and hurt little girl said, "I don't want to cook for myself! I want someone else to cook for me!" But now Christina's appetite was coming back. She said, "The other night I cooked for my Little Girl and when she saw the food, she started crying."

"Love as cooking breaks open your motherless girl's wound and heals it," I said, adding, "It's important for you to love your little girl, to be her good mommy and to cook for her."

Tray 22. Who's HE?

Six months after Tray 21, Christina was still wrestling with her abandonment pain, sorrow, anger, and grief, as represented by the number of *nigredo* figures in this tray: a black panther, black turtle, black snake, and black raven (power animals, both feared and respected); a black mermaid, black witch, and black goddess (the dark side of the feminine); and in the center of the lake, the black cauldron, whose contents have been burned away.

In this tray we also see lots of *albedo*, in the spiral shell at the front of the tray, the crystal, the nine capiz shells, the brain coral, and the oyster with the pearl inside. And *rubedo* has entered the tray in many forms: the red clamshell, the seven red chakras on the tall praying woman, two red treasure chests (one inside the cave), the rosy pink in the Native American woman's blanket, in Glinda the Good' Witch's pink dress, and most obviously in the paradoxical Sacred Heart in the center of the tray. This heart represents, on the one hand, the terrible pain and suffering Christina has undergone (the *rubedo* before it has been cleansed and calcined). However, this heart is more human than the skewered piece of meat over the fire in Tray 17. But, on the other hand, this is not just a bleeding heart pierced with thorns; this is Catholicism's Sacred Heart, with which Christina was familiar. The *ARAS Book of Symbols* says, "The wounded . . . heart of Christ . . . conveys the transformation of Christ's love and sacrifice into the Eucharist . . . So can the deepest pain, when fully held and suffered in the heart's vessel, be gradually distilled into the redemptive."[341]

There are five female figures at the back of the tray. The black witch-mother is still here (more humanized than the purple witch-mother in Tray 1). But there are now four positive mothers, all "holding" her in a protective, mirroring embrace: the tall prayerful goddess, the black goddess (holding a blue butterfly where the pot-smoking Christina

Tray 22. Who's HE?

sat in Tray 18), the gray-haired Grandmother who is wrapped in a blanket and doesn't speak, and the Good Fairy Godmother. With the transformation of the negative mother and the healing of the wounded Chrissie and Christina's wounded feminine self, the positive masculine can come in, as we'll see in a moment.

In the front-right corner of the tray, a healing green snake is going after the two poisonous snakes (Jack and his mother?) near a tombstone (her relationship with Jack was dying). Diagonally opposite the tombstone in the back-left corner of the tray, two mermaids (a black one seated at the entrance to the cave

and a light-skinned one to the right) move freely in and out of the depths. A small green frog sits next to the light-skinned mermaid, reminding us of the story of the Frog Prince. In the story, the frog is actually a prince under a spell; only her love can break the spell. When she truly loves this ugly frog (her inner *animus*), the spell is broken, and the ugly frog becomes her handsome Prince.

At the front of the tray, Christina placed the figure of Neptune (Roman)/Poseidon (Greek). When she had finished, she asked, "Who's *HE*?"

"He's the God of the Sea, your positive *animus*!" I replied.

Just before this session, Christina had taken out a home equity loan on her house and told me she was feeling good, feeling empowered, so it is not surprising to see this healthy male make his appearance. Neptune/Poseidon is a creative god who fashioned the ocean's creatures, but he could be moody, warlike, bold, and unpredictable as well. To make the point that Neptune/Poseidon was a match for Christina's own quite powerful and sometimes overbearing or defended *anima*, I placed Christina's pewter Warrior Woman into the tray next to Neptune/Poseidon, and we stared at the uncanny similarity in stance the two bore to one another.

Christina said, "I wanted to put her in the tray, but she didn't belong in this tray." All the defensive "fight" had been taken out of her.

Finally, glancing back at the photo of Tray 22, we see the broken-heart-shaped blue lake has been replaced by what appears to be a leopard's head, complete with black eye, white ear, red teardrop, and green snaked tongue. The leopard or big cat may represent Christina's natural instinctual self. She had been nurturing her psychospiritual self with weekend workshops and had embarked on a three-year spiritual training with a Native American woman.

Tray 22. Poseidon and Warrior Woman

Tray 23: The Sun Has Risen

Christina continued her inner work in therapy and made several more trays. A year after Tray 22 and almost two years after her triple trauma, Christina came in, radiant. She had been on a month-long Vision Quest and had gained ten pounds. She brought a gift for me, a scarab, which she placed in the position of honor in the center back of the tray.

This tray shows that things in Christina's psyche are shifting. Tree life and color have burst onto the scene. The blue hole in the center of the tray is closing up. There is lots of red and white in this tray, suggesting a *coniunctio* of *albedo* and *rubedo*. Symbolically, this balancing of archetypal masculine and feminine energies is seen in the small white Mayan god and goddess pair on the center-left side of the tray, and even more strikingly in the tall goddess standing on the rim at the center back of the tray, facing the dancing god Shiva balanced on a large green stone at the center front of the tray. All three form a spiritual vertical axis. The last time Christina had put Shiva in her tray was in Tray 1. Shiva destroys the old world and holds the new world in dreamtime, ready for re-creation. The new world has arrived. With all the green trees and color in this tray, more life has come in, Spring is in full bloom, and the apple tree at the back right is heavy with fruit.

On the right side of the tray stand four positive mother-figures: Kwan Yin, the Grandmother, and two mother-figures holding babies. Four is a number of wholeness or completion. Near the woman at the back holding the baby is a nest with two eggs inside, suggesting more good holding. And near the Grandmother rests the black cauldron, its fiery contents burned away. If the cauldron represents our relationship, perhaps its low-burning fires have cleansed away the impurities.

Inside the cave, back left, is a monarch butterfly and a butterfly-shaped shell, mirroring the butterfly-shaped shell she had found on the beach that morning and placed just in front of the scarab. Since the ancient Greek word for butterfly means "soul," we could call this a soulful tray. Just outside the cave, the pearl inside the oyster shell is a symbol of the Self. Next to it, the black snake (her clairsentient body-based wisdom) with its mammalian head raised, counterbalances the rattlesnake, ready to strike, on the opposite side of the tray.

The intelligent, playful air-breathing dolphin, like the mermaids in the last tray, is comfortable in the depths and in the upper world, and may, unlike the fierce leopard in the last tray, represent the playful side of her embodied instinctual self.

Christina had used a black scarab in one of her trays (not presented), which became the subject of my article on the scarab.[342] According to ancient Egyptian mythology, when the sun sets each evening and descends into the underworld, it undergoes a life-and-death struggle. In the morning, the moment the scarab pushes the sun up symbolizes rebirth

Tray 23: The Sun Has Risen

and transformation: spiritual emergence out of the darkest struggles of life. After Christina's dark night of the soul, the sun has risen. It is fitting that the scarab is the ruling principle of this tray.

When Christina gave me the scarab, she said, "I didn't think of it as a parting gift, but," she shrugged, "maybe it is."

"Are you thinking of leaving therapy?" I asked.

"I don't need you anymore, but I'm not ready to give you up. I'd like to see you in two months."

Tray 24. Resolution and Integration

Tray 24. Resolution and Integration

Tray 24, detail. Cave

Tray 24, detail. Native American in Canoe

Two months later, Christina came in for a last session. She was now spending less time at Jack's and more time cultivating her own garden. She was also thinking of cutting back on her demanding extraverted *rubedo* career and working less. Deep into her feelings, she smoothed out the beginnings of a heart-shaped lake.

At the center back of the tray she placed a black-clay mother holding a child, flanked by a phallic male god to the left and a black African goddess to the right. At the center front of the tray Christina added two red roses in a vase near a pair of cupped hands holding a pink crystal heart and facing outward, suggesting that she had internalized my maternal holding and could now give back.

The four corners of the tray are very interesting. In the front-right corner sits a fiery volcano with a gold sphinx on top and a cowboy running away from the fire. We might see the volcano as primal feminine rage or the bad breast.

The sphinx (also in Tray 23), with the body of a lion and the head and breasts of a woman, would ask passersby a riddle. Those who could answer her riddle were spared. "And if they can't [understand the 'riddle' of me]," said Christina, looking at the running cowboy, "they'd better run for their lives!" Christina was no longer going to put up with men who didn't "get" her. Then she asked quietly, "Where does the [volcanic] fire go? . . . It goes over here!" And she pointed to the small contained cooking

fire in the right-back corner. Her rage had been transformed into manageable proportions.

Diagonally opposite the volcano, in the left-back corner, sits a cave, symbolic of the maternal womb. On top of the cave sits a vulture, her spirit-bird, and inside is a large white crystal. Outside the cave, the contained fires of the cauldron have burned away and transformed her wounds. Nearby, the mermaid, her dog at her side, is able to dive into her depths. Flanking these three figures are two women tending to their babies, suggesting good maternal holding of her inner child.

On the opposite diagonal, in the right-back corner, a woman in her boat filled with nourishing food has landed on the shore of a village with two tepees and a hearth-fire cooking away. She is connected and able to give to her community. Following this diagonal to the front-left corner of the tray we see Christina's Native American woman with her travois leaving the tray, heading "home" to her own, much larger tepee. It contains two pieces of iron pyrite, a reminder of her old defended feminine self, melted and transformed through her painful inner journey. Nearby stands a little red fox—a healthy connection to her gifted instinctual body-self.

And in the very center of the tray we see a Native American man paddling a canoe across the lake in her direction, directly toward the entrance to her tepee. In the canoe with him is the third piece of iron pyrite. He is her internalized, very human positive *animus* who can carry the deep wounds without defense. He "gets" her!

Here at last we see the Alchemical Wedding: the sacred marriage of opposites as a *coniunctio*—a healthy inner masculine and healthy inner feminine in balance, which she can take with her into the world.

At the end of her session, Christina said, "You are the container! I teach therapists about holding boundaries and being the container! I'm where I am because of you and all the good work we did together, and now you are in me. I feel calm, grounded, and I can feel my feet on the ground.

This would have been Christina's final session, but a personal disaster two months later brought her back for two more sessions. In one of our many devastating California fires, her home had been burned to the ground. She admitted that immediately after the calamity her terrified infant self lay just below surface and would break to the surface occasionally.

But today she was unable to access that early part of herself. In a fairly calm voice she said, "In the past, in the face of trauma I've resorted to manic coping. Not this time." Being a savvy businesswoman, she had good insurance and short-term catastrophic insurance. Her plan, however, was to take some time off work and heal. Here was her good mother, internalized.

Tray 25. After the Calamity—Christina's Last Tray

Tray 25. After the Calamity—Christina's Last Tray

One month later Christina came in and made her last tray, saying, "I want to keep it simple today."

In the back-left corner she placed a cave, at the entrance of which sits a mermaid. With her fingertips she created an S-curve, brushing away sand down to the blue depths for this crystal ball in the very center of the tray. She added the blue hand with the gold heart, a gold vase with two red roses, and finally a red heart. The buried treasure—the crystal ball, a symbol of the Self—has come out of the cave.

In the face of the disaster of losing her home, Christina showed a remarkable calm and assurance. The fact that she was able to stay within the window of tolerance for stress of this magnitude showed amazing affect regulation and was a good indicator that she was now secure inside herself. She could ask for help, show her vulnerability, and stay calm in the face of the devastating loss. From her ego-Self connection she was able to maintain her basic trust. The Self was right there, helping her weather the storm without having to act out old traumas or resort to manic coping.

After she had finished, quite spontaneously she added, "You're welcome to use my sandplay for your teaching or whatever." I asked if a journal article—and later asked if a book—would be okay, too, and she replied, "I'd be honored."

Reflections on Phase III of Christina's Sandplay Process

The last phase of Christina's analysis brought the *nigredo* back with an intensity experienced as never before. A series of painful setbacks and the traumatic death of her beloved dog—a companion and soulmate—triggered an excruciating, ongoing embodied *nigredo* experience: the visceral sensation that she was being roasted and burned on a spit—a true shamanic initiation experience from which she ultimately emerged triumphant. (I have listed instances of others' shamanic initiations in the Endnotes.)[343] These painful and devastating losses plunged Christina back into even deeper pain and suffering and, paradoxically, the loss of her heroic Warrior Woman defenses for good. But the letting go of her strong defenses created room for the constellation of the Self. This new indestructible center and core of her personality gave her the strength to grieve her losses, cut back on her *animus*-driven extraverted *rubedo* lifestyle, and move closer to the earth in her own garden, thus bringing her *animus* and *anima* into a more equal partnership. In so doing, she had forged the *albedo-rubedo coniunctio*: the marriage of her now-healthy inner masculine and inner feminine, in a balance more in keeping with her authentic Self. Christina had truly come into her own, her alchemical journey complete.

The forging of the inner marriage helped Christina weather the subsequent catastrophic loss of her home and to reexamine how she was living her life. The resolution to her question will be addressed in the next section, the Epilogue.

Balancing White and Red: Resolution of Christina's and the Author's Journeys

THIS BOOK WOULD NOT be complete without an epilogue—a review and comparison of both my journey and Christina's journey of transformation through the three stages, and a look at the surprisingly different ways in which we each resolved the question of how to bring the albedo and the rubedo into balance in our personal lives. I've included suggestions for ways to balance the energies of the white and the red in all of our lives in Appendix D, "Pearls of Wisdom" to put into our knapsacks for the journey ahead.

THE *NIGREDO*

Clients come into therapy because of a problem. The core problem to be worked on is the stuff of the *nigredo*. But many times, the presenting problem is the tip of an iceberg containing other problems that have been submerged in the unconscious, which gradually come to light as the story unfolds.

In Christina's life as an adoptee, the unimaginable early childhood wounds to her core self, of mental, emotional, physical abuse and neglect, mushroomed into serious drug and alcohol abuse and promiscuity in her teens and early twenties. Christina needed a strong, tough self-care system—symbolized

by the strong Warrior Woman she used in her sandplay—to survive. With the help of AA and a loving sponsor, she got clean and graduated from college. After her move to California she sought therapy to deal with the fact that her birthmother did not want to make contact with her or to be contacted. But when she and I began to work together in Phase I, Christina's core anxieties and abandonment terror continued to plague her in the form of anger, rage, and acting-out. It took insight and courage to turn from total immersion in the *nigredo* world of cut-off feeling and extraverted manic defense (the raw, corrosive *rubedo* prior to its cleansing) to the beginnings of the *albedo* experience of reflection on her life and the letting go of her reactivity. It took even greater courage to descend into the deserted castle's dungeon in Tray 4 to encounter her abandoned inner child Chrissie and bring that terribly wounded inner child into the light of consciousness.

While Christina's child-self was forced to live out the nightmare of her family's unconscious, I had repressed mine. My initial presentation was the opposite of Christina's. I began feeling depressed, anxious, fearful, eager to please, and too close to my feelings of hurt and vulnerability. My childhood held many deeply painful and wounding moments, evidenced in my nightmares of tidal waves and huge black trucks bearing down upon me, but my self-care system managed to repress the memory of those recurring nightmares. When I left home for college as a young adult I was unaware that those childhood problems—which I thought I had left behind, when I went away to college—were still alive in my psyche. Until I joined a dream group that is. My dream of the suffocating "Black Hole" and its sequel—a terrifying visualization of falling into an endless abyss followed by the excruciating experience of being crushed under an unbearably heavy cross—shook me to the core and led me to seek therapy. It took years in therapy to peel away the layers of my smiling persona's defenses to reach the core of the masked depression lying buried in the deeper layers of *nigredo* in my soul. But depression is anger turned inward, and that anger needed to be released.

When the unconscious hits with full force, the *nigredo* can feel chaotic and disorienting. From the very start, I was flooded with so many dreams that they became embodied in the dream image of an oncoming tidal wave from which I could not escape. During this period, dreams of setting out upon the vast ocean in a small, leaky boat were common. But I was terrified when I dreamt of falling into an abyss and my sister dreamt of being in space and having the "umbilical cord" to the mother ship severed. And deeper into analysis, when I felt as if I had lost my bearings because my conscious ego was no longer in charge, I had two dreams of disembodied heads—one male and the other female.

Even worse, being in the *nigredo* and having to face our worst shadow qualities is embarrassing, humiliating, and mortifying—the whole experience a kind of torture. Analysands often have mortifying dreams of being exposed, naked, or sitting on a toilet in view of others. To be in the *nigredo* is to suffer, but the silver lining around the dark cloud of suffering is a gradual dawning of the light of consciousness and understanding—the pre-dawn light of the *albedo*.

THE *ALBEDO*

As noted earlier, the *albedo* stage has to do with the archetypally feminine qualities associated with Yin, lunar consciousness, and the right brain, reflecting the primacy of psychic reality as opposed to outer reality. The qualities of *albedo* consciousness are yielding, receptive, allowing, receiving, and taking in, not fighting against or falling victim to; that is, the *albedo* phase of deep interiority involves subjection to a process in which one can "do" nothing but can only "let happen." Existentially, the *albedo* may be experienced as mysterious, ghostly, silent, still, lonely, or as Hillman says, "The dead alive on the moon."[344]

Although Christina and I presented very differently at the outset of therapy, during the *albedo* stage, the process of therapy for each of us was similar. We both became deeply involved in our inner worlds, the stories of our lives, our relationships, our dreams, our sandplay, and our buried feelings. As cherished beliefs or outmoded parts in each of us were dying, images and themes of death were never far away.

During the *albedo* phase, as Christina became more conscious of her anger and acting out and more compassionate toward the wounded child inside, she began to open up to the unimaginably painful feelings of rejection and abandonment when her birth-mother never followed through on her message saying she wanted to talk to Christina. For the first time, Christina began to feel in her body her hurt, pain, and vulnerability, symbolized by the large pools or lakes of water in the center of her sandtrays. The death of her longing to connect to her birthmother and the death of her marriage were both painful experiences akin to actual death. When she had worked through these painful feelings, and the very real feelings of abandonment terror at the prospect of divorce, she was ready for another break. This took courage and strength, but with the aid of Kali, she was succeeding.

And when I finally began to get in touch with my buried anger, what therapy drew out was my so-called individuation rage, so eloquently expressed by Stephen Martin.[345] In one dream during this time, *I threw a large grocery-bag filled with garbage high into the air over the head of my analyst and watched it explode like Fourth of July fireworks.*

Letting go of my persona-driven defenses in order to accept this level of anger was mortifying—a death of the old smiling, eager-to-please persona. But for both Christina and me these felt experiences of torture, mortification, and dying meant paradoxically dying into new life.

THE *RUBEDO*

After the raw, unrefined elements of the *prima materia* (such as obsessive thoughts, manic activity, rage, lust, concupiscence, unbridled greed and desire in all forms, including addictions) have been burned away, the *rubedo* in refined form is the natural flow of ideas, creative action, anger channeled into constructive, purposeful activity and a natural, healthy relationship to the body and its appetites, including unashamed sexuality in the service of true intimacy and love. Or, as Henderson and Sherwood explain in cogent psychological terms,

> Von Franz[346] has applied the symbolism of the *nigredo* and *albedo* to the psychological process of working through a complex: the *nigredo* represents the disturbance, usually projected outwardly onto a person or persons. After "a long process of inner development and realization" the projection is withdrawn, and "... a sort of peace establishes itself—one becomes quiet and can look at the thing from an objective angle ... that corresponds to the *albedo*."[347] The *rubedo* would then refer to the new life that appears spontaneously after libido is freed from the complex."[348]

This new life, which appeared spontaneously for both Christina and me, was charged with energy and enthusiasm.

Christina's working through of the painful death of her wish to connect to her birthmother and the anxiety-provoking prospect of ending her marriage ushered in the *rubedo* phase with its "huge new energy" and sacred sexuality. While enjoying a connection to the kink community, she bought herself a red sports car, worked hard developing her career to its fullest, and eventually was earning enough money to own three vehicles and to buy herself a home. Christina's naturally fiery energy and expansive spirit were on a roll.

After my own four years of intense analysis into the heart of the *nigredo* and *albedo* phases, working through the painful realities of childhood and adolescence, I began to feel alive, happy, and attractive for the first time. As my energy returned, I began to consider going back to school. The following year—ushered in by the four *rubedo* dreams of red-headed boys and men—I applied to graduate school in psychology. Being around like-minded classmates, the Ugly Duckling in me suddenly felt that I had arrived "home" to a pond of swans, and I was one of them. A voice in a dream declared, "You were meant to be a therapist," and I knew without a doubt it was true. Graduating and beginning private practice were the fulfillment of my dream. I was finally coming into my own. But Christina's and my journeys were not complete; something was missing.

BALANCING THE *ALBEDO* AND *RUBEDO*

Once the hard work of separating the opposites is complete—making possible the marriage of the feminine *albedo* and the masculine *rubedo* energies we all carry—there remains one last task: striking the balance between these two: work and play, "doing" and "being," "head" and "heart." Given our extraverted culture with its seductive rewards for "doing," accomplishment, and success, this is not easy.

For Christina, with her outgoing fiery energies and lust for life, and her earlier tendencies toward manic coping, striking the right balance between work and play, or between "doing" and "being" meant leaving her busy, successful, demanding career and over-charged *rubedo* lifestyle and embracing a quieter life, closer to the earth and nature.

After the loss of her home, over a two-year period, Christina gradually let go of her demanding, extraverted career altogether, sold her property, and having been a lifelong sun-worshipper, moved to a warm earthly paradise. Here she has created a new, quieter life close to the earth and to her inner feminine intuitive, clairsentient gifts and earth-based body-wisdom, helping others realize their potential by developing her own talents as a gifted clairsentient, shaman, mystic, and healer, practicing peace, love, compassion, and openness. She shifted her inner balance from too much *rubedo* to more *albedo*, more in line with her soul's purpose.

Christina adds that the only man she would consider at this point in her life would be someone following a spiritual path.

For me, an Introverted Intuitive-Feeling Type,[349] a Highly Sensitive Person (HSP),[350] and Empath,[351] with an early tendency to daydream and withdraw into invisibility, striking the right balance in my life meant doing the opposite: challenging myself to venture out of my *albedo* comfort zone, focused on the inner life, into the more uncomfortable territory of the *rubedo* world "out there." As much as I love my work as a therapist, for years after beginning my career, I had a subtle, nagging feeling that something else was missing: creativity and joy! It took the *nigredo* experience of a broken foot and the *albedo* injunction that I sit as many hours of the day as possible with my foot raised above the level of my heart, to unlock it. Sitting on my bed with my foot propped high on pillows, I gathered the hundreds of images I had collected and photographed, sorted them into coherent groups and began to weave them together with their symbolic meanings to create material for a year-long course on dream symbolism. Given my terror of public speaking, putting myself "out there" for teaching had always been anathema. And being an Intuitive-Feeling Type with little natural propensity for analyzing, thinking, or writing, it has taken patient, sustained effort to do both. But once I can relax into what I am teaching or writing, I genuinely enjoy doing both.[352] Challenging myself out of my comfort zone has not been easy, but the rewards have been enormous.

And a last reflection. As joyful and hopeful as the 1984 Citadel dream was, the dream's message that the journey was not yet over was disconcerting. What did it mean, that the last obstacle (the widest river and the deepest canyon yet) could not be crossed directly? That I still needed to walk "halfway around the world"? Did this mean that I would have to wait another thirty or forty years? Despite my ego-driven (*rubedo*) desire to turn my dissertation into a book immediately after it was accepted in 1992, in literal and figurative 2020 hindsight, the dream was saying that in order for my life and my book to have soul, depth, and deeper meaning, I would have to continue to grow and "ripen" into a maturity where a true *coniunctio* of inner masculine and feminine energies would be possible. Neumann's words come echoing back: "The ego of matriarchal consciousness is used to keeping still till the time is favorable, till the process is complete . . . It must wait for time to ripen, while with time, like sown seed, comprehension ripens too. Only when the time is 'fulfilled' does understanding come as an illumination."[353] As I put the finishing touches on this book, the illumination comes to me as two precious gifts from the dream world.

April 2, 2021. *IMPERFECT PEARL. I hold in the palm of my hand a large, irregularly heart-shaped pearl with a smooth, pearly luster. It has a small, rough cavity on its surface, so it's not perfect, but it is too precious to discard.*

The dull, hard, spiky metallic jewelry in my own jewelry box that I wished to exchange for Amelia's softer, smoother jewelry brings my 1974 dream full circle. This by no means perfect self, growing for 47 years within the womb of my wounded soul, has become who I am.

And the night after a particularly enjoyable work project with my husband...

July 17, 2020. *NEW MAN IN MY LIFE. I am with a man I have never met before. He is Asian. Although it's unclear in what capacity, it seems we have had a longstanding collaborative relationship from afar. And now I have traveled across the globe to his land to meet him in person. He is the most completely natural, unselfconscious man I have ever met, physically unremarkable in that he is neither tall nor short, neither thin nor fat, but has a just-rightness to him that's hard to describe: muscular without being overly so; broad-shouldered, with arms and largish hands used to physical labor. His skin is a clear light brown. His face is rather broad and flat, with beautiful wide eyebrows, but his features, too, are unremarkable, with a just-so quality to them. He appears ageless, neither young nor old. But it is hard to place him: he could be a Nepalese Sherpa, a Mongolian horseman, an Inuit seal hunter, or a Japanese man used to the outdoors and to working, but too well-spoken and refined to be a village farmer. This man works collaboratively with others, perhaps one who travels from village to village like a field agent, to coordinate the donation of livestock to the neediest families and train them in the care of those precious sources of food and livelihood. With a promise to donate the first offspring of the livestock to the next-neediest family, the gift ultimately raises the prosperity of the whole village.[354] During these years, I have been coordinating the efforts of the organization on my end to see that donations reach their intended recipients. And finally I have arrived on his turf. Although he is ostensibly showing me around, I am neither the guest nor is he the guide; rather, I am simply accompanying him as he goes about his business. Our conversation flows easily, fluidly. He is earnest, serious, pleasant, but he doesn't need to smile to win my approval or admiration. It's not clear how long we have been in the field together, perhaps a week, a month, or just a day. But his physical presence is something I cannot deny. The hot burning desire I have begun to feel for him increases to such an extent I feel ecstasy just imagining being with him, and I sense that the feeling is mutual. I WANT this man.*

This man with whom I've fallen deeply in love is my life's partner, my soulmate, my inner animus. The monetary donations (energy) exchanged between us mean that we have been working together to serve the same end for years! It is a great mystery, touching and deeply comforting to know that this man, my animus, has been there all along, steadfast and strong, doing his job on his end as I have on my end.[355]

Having traveled in this dream halfway around the world, thirty-six years and half a lifetime later, the Citadel dream's message is clear: living my life and writing this book today, with the collaborative efforts of my solar analytic thinking function (the left brain) and lunar capacities to express myself with heart and feeling (the right brain) in good balance, has made this a joyful experience.

I would like to give the last word to Christina, which she sent to me in a letter:

Using the metaphor of the well as core wounds, I always thought we went in to get one toxic bucket of water out at a time. Who knew that well could be the portal into somewhere magical, mystical and beyond what I sought? All those years of work have given me amazing freedom. I feel the love filling my beautiful ruby heart. Thanks again for sharing your love with me. May it always circle around and heal us all.

Figure 29. The Scarab as the Rising Sun

ACKNOWLEDGMENTS

To Christina ~ for your courage and tenacity, and for graciously allowing me to share your story.

To Dyane ~ for your vision, dedication and generosity, expertly guiding me through the process to bring my Magnum Opus into the world; how lucky I've been to have you as my editor and publisher.

To LeeAnn ~ for your copy-editing wizardry; you are a magician.

To Loren ~ for holding high a lantern to light my way through many years of darkness.

To Betty and Suzanne ~ for being the Wise Women I needed to guide me through the narrows.

To Maria ~ for being both mentor and friend.

To John ~ for shepherding me through the challenges of research and scholarly endeavor.

To Mary ~ for so enthusiastically asking when my presentation would become a book; you lit the candle which has been burning brightly ever since.

To Linda ~ for the many fine hours we spent early on, sifting, sorting and putting together the pieces of this Opus, and for your knowledge, wisdom and steadfast friendship.

To Susana ~ for your keen interest, penetrating questions, thought-provoking ideas and inspiring conversations regarding this book and the mysteries of this journey.

To Karen ~ for your insight, compassion and sisterly companionship through thick and thin over many years.

To MarthaElin ~ for your interest in this book and for sharing your tender, radiant soul.

To my real sisters Nicole, Stephanie and Laurie and my soul sisters Adrianne, Agnes, Annette, Barbara, Beth, Bev, Carrie, Corinne, Dianne, Ginger, Gretchen, Jan, Jenness, Joan, Joy, Karin, Lani, Marilyn, Nancy, Sarah, Shirley, Sue, Susan, Vicky and so many others ~ for your friendship, support and loving kindness as we walk this sacred path hand in hand.

To my clients ~ for your commitment and courage to search in the darkest corners, I feel honored to have accompanied you on your journeys; you have taught me so much.

And last but not least, to my dear companions Dave, Becky, Carlos and Ryan ~ for being the warm and steady wind beneath my wings, helping me to soar.

And for the love each of you have showered upon me, my heartfelt gratitude.

Appendix A

Last Will and Testament of Basil Valentine

The first paragraph of *The Last Will and Testament of Basil Valentine* states:

The Last Will and Testament of Basil Valentine

Monke of the Order of St. Bennet: Which, Being Alone, he hid Under a Table of Marble, Behind the High-Altar of the Cathedral Church, In the Imperial City of Erford: Leaving it There to be Found by him, Whom Gods Providence Should Make Worthy Of It: To Which Is Added Two Treatises, The First Declaring his Manual Operations, the Second Shewing Things Natural and Supernatural.

This document by Basilius Valentinus, ostensibly a 15th century German alchemist and possibly a Canon of the Benedictine Priory of Saint Peter in Erfurt, Germany, was hidden under the marble table behind the Altar of his church and not discovered until lightning struck the table. This page among his papers is one example of the elaborate alchemical symbol-systems developed by European alchemists during the Middle Ages. (See the next page for a copy of "A Table of Chymicall & Philosophicall Chareccters in their signnifications as they are usually found in Chymical Authors both printed & in manuscript.")

As explained in the Introduction, the baffling use of hieroglyphics and symbols was necessitated by the alchemists' manifold need for secrecy: not only to keep their secrets from the unwise, but also to protect themselves from very real threats upon their persons to steal the gold, from the ransacking of their laboratories or homes and the very real threat of death if accused of heresy by the Church (cf Appendix B).

Appendix A: The Last Will and Testament of Basil Valentine 177

APPENDIX B

TWO LAWS REGARDING HERETICS IN GERMANY AND FRANCE

These laws remained valid for the persecution of heretics throughout the Middle Ages.

Laws for Germany by Frederick II, 1232 CE[359]

1. Everyone who is condemned by the Church as a heretic is to be punished with death by the civil judges.

2. Those who return to the bosom of the Church through fear of death are to be punished with imprisonment for life.

3. All suspected persons must be kept in close custody during the investigation.

4. Supporters of heretics meet with the same punishment as the heretics themselves.

5. Heretics are to be punished in every place, also when they have left their homes.

6. Relapsing heretics are to be condemned to death without further ado.

7. Heretics as well as their supporters have no right of appeal or proclamation, in order that the disgrace of heresy may be removed by every means from faithful orthodox Germany.

8. The descendants and heirs of heretics and their supporters shall be deprived of all their worldly privileges and public honors, unto the second generation, with the exception of orthodox children who denounce their heretical parents.

Regulations of the Synod of Toulouse, in the Year 1229 [CE][360]

1. In every parish, inside as well as outside a city, the Bishops must appoint one priest and two, three or more laymen of good repute and if necessary bind them by oath to search diligently, faithfully and frequently for heretics in these parishes; and to examine individually suspicious houses, underground cellars, annexes, and other hidden corners, which must all be destroyed. If they discover any heretics, credentes (those who believe in heretics), patrons or protectors of heretics, they must (taking every precaution that the heretics may not escape) immediately denounce them to the Bishop, or to the Lord of that place, or his bailiffs, in order that they may be suitably punished.

2. The exempted Abbots, who are not under episcopal jurisdiction, must do the same (as the Bishops) in their districts.

3. The Lords of the various districts must have the estates, houses and woods diligently searched for heretics and must destroy their hiding places.

4. In future he who harbors a heretic in his territory, whether for money or for any other reason will lose his possessions for ever (whether he pleads guilty or is convicted) and his body will be delivered to his supporters for suitable punishment.

5. But he also, whose territory has become (even without his knowledge, but through his carelessness) a frequent refuge for heretics, will be liable to the punishments of the law.

6. The house in which one has found a heretic must be torn down, and the place or ground must be confiscated.

7. The bailiff who lives in a suspicious place and is not diligent in searching for heretics shall lose his post and may not be installed elsewhere.

8. But in order that innocent persons may not be punished and that no one shall be wrongfully accused, we decree that no heretic or credent shall be punished until a Bishop or other authorized clerical person has declared him to be a heretic or credent.

9. Everyone is permitted to search for heretics in the territory of another, and the bailiffs of the place in question must give every assistance. So, the King may search for heretics in the domain of the Count of Toulouse and vice versa.

10. When a clerical heretic voluntarily renounces his heresy, he may not remain on the estate where he lived before, if this is suspected of heresy, but must be transplanted into a Catholic, wholly unsuspected estate. In addition, he must wear two crosses on his clothes, one on the right and one on the left, and they must be of a different color to that of the clothes. Also, such persons must not have access to public offices or legal action, unless after suitable penances they are reinstated in integrum by the Pope or his legates.

11. Whoever does not return voluntarily to the Church, but only through fear of death or for some other reason, must be imprisoned by the Bishop to complete his penance and in order to prevent him from misleading others.

APPENDIX C

SPLENDID EXAMPLE OF AN ALCHEMICAL TEXT, 1645 CE
Extract from *An Open Entrance to the Closed Palace of the King*
by *"An Anonymous Sage and Lover of Truth"* (Eirenaeus Philalethes)

WHOEVER WISHES TO POSSESS this secret Golden Fleece, which has virtue to transmute metals into gold, should know that our Stone is nothing but gold digested to the highest degree of purity and subtle fixation to which it can be brought by Nature and the highest effort of Art; and this gold thus perfected is called "our gold," no longer vulgar [common gold], and is the ultimate goal of Nature . . . Take your substance and place it in the furnace, regulate the fire properly . . . till dews and mists begin to ascend, and the moisture is diminished night and day without intermission. The whole operation lasts about 40–50 days, and is called the Regimen of Mercury, because the body is passive throughout, and the spirit, or Mercury, brings about all the changes of colour, which begin to appear about the 20th day, and gradually intensify till all be at last completed in black of the deepest dye . . . The Regimen of Mercury, the operation whereof despoils the King of his golden garments, is followed by the Regimen of Saturn. When the Lion dies the Crow is born. The substance has now become of a uniform colour, namely, as black as pitch and neither vapours, or winds, or any other signs of life are seen; the whole is dry as dust, with the exception of some pitch-like substance, which now and then bubbles up; all presents an image of eternal death. Nevertheless, it is a sight which gladdens the heart of the Sage. For the black colour which is seen is bright and brilliant; . . . it is the work

of the quickening spirit, which will soon restore the dead bodies to life . . . Black Saturn is succeeded by Jupiter . . . After the putrefaction . . . there is once more a change of colours and a circulating sublimation. This Reign, or Regimen, lasts only three weeks. During this period, you see all conceivable colours concerning which no definite account can be given. When the Reign of Jupiter comes to an end (towards the close of the fourth month), you will see the sign of the waxing moon (Crescent) and know that the whole Reign of Jupiter was devoted to the purification of the Laton [copper or brass?]. The mundifying spirit is very pure and brilliant, but the body that has to be cleansed is intensely black. While it passes from blackness to whiteness, a great variety of colours are observed; nor is it at once perfectly white; at first it is simply white—afterwards it is of a dazzling, snowy splendour. Under this Reign the whole mass presents the appearance of liquid quicksilver . . . its intermediate colours are more white than black, just as in the Reign of Jupiter they were more black than white. The Reign of the Moon lasts just three weeks; but before its close, the substance exhibits a great variety of forms; it will become liquid, and again coagulate a hundred times a day; sometimes it will present the appearance of fishes' eyes, and then again of tiny silver twigs and leaves. Whenever you look at it you will have cause for astonishment, particularly when you see it all divided into beautiful but very minute grains of silver, like the rays of the Sun. This is the White Tincture, glorious to behold, but nothing in respect of what it may become. Of the Regimen of Venus . . . you should also give careful attention to your fire . . . The heat should be gentle, so as to melt the compound very slowly and gradually; it will then raise bubbles and receive a spirit that will rise upward . . . imparting to it new colours, especially a copper-green colour . . . When you see the green colour, know that the substance now contains the germ of its highest life. Do not turn the greenness to blackness by immoderate heat . . . The next change is to blue and livid, and at the close of this Reign the colour is a pale purple . . . When the Regimen of Venus is over, and therein has appeared the philosophical tree, with all its branches and leaves, the Reign of Mars begins with a light yellow, or dirty brown colour, but at last exhibits the transitory hues of the rainbow and the peacock's tail. At this stage the compound is drier, and often shews like a hyacinth with a tinge of gold. The mother being now sealed in her infant's belly, swells and is purified, but because of the present great purity of the compound, no putrid-ness can have place in this regimen. Our Virgin Earth is now undergoing the last degree of cultivation, and is getting ready to receive and mature the fruit of the Sun. Hence you should keep up a moderate tempera-ture . . . As you are now approaching the end of the work, the substance receives a golden tinge. Pray to God to keep you from haste and impatience at this stage of the work; consider that you have now waited for seven months, and that it would be foolish to let one hour rob you of the fruits of all your labour. Therefore, be more and more careful the nearer you approach perfection. Then you will first observe an orange-coloured sweat breaking out on the body; next there will be vapour of an orange hue. Soon the body below becomes tinged with violet and a darkish purple . . . At length an unexpectedly glorious light will burst from your substance, and the end will arrive three days afterwards. The substance will be granu-lated, like atoms of gold (or motes in the Sun) and turn a deep red—a red the intensity of which makes it seem black like very pure blood in a clotted state. This is the Great Wonder of Wonders which has not its like on earth . . . You now possess the incombustible red Sulfur which can no longer be affected in any way by fire . . . Then you have the true Stone of the third order, one part of which will perfectly tinge 1,000 parts of any other metal . . . Then kneel down and render thanks to God for this precious treasure . . . He that has once found this Art, can have nothing else in all the world to wish for . . . He will not care for pomp or dazzling outward show. But if he lived a thousand years, and daily entertained a million people, he could never come to want, since he has at hand the means of indefinitely multiplying the Stone both in weight and virtue, and thus of changing all imperfect metals in the world into gold. In the second place, he has it in his power to make stones and diamonds far more precious than any that are naturally procured. In the third place, he has a Universal Medicine, with which he can cure every conceivable disease, and, indeed, as to the quantity of his Medicine, he might heal all sick people in the world. Now to the King Eternal, Immortal, and sole Almighty, be everlasting praise for these His unspeakable gifts and invaluable treasure.[361]

Appendix D

Balancing White and Red

Pearls of Wisdom for the Journey Ahead

I AM OFTEN ASKED by clients how to bring the energies of our inner feminine into alignment with our inner masculine. The idea of offering some pearls of wisdom brought to mind a dream that came to me thirty-eight years ago. Today it seems uncannily relevant:

I'm standing in front of Tiffany's. Suddenly I see something dropping from above, some very tiny gold beads. By their shine I can tell that they are pure gold. I bend over to pick them up. At first, they are elusive, hard to find and hard to pick up. But as I search in the dirt and rubble for them, more appear, many more, and larger, ever larger, some the size of quarters, but uneven, more like real gold nuggets than perfect spheres. I eagerly reach for the largest ones and put them in my pocket or purse.

Then I am inside Tiffany's on the ground floor, in what appears to be an atrium—a light-filled space with plants and a jungle-like atmosphere. People are seated here, taking a class. Again, something falls from above, but this time I am picking up pearls! At first there are just a few and they are small, but as I get into it, pearls are lying in heaps in front of me and I am scooping them up by the handful—all colors, all sizes, all shapes, pearls by the hundreds, by the thousands! I am even scooping them up under the feet of people sitting in the class. They must not have noticed these pearls. It is an experience of awe, excitement, and reverence.

There are hundreds, even thousands of pearls of wisdom lying right at our feet, in the form of ideas, books, CDs, lectures, programs, and activities designed to enhance our physical, mental, emotional, and spiritual well-being. I will mention a few.

Given the dominance in our Western culture of the archetypally active masculine energies of the *rubedo*, of "doing" versus "being," in the head rather than in the heart, it is crucial to encourage and enhance the opposite: archetypally feminine *albedo* qualities. Ornstein's list of right hemisphere qualities (Table 4) gives us a start: Yin, Earth, Feminine, Dark, Night, Intuitive, Receptive, Sensuous, Gestalt, Tacit, Non-lineal, Spatial, Simultaneous, Space, Eternity/Timelessness, Acausal. To the list I would add "being" as opposed to "doing," keeping still, in the body rather than in the head. In Western culture, which does not understand, much less value, these archetypally feminine *albedo* qualities, it is difficult to grasp what these words even mean and more difficult still to put them into practice. For example, the *albedo* quality of stillness does not mean becoming a couch potato, assuming an attitude of passivity or doing nothing. It means establishing a way of being in the world more in line with the Taoist notion of wu-wei—going with the flow, with a calm acceptance of what is, in a way that ultimately feels effortless. However, getting to this point is not easy! It requires consciousness and patient effort.

Gems to Enhance *Albedo* Consciousness and Inner Balance

The Physical Body. A good place to begin is to become the Good Mother/Father to your physical body. Think of it as a sacred temple. Are you honoring it or desecrating it? What are you putting into your body? Is it nourishing and healthy? Are you creating an environment for yourself in which a good night's sleep is nonnegotiable? Are you exercising? Are you striking the right balance between work and play? Bringing our physical bodies into harmony is the first step toward bringing our mental, emotional, and spiritual selves into harmony.

To be out of our heads and into our bodies means to focus on the sensuous as opposed to the intellectual. How can you enhance sensuous awareness and pleasure in your body? You might begin in the shower or bath, bringing your attention to the now: the colors and shapes of your visual surroundings, the sound of the water, how it feels on your skin, the smell of soap, the feel of washcloth or sponge, the pleasure of cleansing this temple, which is your body, and the contentment that comes from appreciating your body for exactly its shape and size right now.

Dreams. Pay attention to your dreams. Dreams are like letters from the unconscious with important messages inside. If you do not write them down or think about them, they are thrown into a Dead Letter pile. You might begin a dream practice by placing a pad and pencil or a small tape recorder next to your bed. As you are falling asleep, set an intention to remember your dreams. We all fall into REM (rapid eye movement) dreaming states three to four times a night. As you become aware of dreaming, without moving, try to recall as much detail of the dream as you can, before you turn to write it down or tell it to a tape recorder.

Regardless of whether you are able to interpret your dreams, the very act of writing them down will help your conscious ego begin to process the energies and messages your dreams are sending. If you want to learn more, there are countless books on dreams and dreaming. If you are interested in what certain images in your dreams mean, there are many symbol dictionaries on the market although more and more people are turning to the internet as a resource. Or you may want to seek a therapist or counselor skilled in working with dreams.

Meditation. Meditation, either walking or sitting, is another way to access the inner world and quiet the too-busy activity of your mind. There are meditation centers in many cities, as well as CDs available to help you begin your meditation practice. For walking meditation, try walking a unicursal (one-way) labyrinth, an increasingly popular activity championed by Lauren Artress.

Active Imagination. Active imagination is an excellent technique for activating the dreaming mind while conscious. Barbara Hannah's book is a wonderful introduction to the practice. However, after my unguided visualization into the Black Hole, I recommend that you attempt this under the guidance of a trained professional.

EMDR and Tapping In. EMDR (Eye Movement Desensitization and Reprocessing), pioneered by

Francine Shapiro, and its more recent offshoot Tapping In, by Laurel Parnell, are excellent and efficient ways to activate the brain to heal trauma and strengthen your psyche.

Movement. Movement of any kind, such as walking, running, swimming, dancing, hiking, yoga—if not done to excess—promotes health and can help you feel alert and energized. Authentic Movement is a unique form of movement that accesses the deepest layers of the right brain. Several women who have pioneered this approach to the unconscious include Joan Chodorow, Janet Adler, Patrizia Pallaro, and Mary Starks Whitehouse. I highly recommend their books, which you can find at the end of this appendix in my "Pearls of Wisdom Bibliography."

Dance. Another way of getting in touch with the joyful sensuality in your moving body is though dance. Ballet, ballroom, jazz, tap, hip-hop, folk, Zydeco, Hula, African, circle- or square-dancing—to name but a few—are a source of release and pleasure. When certain songs are played on the radio, getting up and dancing around feels great.

Voice Work and Singing. Other ways of activating the right hemisphere of the brain is through voice work and singing. Brownell says that Voice Movement Therapy (VMT) is "both a creative and a therapeutic modality. . . requiring an exploration of oneself and one's issues through the contours of the voice and through the creative enactment of one's story in movement and song." Singing itself is therapeutic. Join a choir. Take singing lessons. Try karaoke. Or just sing along with your favorite music on the radio or on your phone while on a hike, cooking, washing dishes, or folding laundry.

Creative Arts. The creative arts, both artistic and playful, are a wonderful way to access the right side of the brain. Try working with clay, either on the wheel or sculpting. Try drawing, painting, or collage. Quilting, sewing, embroidery, macramé, flower arranging such as Ikebana, gardening, cooking, writing music, poetry, or books can be deeply engaging, meditative activities. Jill Mellick's books, *The Natural Artistry of Dreams* and *The Art of Dreaming*, combine dreamwork with art: drawing, collage, movement, wordplay, voice, mask-making, and writing. Any of these can be inspirational.

Music. Music puts us in harmony with our souls. If you know how to play an instrument, get it out and play it. If you don't, try learning to play an instrument. As we age, learning to play a new instrument is a way of keeping the brain supple and active. Music is also good therapy. The following is a passage from Mary Lynn Kittelson's book *Sounding the Soul.*

In old age, in 1956, Jung had an apparently isolated yet emotional meeting with Margaret Tilly. As she played for him, with the intent of showing him what music therapy was like, she said that he appeared deeply moved. They discussed what she would do in different types of cases. Finally, she said, he burst out with this speech: "This opens up whole new avenues of research I'd never even dreamed of. Because of what you've shown me this afternoon—not just what you've said, but what I have actually felt and experienced—I feel that from now on music should be an essential part of every analysis. This reaches the deep archetypal material that we can only sometimes reach in our analytical work with patients. This is most remarkable."

The Mystical Branch of Religions. Finally, the mystical branch of all religions, involving prayer, fasting, meditation, drumming, chanting, labyrinth-walking, pilgrimage, or Sufi dancing—all *albedo* activities—can lead to a direct encounter with the Self, where the intuitive, the acausal, the nonlineal, the eternal and timeless—all aspects of the right brain—reside. I particularly enjoy the poetry of mystics such as Rumi and Hafiz—a way to stay closer to the soul.

Soul Tending. Everything on this list has to do with soul tending. It is no accident that Thomas Moore's *Care of the Soul* and Eckhart Tolle's *The Power of Now* became instant bestsellers, along with many of their other books on deepening soul and cultivating a mature spiritual life. For insight into how to move beyond ego to awaken to our life's purpose, I recommend Tolle's *A New Earth*. And for inspirational ideas on healthy aging, read Thomas Moore's *Ageless Soul*.

A Vision. Synchronistically, on a wintry January day as I was writing this appendix, my friend Vicky Semones called to share a vision that had recently come to her. Because of recent health challenges, this woman of action described having totally surrendered to winter, with quiet hearth-fires, rest, and slumber, telling herself, "It's okay to rest, to nap, and be in the depths of winter, not always "doing-doing-doing." Then, she went on to describe her vision:

As I was slipping into slumber, I saw a small female figure, all in silver, shimmering radiantly. Her long silver gown was pulsing, radiating a soft brilliance. And the silver candle she was holding was emitting its own luminous light. The silver woman, perhaps three to six inches tall, was just "there" in the near distance, floating, her shimmering presence at once powerful, soft and comforting. I felt a sense of awe and reassurance.

Surrendering to the *albedo* energies of quiet, rest, and just "being," allowed this numinous image of the archetypal feminine to appear unbidden in Her shimmering radiance, holding the light of consciousness. When we allow the feminine energies of the *albedo*, of just "being" into our lives, She is there, waiting for us.

Gems from the World of the Rubedo to Enhance Inner Balance

The previous section focused on ways to access the personal unconscious—through dreams, meditation, active imagination, visualization, movement, singing, voice-work, creative arts, music, and the mystical side of religion—all ways to nurture the inner world. This section focuses on the outer world of nature and the great creations of the ages—the collective unconscious made manifest in the outer world of the *rubedo*—in particular, religion and the great art masterpieces of the world, and how these, too, may help us maintain inner balance and lead us closer to our own true center.

Nature. The natural world is filled with wonders that can bring us closer to the eternal and the timeless in ourselves. Mother Nature is just waiting for us to venture outside and experience the vast wild beauty of her oceans, majestic mountains, fertile valleys, thundering waterfalls and gorges, wild rivers, towering trees, exquisite flowers and plants, and animals large and small. It takes little to glory in her seasons with their changes of color, temperature, and mood; to marvel at the peregrinations of birds, mammals, and the creatures of the sea; to witness the awesome power of thunder and lightning; and to bow before the mighty energies of her hurricanes and floods, cyclones and typhoons, wildfires and volcanic eruptions, earthquakes and tsunamis.

Go outside and watch the sun set, as rosy fingers of light poking up from the horizon turn green. Or after dark, admire the stars as they twinkle and twirl in their eternal circle dance around the Pole Star. The moon, that radiant white orb, connects us to the night and to the archetypal feminine. Look carefully at her; have you ever seen the "woman" in the Moon? She's there. Become aware of her phases and how they affect your energies, your moods, and the tides in your body. More violent crimes are committed during the dark of the moon and more babies born during the full moon than at any other times of the month.

Religion and Spirituality. Whether we call it the Tao, the Buddha, Mohammed, Jesus, the Divine Spirit, the All, or the One, at the heart of all religions lies the archetype of the Self. For many, deep connection to a religion or to a spiritual practice is a way to stay grounded, calm, connected to the inner center as we make our way in the world.

Art. The world's greatest art—the language arts, performing arts, and visual arts—arising from the cultural unconscious, connect us with eternity and timelessness. These all have the potential to move us, to bring us closer to Self, and thus into balance.

Reading poetry such as Dante's *Divine Comedy*, the Romantic poets, Walt Whitman, Rainer Maria Rilke, T. S. Eliot, and Mary Oliver's "The Journey" and "Serengeti," or literature like *The Bhagavad Gita*, the *Ramayana*, and Shakespeare allows us to reflect upon social and cultural issues and the human condition. Attending, or watching online, performing arts events such as symphonies, especially those by Mozart, Beethoven, Bach, Brahms, and Vivaldi; operas sung by Luciano Pavarotti and Beverly Sills; ballets performed by Nijinski, Pavlova, Baryshnikov, or Makarova; and theater, Greek or modern, can move us to laughter or tears, drawing us closer to our souls. Take time to experience the visual arts, the cave paintings of Lascaux, Tibetan mandalas, the paintings of da Vinci and others; the splendid architecture of gothic cathedrals, the Great Pyramids, the Taj Mahal; or amazing sculptures such as those by Michelangelo, Bernini, and Rodin. Many of these are available online to view or listen to. Your choices, like the thousands of pearls, are endless. Each of these has the potential to connect us with eternity and timelessness—and all are ways of attending to the mystery in our souls.

Online Sources of Spiritual Inspiration and Awareness.

Jung Platform, https://www.jungplatform.com
New York Center for Jungian Studies, includes Jung on the Hudson, Jung in Ireland, and Jung in other countries, https://nyjungcenter.org
Marion Woodman Foundation, https://mwoodmanfoundation.org
The Shift Network, https://theshiftnetwork.com
Sounds True, https://www.soundstrue.com

Esalen, https://www.esalen.org/learn/workshops/all
Holotropic Breathwork, http://www.holotropic.com/
    holotropic-breathwork/about-holotropic-breathwork/
Mindfulness Based Stress Reduction (MBSR),
    https://www.livingmindfully.org or http://www.
    mindfullivingprograms.com
Creativity Workshop, https://creativityworkshop.com
Veriditas (Lauren Artress and the Labyrinth programs),
    https://www.veriditas.org

Books. Any book under the Colophon Inner City Books—studies in Jungian Psychology by Jungian analysts—is excellent. Other favorite Jungian authors published elsewhere include Jean Shinoda Bolen, Edward F. Edinger, Robert Johnson, and Marion Woodman, to name but a few.

For working with traumatized clients, no books have been more instructive for me than Donald Kalsched's *Inner World of Trauma: Archetypal Defenses of the Personal Spirit*, his later volume, *Trauma and the Soul: A Psycho-Spiritual Approach to Human Development and Its Interruption*, and Bessel van der Kolk's *The Body Keeps the Score*. For sandplay therapists with traumatized clients, I recommend Linda Cunningham's *Sandplay and the Clinical Relationship*.

Many clients with especially sensitive souls are astounded and relieved to learn that they are not "too sensitive" and that being highly sensitive is a gift. I highly recommend Elaine N. Aron's *The Highly Sensitive Person: How to Thrive When the World Overwhelms You*, and her companion volumes, *The Highly Sensitive Person in Love*, *The Highly Sensitive Child*, and *The Highly Sensitive Parent*. Judith Orloff's *Thriving as an Empath: 365 Days of Empowering Self-Care Exercises* contains excellent suggestions on how to care for ourselves whether we are empaths (her word for highly sensitive individuals) or just stressed out.

There is nothing wrong with being a puer (Latin for "boy") or a puella (Latin for "girl"), someone in whom the joyful and spontaneous child-spirit is strong, if they are able to grow up and lead a productive life. But the eternal puer or puella, unable to move into a productive adulthood, is stuck. Peter Pan, one of the Lost Boys who chants, "I never want to grow up!" is the perfect example. The female version, the puella, is captured in Collette Dowling's *The Cinderella Complex*. Marie-Louise von Franz declares that the best antidote for the puer (and I would add, for the puella), and she capitalizes it, is WORK! We cringe, but she's right: work—whether it be a job or work on a relationship or a creative project—grounds us in reality and helps us to become masters rather than passive participants in our fate. See the "Pearls of Wisdom Bibliography" for more titles.

THE STILL POINT MEDITATION

At the still point of the turning world. Neither
    flesh nor fleshless;
Neither from nor towards; at the still point, there
    the dance is,
But neither arrest nor movement. And do not call
    it fixity,
Where past and future are gathered. Neither
    movement from nor towards,
Neither ascent nor decline. Except for the point,
    the still point,
There would be no dance, and there is only the
    dance.

—T. S. Eliot, excerpt from "Burnt Norton,"
    in *Four Quartets*, lines 62-67

I meditate daily on the still point. I feel it in my body,

around the solar plexus. I want to focus on it until it becomes a part of me, moment to moment, as I move through my day. I close my eyes and focus on this still point. It is calm. Quiet. Still. Centered. It is nonaction. No striving. No push. No effort. But the still point is paradoxical: it also carries Weight, Authority, Presence, Gravitas, Power. It's not "power over"; rather it is a quiet, self-contained power carried in the expression on my face, my direct, unwavering gaze saying, "Here I stand my ground, don't mess with me."

A client protests that if she stands up to push back she will come across as loud, bitchy, angry, or mean. Blessed are the children who received enough good mirroring that this still point resides in them naturally. But if we have lived at the pole of the pendulum's swing demanding that we erase ourselves in order to put others' interests ahead of our own, the desired shift toward the still point in the center doesn't stop there. The momentum created by years of repressed expression carries us toward its polar opposite: repressed rage, resentment or bitterness, whose expression suddenly feels pushy, strident, bitchy, or mean. This cannot be suppressed; it must come out, hopefully in moderation, before we find our way back to the center, the still point.

Again, I close my eyes and focus on the still point in my body. It is calm. Quiet. Still. Centered. Peaceful. But also powerful.

Resources for Those Interested in Learning More

International Association for the Study of Dreams (IASD), https://www.asdreams.org. Contact is Richard Wilkerson, office@asdreams.org.

Sandplay Therapists of America (STA), https://www.sandplay.org, P.O. Box 4847, Walnut Creek, CA 94596. Contact is Ritu Tandon, sta@sandplay.org.

Pearls of Wisdom Bibliography

Adler, Janet. *Arching Backward: The Mystical Initiation of a Contemporary Woman*. Rochester, VT: Inner Traditions, 1996.

———. *Offering of the Conscious Body: The Discipline of Authentic Movement*. Rochester, VT: Inner Traditions, 2002.

Aron, Elaine N. *The Highly Sensitive Child: Helping Our Children Thrive When the World Overwhelm Them*. New York: Broadway Books, 2002.

———. *The Highly Sensitive Person: How to Thrive When the World Overwhelms You*. New York: Birch Lane Press, 1996.

———. *The HSP in Love: Understanding and Managing Relationships When the World Overwhelms You*. New York: Harmony Books, 2001.

Artress, Lauren. *Walking a Sacred Path: Rediscovering the Labyrinth as a Spiritual Tool*. New York: Riverhead Books, 1995.

Brownell, Anne. *International Association of Voice Movement Therapy (IAVMT)*. https://www.iavmt.org/dive-deeper

Chodorow, Joan. *Dance Therapy and Depth Psychology: The Moving Imagination*. New York: Routledge, 1991.

Cunningham, Linda. *Sandplay and the Clinical*

Relationship. San Francisco: Sempervirens Press, 2013.

Dowling, Colette. *The Cinderella Complex: Women's Hidden Fear of Independence*. New York: Simon & Schuster, 1981.

Hafiz of Shiraz. *The Illuminated Hafiz: Love Poems for the Journey to Light*. Translated by Coleman Barks, Robert Bly et al. Boulder, CO: Sounds True, 2019.

Hannah, Barbara. *Encounters with the Soul: Active Imagination as Developed by C. G. Jung*. Boston: Sigo Press, 1981.

Kalsched, Donald. *The Inner World of Trauma: Archetypal Defenses of the Personal Spirit*. London and New York: Routledge, 1996.

———. *Trauma and the Soul: A Psycho-spiritual Approach to Human Development and Its Interruption*. London & New York: Routledge, 2013.

Kittelson, Mary Lynn. *Sounding the Soul*. Einsiedeln, Switzerland: Daimon, 1996.

Moore, Thomas. *Ageless Soul: My Lifelong Journey Toward Meaning and Joy*. New York: St. Martin's Press, 2017.

———. *Care of the Soul: A Guide for Cultivating Depth and Sacredness in Everyday Life*. New York: HarperCollins Publishers, 1992.

Orloff, Judith. *Thriving as an Empath: 365 Days of Empowering Self-Care Exercises*. Boulder, CO: Sounds True, 2019.

Pallaro, Patrizia, ed. *Authentic Movement: Essays by Mary Starks Whitehouse, Janet Adler and Joan Chodorow*, Vol. 1. London and Philadelphia: Jessica Kingsley Publishers, 1999.

———. *Authentic Movement: Moving the Body, Moving the Self, Being Moved, a Collection of Essays*. Vol. 2. London and Philadelphia: Jessica Kingsley Publishers, 2007.

Parnell, Laurel. *Tapping In: A Step-by-Step Guide to Activating Your Healing Resources Through Bilateral Stimulation*. Boulder, CO: Sounds True, 2008.

Richards, Mary Caroline. *Centering in Pottery, Poetry, and the Person*. 2nd ed. Hanover, NH: Wesleyan University Press, 1989.

Rumi, Jalal Al-Din. *The Illuminated Rumi*. Translated by Coleman Barks. New York: Broadway Books, 1997.

Shapiro, Francine. *Eye Movement Desensitization and Reprocessing [EMDR] Therapy*. 3rd ed. New York: Guilford Press, 2018.

Tolle, Eckhart. *A New Earth: Awakening to Your Life's Purpose*. New York: Penguin Books, 2005.

———. *The Power of Now: A Guide to Spiritual Enlightenment*. Novato, CA: New World Library, 1999.

van der Kolk, Bessel. *The Body Keeps the Score*. New York: Viking, 2014.

von Franz, Marie-Louise. *Puer Aeternus*. 2nd ed. Zürich: Spring Publications, 1997.

GLOSSARY OF ALCHEMICAL WORDS AND PHRASES

Where indicated, "Fr." indicates French terms; "Gk." indicates Greek; and "L." indicates Latin.[362]

adept   the alchemist

alba   L. for "white"

albedo   a) whitening; b) name given by Jung for a psychological process, as distinct from a chemical process

alembic   vessel, retort, or container

alkimia   Arabic name for the art (of alchemy)

androgyne   male and female in one body

anima mundi   L. for "soul of the world"

athanor   alchemical furnace

Aurora   a) L. for "dawn"; b) Roman goddess of dawn

bain marie (**Fr.**) or *balneum mariae* (**L.**)   a) "Mary's bath"; b) water bath for the retort

caeruleus   L. for "blue"

cauda pavonis   a) L. for "peacock's tail"; b) iridescence; c) many colors

citrinitas   yellowing of the work

citrus   L. for "yellow"

coniunctio   a) L. for "union" of opposites; b) the Sacred Marriage; c) marriage of the Sun and Moon, King and Queen

curcurbit   alchemical alembic, retort, vessel, or container

ego-Self Axis   the conscious ego recognizes the greater power of the Self and works in harmony with it

elixir vitae   a) L. for "elixir of life"; b) name given by Arab alchemists to the *quintessence* or *Precious Essence*

Eros   a) Gk. god of "love"; b) "transforms feeling into relatedness"[363]

filius philosophorum   a) L. for "son of the philosopher"; b) archetype of the divine child; c) symbol of the goal of the alchemical process

grand arcanum   the *Great Work*, the opus of alchemy

heiros gamos   Gk. for "sacred marriage"

hermaphrodite   a) being with one body and two heads: one female, one male; b) *Rebis* or *androgyne*

Hermetic art   name for alchemy, after Hermes Trismegistus, the legendary founder of alchemy

individuation   the process of inner transformation and growth

iosis   Gk. for "reddening"

lapis philosophorum   L. for "Philosopher's Stone" (from *lapis lazuli*)

laton   brass or copper

leukosis   a) Gk. for " white"; b) whitening of the work

Logos   a) Gk. for "logic," "reason"; b) "transforms thinking into 'word'"[364]

medicina catholica   a) L. for "universal medicine"; b) that which "cures all ills"

melanosis   a) Gk. for "black"; b) blackening of the work

niger   L. for "black"

nigredo   a) "blackness"; b) name given by Jung for a psychological process

operations   a) the physical work on the *prima materia*; b) varied widely but included *solution* (water), *calcination* (fire), *coagulation* (earth), *sublimation* (air), *mortification* (death), *separation*, *conjunction, congelation, fixation, digestion, distillation, ceration, fermentation, multiplication, projection,* and so on

opus a) the "work" of alchemy; b) the transmutation of matter into the Philosopher's Stone

opus contra naturam L. for "the work against nature"

opus magnum L. for the "Great Work"

Philosopher's Stone a) the transcendent miraculous substance; b) the supreme and ultimate value, variously called the *lapis philosophorum, elixir vitae, aurum nostrum, infans, puer, filius philosophorum, Hermaphroditus, lapis,* and so on; c) synonym for Jung's concept of the Self

prima materia a) L. for "first matter"; b) primal matter, that which is to be worked upon

psychopomp a) a person who conducts spirits or souls to the other world; b) spiritual guide

puella L. for the "inner girl who doesn't want to grow up"

puer L. for the "inner boy who doesn't want to grow up"

quintessence the miraculous substance of the Philosopher's Stone

Rebis a) a being with one body and two heads; b) hermaphrodite; c) androgyne

rubedo a) reddening; b) Jung's term for the last stage of the work

ruber L. for "red"

Self the center and circumference of the personality, consisting of conscious and unconscious

shadow a) the rejected, disowned parts of ourselves; b) "the unrecognized dark half of the personality"[365]

solutio a) L. for "dissolving"; b) one of the alchemical operations

soror mystica L. for "mystical sister"

spagyric art name for alchemy coined by Paracelsus

tincture a) a dye; b) to color, tint, or tinge

unio mentalis L. for "mental union"

unus mundus a) L. for "unity of the world"; b) unity of the psyche

universal medicine synonym for the Philosopher's Stone

vas Hermeticum a) synonym for alembic, curcurbit, or container; b) symbol for the womb; c) place of creation, incubation, and transformation

viriditas L. for "green"

xanthosis Gk. for "yellowing"

NOTES

Many of Jung's articles and books were collected in 20 volumes. The English editions are published by Routledge in the UK and by Princeton University Press in the US.

References to Jung's *Collected Works* (CW) will be indicated by title, date, volume number, and page or paragraph number. They refer to the US edition: C. G. Jung, *The Collected Works of C. G. Jung*, ed. William McGuire, trans. R. F. C. Hull (Princeton: Princeton University Press)

INTRODUCTION

1. Marie-Louise von Franz, *Alchemy: An Introduction to the Symbolism and the Psychology* (Toronto: Inner City Books, 1980), 83.

2. von Franz, *Alchemy*; Robert Grinnell, *Alchemy in a Modern Woman* (New York: Spring, 1973); Johannes Fabricius, *Alchemy: The Medieval Alchemists and their Royal Art* (Copenhagen: Rosenkilde & Bagger, 1976): James Hillman, "Silver and the White Earth: Part One," *Spring*, no. 1 (1980): 21–48; "Silver and the White Earth: Part Two," *Spring*, no. 1: 21–66; and "The Yellowing of the Work," *Proceedings of the 11th International Congress for Analytical Psychology, August 28 to September 2, 1989*, ed. Mary Ann Matton (77–96) (Einsedeln, Switzerland: Daimon-Verlag, 1991); Gerard D. Astrachan, "King Solomon and the Queen of Sheba in Alchemy" (Diploma thesis, C. G. Jung Institute, Zurich, 1982); Edward Edinger, *Anatomy of the Psyche: Alchemical Symbolism in Psychology* (La Salle: Open Court, 1985); Joseph L. Henderson and Dyane N. Sherwood, *Transformation of the Psyche: The Symbolic Alchemy of the Splendor Solis* (New York: Brunner-Routledge, 2003).

3. By entering 2500 dreams in the software program FileMaker and using the search words for *black, white, yellow,* and *red,* the program produced separate files of 184 *black* dreams, 150 *white* dreams, 23 *yellow* dreams, and 104 *red* dreams. Clifford C. Clogg, chair of the Statistics Department at Pennsylvania State University, suggested that I consult with Terry Speed, professor of Statistics at U.C. Berkeley; both suggested chi-square using residual components as the statistic required to analyze the four groups.

4. Lynne Ehlers, "The Alchemical *Nigredo, Albedo, Citrinitas* & *Rubedo,* Stages of Transformation: A Case Study" (PhD diss., California School of Professional Psychology, 1992).

5. Edward Edinger, "Alchemy and the Individuation Process," cassette recording (Centerpoint, 1976).

CHAPTER 1

6. Stewart Berg Flexner, ed., *Random House Dictionary of the English Language,* 2nd ed. (New York: Random House, 1987), 49.

7. Eric John Holmyard, *Alchemy* (Baltimore, MD: Penguin Books, 1957), 19; John Read, *Prelude to Chemistry: An Outline of Alchemy* (Cambridge, MA: MIT Press, 1936/1966), 4.

8. Mircea Eliade, *The Forge and the Crucible: The Origins and Structures of Alchemy,* 2nd ed., trans. by S. Corrin (Chicago: University of Chicago Press, 1956/1978); Homer H. Dubs, "The Origins of Alchemy," *Ambix* IX, no. 1 (1961), 23.

9. Marie-Louise von Franz, "Psyche and Matter in Alchemy and Modern Science," *Quadrant* 8, no. 1 (1975), 33–49.

10. Read, *Prelude to Chemistry;* Eliade, *The Forge and the Crucible.*

11. Tenney Lombard Davis, "The Dualistic Cosmogony of Huai-nan-tzu and Its Relations to the Background of Chinese and European Alchemy," *Isis* XXV, no. 2 (1936), 333.

12. F. Sherwood Taylor, "The Origins of Greek Alchemy," *Ambix* I, no. 1 (1937), 37.

13. Read, *Prelude to Chemistry,* 4.

14. Holmyard, *Alchemy,* 19.

15. Syed Mahdihassan, "The Chinese Origin of Three Cognate Words, Chemistry, Elixir and Genii," *Journal of the University of Bombay* 20, no. 2 (1951), 107, quoted in H. J. Sheppard, "Alchemy: Origin or Origins?" *Ambix* XVII, no. 2 (1970), 71.

16. Titus Burkhardt, *Alchemy: Science of the Cosmos, Science of the Soul,* trans. W. Stoddart (Baltimore, MD: Penguin Books, 1967/1971), 27.

17. C. G. Jung, "The Process of Individuation: Alchemy II," vol. 8, *E.T.H. Lectures: Notes on a Series of Unpublished Lectures Given at the Eidgenössische Technische Hochschule, Zurich, May–July 1941* (Privately printed, 1960), 15.

18. Read, *Prelude to Chemistry,* 35, 41; Dubs, "The Origin of Alchemy," 34.

19. Holmyard, *Alchemy,* 60–104; Read, *Prelude to Chemistry,* 17.

20. Charles H. Haskins, "Arabic Science in Western Europe," *Isis* VII, no. 3 (1925), 482.

21. Holmyard, *Alchemy,* 105; Read, *Prelude to Chemistry,* 41.

22. Ibid., 105.

23. Taylor, *The Origins of Greek Alchemy,* 41.

24. Holmyard, *Alchemy.*

25. Richard K. Payne, "Sex & Gestation, the Union of Opposites in European & Chinese Alchemy," *Ambix* 36, no. 2 (1989), 75.

26. C. G. Jung, "Psychology of the Transference," CW 16. ¶505.

27. Holmyard, *Alchemy,* 273.

28. C. G. Jung, "The Process of Individuation: Alchemy I, vol. 7, *E.T.H. Lectures, Notes on a Series of Unpublished Lectures Given at the Eidgenössische Technische Hochschule, Zurich. Nov.–Feb. 1940–1941* (Privately printed, 1960), 148.

29. Manley P. Hall, *The Secret Teachings of All Ages: An Encyclopedic Outline of Masonic, Hermetic, Kabbalistic and Rosicrucian Symbolical Philosophy* (Los Angeles: Philosophical Research Society, 1975), 6.

30. Jung, "The Process of Individuation: Alchemy I," 15.

31. Chakrapani Ullal, personal communication, June 22, 1992.

32. Arthur J. Hopkins, *Alchemy: Child of Greek Philosophy* (New York: AMS Press, 1934/1967).

33. Eliade, *The Forge and the Crucible,* 146.

34. Holmyard, *Alchemy,* 26.

35. Francis Llewellyn Griffith and Herbert Thompson, eds., *The Leyden Papyrus: An Egyptian Magical Book* (San Diego, CA: The Book Tree, 1904/2017), 15–17.

36. Holmyard, *Alchemy,* 26.

37. Taylor, "The Origins of Greek Alchemy," 88–92.

38. H. J. Sheppard, "Gnosticism and Alchemy," *Ambix* VI, no. 2 (1957), 96.

39. Read, *Prelude to Chemistry,* 41.

40. Holmyard, *Alchemy,* 35.

41. Jung, "Alchemy I," 41.

42. Roger Bacon, in Holmyard, *Alchemy,* 120.

43. Sheppard, "Gnosticism and Alchemy," 87.

44. Maier, in Waite, *The Hermetic Museum,* vol. 1, 309.

45. Burkhardt, *Alchemy,* 17–18.

46. Holmyard, *Alchemy,* 15.

47. Jung, Alchemy I, 74.

48. Eliade, *The Forge and the Crucible,* 142.

49. Jung, "Alchemy I," 74–75. Italics added.

50. Read, *Prelude to Chemistry,* 91.

51. Antoine-Joseph Pernety, *Dictionnaire mytho-hermetique* (Paris: Delalain, 1787).

52. Read, *Prelude to Chemistry,* 91.

53. Molly Tuby, *The Search and Alchemy* (London: Guild of Pastoral Psychology, 1982), 19.

54. Holmyard, *Alchemy,* 247.

55. Jung, "Alchemy I," 150–152.

56. Synesios, quoted in Burkhardt, *Alchemy,* 29.

57. Ibid., 29.

58. Holmyard, *Alchemy,* 259–272.

59. Tuby, *The Search and Alchemy,* 19.

60. Fabricius, *Alchemy: The Medieval Alchemists and their Royal Art,* 12.

61. Read, *Prelude to Chemistry,* 116.

62. Edinger, *Anatomy of the Psyche,* 14.

63. Jung, "Alchemy I," 61.

64. Edinger, "Alchemy and the Individuation Process."

65. C. G. Jung, *Mysterium Coniunctionis,* CW 14, ¶792.

66. Herbert Silberer, *Hidden Symbolism of Alchemy & the*

Occult Arts, trans. Smith Ely Jeliffe (New York: Dover, 1917/1971), 151.

67. Ethan Allan Hitchcock, *Alchemy and the Alchemists* (Los Angeles: Philosophical Research Society, 1857/1976), 18.

68. Ibid., 225.

69. Ibid., 155.

70. Fabricius, *Alchemy: The Medieval Alchemists and their Royal Art,* 12.

71. James Kirsch, "Jung & Alchemy," in *International Encyclopedia of Neurology, Psychiatry, Psychoanalysis and Psychology,* 12 vols. (New York: Van Nostrand Reinhold, 1977), 357.

72. C. G. Jung, "The Philosophical Tree," *Alchemical Studies* (1967), CW 13, ¶393.

73. Jung, CW 14, ¶792.

74. Edinger, "Alchemy and the Individuation Process."

75. Edinger, *Anatomy of the Psyche,* 2–9.

76. Ibid., 69.

77. Holmyard, *Alchemy,* 26.

78. Heraclitus (c. fifth-century CE) in C. G. Jung, *Psychology and Alchemy* (1968), CW 12, ¶333.

79. Arthur John Hopkins, "A Modern Theory of Alchemy," *Isis* VII, no 1 (1925), 66.

80. Read, *Prelude to Chemistry,* 146.

81. Brent Berlin and Paul Kay, *Basic Color Terms: Their Universality and Evolution* (Berkeley, CA: University of California Press, 1969/1999).

82. Christopher Rowe, "Concepts of Colour and Colour Symbolism in the Ancient World" in *Color Symbolism* (Dallas, TX: Spring Publications, 1972/1977), 37–38.

83. Rowe, "Concepts of Colour and Colour Symbolism," 43.

84. Jamsthaler, *Viatorium spagyricum,* Frankfurt, 1625, in Gareth Roberts, *The Mirror of Alchemy* (Toronto: University of Toronto Press, 1994), 47.

85. Marie-Louise von Franz, *The Feminine in Fairy Tales* (Irving, TX: Spring Publication, 1972), 64.

86. Lynne Ehlers, "The Scarab," *Journal of Sandplay Therapy* 20, no. 2 (2011), 85–94.

CHAPTER 2

87. Anonymous, in Waite, *Hermetic Museum,* II, 198.

88. Benedictus Figulus, *A Golden and Blessed Casket of Nature's*

Marvels (seventeenth century), trans. A. E. Waite (London: Vincent Stuart, 1963), 298.

89. Edinger, *Anatomy of the Psyche,* 10.

90. John Beebe, personal communication, May 4, 1992.

91. Martin Ruland the Elder, *A Lexicon of Alchemy* or *Alchemical Dictionary* (New York: Samuel Weiser, 1984), 220–225.

92. Jung, "Alchemy II," 89.

93. Edinger, *Anatomy of the Psyche,* 10.

94. Hillman, "Salt, A Chapter in Alchemical Psychology," in *Images of the Untouched,* eds. J. Stroud and G. Thomas (Dallas: Spring, 1982), 118.

95. Jung, CW 14, ¶552.

96. Jung, CW 14, ¶404.

97. Jung, CW 14, ¶696.

98. Edinger, *Anatomy of the Psyche,* 157.

99. Ruland, *A Lexicon of Alchemy,* 34.

100. Edinger, *Anatomy of the Psyche,* 148.

101. Jung, CW 16, ¶472.

102. Edinger, *Anatomy of the Psyche,* 171.

103. Ibid., 148.

104. Jung, "Alchemy I," 96.

105. Allison Coudert, *Alchemy, the Philosopher's Stone* (London: Wildwood House, 1980), 198.

106. Jung, CW 14, ¶646.

107. C. G. Jung, "On the Psychology of the Unconscious," *Two Essays on Analytical Psychology,* CW 7, ¶152.

108. Jung, CW 14, ¶708.

109. Ibid., ¶730.

110. *Artis auriferae* II, 258, quoted in Jung, CW 14, ¶729n.

111. Scholia to "The Golden Treatise of Hermes," quoted in Edinger, *Anatomy of the Psyche,* 149.

112. Arthur Edward Waite, ed., *The Hermetic Museum,* 2 vols. (New York: Weiser, 1893/1974), II, 191–192.

113. Hitchcock, *Alchemy and the Alchemists,* 255.

114. Silberer, *Hidden Symbolism of Alchemy and the Occult Arts,* 102.

115. Ibid., 294.

116. Jung, "Paracelsus as a Spiritual Phenomenon," CW 13, ¶199.

117. Jung, CW 14, ¶306.

118. Jung, CW 14, ¶741.

119. Jung, CW 14, ¶346.

120. Edinger, *Anatomy of the Psyche,* 149.

121. Ibid., 150.

122. Ibid.

123. The text accompanying this image says, "If any man cut off his [the dragon's] head, / His blackness will disappear, / And give place to snowy white."

124. Edinger, *Anatomy of the Psyche,* 151.

125. *Theatrum Chemicum* IV, 569, quoted in Jung, CW 14, ¶733.

126. Edinger, *Anatomy of the Psyche,* 152.

127. Jung, CW 14, ¶670ff.

128. Edinger, *Anatomy of the Psyche,* 178.

129. Ibid., 146.

130. Hillman, "The Yellowing of the Work," 86.

131. Stephen A. Martin, "Anger as Inner Transformation," *Quadrant* 19, no. 1 (1989), 40–41.

132. Anonymous German Philosopher, "The Golden Tract Concerning the Stone of the Philosophers," in *Museum Hermeticum,* I,24, quoted in Jung, "Alchemy II," 105.

133. Salomon Trismosin, *Splendor Solis,* 16th century, Alchemical Tree of Life, folio 15, Harley MS 3469, British Library, London. See also Salomon Trismosin, *Splendor Solis: Alchemical Treatises of Solomon Trismosin, Adept and Teacher of Paracelsus,* trans. Julius Kohn (London: Kegan Paul, Trench, Trubner, 1582/1921).

134. P'u Ming, *Oxherding Pictures & Verses,* trans. Red Pine (Townsend, WA: Empty Bowl, 1987), 1–20.

135. Bradway, *Sandplay Bridges and the Transcendent Function* (San Francisco: The C. G. Jung Institute of San Francisco, nd).

136. Kate Amatruda, personal communication, October 8, 2019.

137. Ibid.

138. Donald Kalsched, *The Inner World of Trauma: Archetypal Defenses of the Personal Spirit* (London and New York: Routledge, 1996), 41.

139. Lynne Ehlers, "Kali," *Journal of Sandplay Therapy* IX, no. 1 (2000), 67–78.

140. Harry Harlow, "The Nature of Love," *American Psychologist* 13 no. 12 (1958), 673–685.

141. Joseph Henderson, "Shadow and Self," lecture given at the C. G. Jung Institute of San Francisco, February 27, 1982.

142. Pratibha Eastwood, *Nine Windows to Wholeness: Exploring Numbers in Sandplay Therapy* (Honolulu: Sanity Press, 2002), 156.

143. Dora Kalff, *A Psychotherapeutic Approach to the Psyche* (Boston: Sigo Press, 1980).

144. Ibid., 10.

CHAPTER 3

145. *Theatrum Chemicum* I, 424, quoted in Jung, CW 14, ¶434.

146. Waite, *The Hermetic Museum,* II,267.

147. *Le Texte d'Alchymie,* quoted in Davis, "The Dualistic Cosmogony," 81.

148. Sherwood F. Taylor, "The Alchemical Works of Stephanos of Alexandria," *Ambix* II, no. 1 (1938), 41.

149. Senior, *De Chemia,* quoted in Jung, CW14, ¶319n.

150. Jung, CW 14, ¶630.

151. Hillman, "Silver and the White Earth II," 61.

152. Mylius, *Philosophia reformata,* 20, quoted in Jung, CW14, ¶620.

153. Jung, CW 14, ¶330.

154. Jung, CW 14, ¶¶234-255.

155. Hillman, Silver and the White Earth II," 118.

156. Ibid., 130.

157. Ibid., 132.

158. John Pordage (1607–1681), quoted in Jung, CW 16, ¶¶512–515.

159. Pordage, quoted in Jung, CW 16, ¶¶512–515.

160. Jung, "Religious Ideas in Alchemy," CW 12, ¶334.

161. Ibid.

162. von Franz, *Alchemy,* 220.

163. Edinger, *Anatomy of the Psyche,* 72–73.

164. Maier, *Atalanta Fugiens* (1618), quoted in Connie Zweig, "To Be a Woman: The Birth of the Conscious Feminine," *The San Francisco Jung Institute Library Journal* 10, no. 4 (1992), 4.

165. Jung CW 14, ¶307.

166. Jung, CW 12, ¶334.

167. Neumann, "On the Moon and Matriarchal Consciousness," 84–85.

168. Ibid., 86.

169. Ibid., 83.

170. Ibid., 86.

171. Ibid., 88.

172. Ibid., 89.

173. Ibid.

174. Ibid.

175. Ibid., 90.

176. Ibid., 91.

177. Neuman says "This heart-center … with its relation to moon-time, is still the valid orienting factor in all processes of growth and transformation. Its dominance is also typical of the processes of the creative spirit, in the course of which contents are slowly constellated in the unconscious, more or less independent of conscious participation, until they flow up into a consciousness which is neither systematized nor insulated, but open and ready to expand." Ibid., 90.

178. Ibid.

179. Ibid., 92.

180. Ibid., 94.

181. Ibid.

182. Ibid., 95.

183. Ibid., 96–97.

184. Ibid., 98.

185. Ibid., 99.

186. Hitchcock, *Alchemy and the Alchemists,* 76.

187. Silberer, *Hidden Symbolism of Alchemy and the Occult Arts,* 401.

188. Hillman, "The Yellowing of the Work," 83–86.

189. T. S. Eliot, "Burnt Norton," in *The Four Quartets* (New York: Harcourt, 1968), 15–16.

190. Jack London, *To Build a Fire and Other Stories* (New York: Bantam, 1988), 14–15.

191. James Kirsch, "The White Silence: Psychological Interpretation of a Story by Jack London" (Paper presented to the Analytical Psychology Club, Los Angeles, 1955), 26.

192. Martin, "Anger as Inner Transformation," 42.

193. "For Marion," a poem written by the board of the Marion Woodman Foundation read at her memorial on July 16, 2018.

194. Phillip Rawson, *The Art of Tantra* (Greenwich, CT: New York Graphic Society, Ltd., 1973), 194.

195. Donald Sandner, *Navaho Symbols of Healing* (Rochester, VT: Healing Arts Press, 1991), 207.

196. Herder Freiburg, *The Herder Symbol Dictionary,* trans. B. Matthews (Wilmette, IL: Chiron, 1978/1986), 214.

197. Gertrude Jobes, *Dictionary of Mythology, Folklore and Symbols,* 2 vols. (New York: Scarecrow, 1962), 262.

198. Jean C. Cooper, *An Illustrated Encyclopedia of Traditional Symbols* (London: Thames & Hudson, 1978), 42.

199. C. G. Jung, *C. G. Jung Speaking,* eds. William McGuire and R. F. C. Hull (Princeton: Princeton University Press, 1977), 228.

200. Eirenaeus Philalethes, "An Open Entrance to the Closed Palace of the King" (1645), in A. E. Waite, *The Hermetic Museum,* II, 193.

201. Loren Pedersen, personal communication, 1988.

202. Arnold of Villanova. Figures 1–10 are full page reproductions from the *Rosarium Philosophorum* (Frankfurt, 1550), 113. These images provide the basis of Jung's essay on "The Psychology of the Transference" in CW 16, ¶¶402–564; the text accompanying the figures is found in the version of the *Rosarium* found in *Artis Auriferae* II (Basel, 1593).

203. London, *To Build a Fire and Other Stories,* 14–15.

204. Richard Tarnas, "Depth Psychology's Deepening Journey: From the Unconscious to the *Anima Mundi,*" Public Program in Depth Psychology, Sonoma State University, February 28, 2009.

205. von Franz, *Alchemy,* 220.

206. Ctesias, *Indica,* 5th century BCE, in Robert Graves, *The White Goddess* (New York: Farrar, Strauss & Giroux, 1948), 410.

207. Cooper, *An Illustrated Encyclopedia of Traditional Symbols,* 183.

208. Hillman, "The Yellowing of the Work," 86.

209. Fibber McGee's closet alludes to the overstuffed hall closet in the US radio comedy series *Fibber McGee and Molly* (1935–1956). Google internet reference, August 25, 2019.

210. *De Chemia,* quoted in Jung, CW 14, ¶319n.

211. Stephanos of Alexandria, translated by Taylor, "The Alchemical Works of Stephanos of Alexandria," 41.

212. Gerhard Dorn, "Philosophia Meditativa," *Theatrum Chemicum,* 451, quoted in Jung, CW 14, ¶670ff.

213. Kalff, *A Psychotherapeutic Approach to the Psyche.*

214. Heinz Kohut, *The Restoration of the Self* (New York: International Universities Press, 1977), 104.

215. This flesh-colored Warrior Woman is more embodied and human than her pewter Warrior Woman, but she was also a substitute for the pewter Warrior Woman in my other office.

216. Estelle Weinrib, *Images of the Self: The Sandplay Therapy Process* (Hot Springs, AR: Temenos Press, 2004), 83.

217. Eastwood, *Nine Windows to Wholeness,* 160; 166.

CHAPTER 4

218. Fabricius, *Alchemy: The Medieval Alchemists and their Royal Art,* 147.

219. Hillman, "The Yellowing of the Work," 77–96.

220. Ibid., 85.

221 St. Thomas Aquinas, *Aurora Consurgens* (13th c.), quoted in von Franz, *Alchemy,* 196.

CHAPTER 5

222. Tenney Lombard Davis, "Pictorial Representations of Alchemical Theory," *Isis* XXVIII, no. 1 (1938), 74.

223. Dorn, *Theatrum Chemicum* I, 423, quoted in Jung, CW 14, ¶137.

224. Pordage, quoted in Jung, CW 16, ¶¶516–517.

225. H. J. Sheppard, "Colour Symbolism in the Alchemical Opus," *Scientia (Rivista de Scienza)* IC, N. DCXXXI (VI), (1964), 235.

226. Jung, CW 14, ¶118.

227. Waite, *The Hermetic Museum,* 26.

228. Arthur Edward Waite, *The Turba Philosophorum* (New York: Samuel Weiser, 1602/1896/1973), 201.

229. Irenaeus Philalethes (1645), quoted in Hitchcock, *Alchemy and the Alchemists,* 247–248.

230. "Compositum de Compositis," quoted in Hopkins, *Alchemy, Child of Greek Philosophy,* 117.

231. Marcellin Berthelot, *Collection des anciens alchimistes grecs,* 3 vols. (Paris: G. Steinheil, 1887-1888) III,xlix, 4–12, quoted in Jung, CW 12, ¶456.

232. Berthelot, III, xxix, 24, quoted in Jung, CW 12, ¶456.

233. Sheppard, "Egg Symbolism in Alchemy," *Ambix* VI, no 3, 143.

234. Hargrave Jennings, *The Rosicrucians: Their Rites and Mysteries* (New York: Arno Press, 1976), 182, 186.

235. Hitchcock, *Alchemy and the Alchemists,* 76.

236. Silberer, *Hidden Symbolism of Alchemy and the Occult Arts,* 316–318.

237. Jung, CW 12, ¶334.

238. Hillman, "Silver and the White Earth II," 29.

239. Martin, "Anger as Inner Transformation," 44.

240. Ibid., 44.

241. Hillman, "The Yellowing of the Work," 87.

242. C. G. Jung, "The Psychological Aspects of the Kore," *The Archetypes and the Collective Unconscious* (1968), CW 9i, ¶331.

243. Jung, CW 9i, ¶312.

244. Revelations 7:4.

245. Isaiah 1:18, quoted in Jung, CW 14, ¶421f.

246. Joseph Needham, *Science and Civilization in China,* vol. 3, *Chemistry and Chemical Technology, Part II: Spagyrical Discovery and Invention, Magisteries of Gold and Immortality* (Cambridge, MA: Cambridge University Press, 1974), 5ff.

247. Gabrielle Wilson, personal communication, January 1992.

248. Jennings, *The Rosicrucians: Their Rites and Mysteries,* 150.

249. Rawson, *The Art of Tantra,* 181.

250. Rowe, "Concepts of Colour and Colour Symbolism," 46.

251. London, *To Build a Fire and Other Stories,* 363–385.

252. James Kirsch, "The Red One: Psychological Interpretation of a Story by Jack London" (Paper presented to the Analytical Psychology Club, Los Angeles, 1955), 12.

253. Max Lüscher, *The Lüscher Color Test,* trans. Ian A. Scott (New York: Random House, 1948/1969), 60–61.

254 Henderson and Sherwood, *Transformation of the Psyche,* 43.

255. Ad de Vries, *Dictionary of Symbols and Imagery* (Amsterdam: North-Holland, 1984), 469.

256. Many of the figures here are different than ones previously used because Christina began seeing me in my East Bay office, with a somewhat different collection of sandplay figures.

257. Philalethes, "An Open Entrance to the Closed Palace of

the King," in Waite, *The Hermetic Museum,* II, 165.

CHAPTER 6

258. Christian Rosenkreutz, *The Chymical Wedding of Christian Rosenkreutz,* trans. Joscelyn Godwin, ed. Adam McLean (Grand Rapids, MI: Phane, 1616/1991).

259. Thomas Norton, "Ordinal of Alchemy," Waite, *The Hermetic Museum,* I, 12, quoted in Jung CW 14, ¶655n.

260. Ehlers's adaptation of C. G. Jung's *Mysterium Coniunctionis,* CW 14. See also Charles Poncé, *Papers Toward a Radical Metaphysics: Alchemy* (Berkeley, CA: North Atlantic Books, 1983).

261. Archelaos, "Upon the Sacred Art," translated by C. A. Brown, "Rhetorical & Religious Aspects of Greek Alchemy II," *Ambix* II, nos. 3 and 4 (1946), 129–137.

262. Jung, CW 14, ¶1.

263. Waite, *The Hermetic Museum,* I, 272.

264. Ibid., 285.

265. Ibid., 281.

266. Ibid., 283; Mylius, *Philosophia reformata,* 190.

267. Jung, CW 14, ¶4.

268. Charles Poncé, *Working the Soul: Reflections on Jungian Psychology* (Berkeley, CA: North Atlantic Books, 1988), 92.

269. Thomas Ogden, *The Matrix of the Mind* (Northvale, NJ: Jason Aronson, 1986), 41–65.

270. Jung, CW 14, ¶4.

271. Waite, *The Hermetic Museum,* 351; Mylius, *Philosophia reformata,* 190.

272. "Consilium coniugii," *Ars chemica,* 1566, 136, quoted in Jung, CW 14, ¶22.

273. Grinnell, *Alchemy in a Modern Woman,* 1973.

274. Ripley, *Theatrum Chemicum* II, 1602, 128, quoted in Jung, CW 14, ¶1n. Emphasis added.

275. Hillman, "Silver and the White Earth II," 56–57.

276. Marie-Louise von Franz, "Macro- and Microcosmos in the Light of Jungian Psychology," *Ambix* XIII, no. 1 (1965), 30.

277. Poncé, *Working the Soul,* 93.

278. Henderson and Sherwood, *Transformation of the Psyche,* 137-142.

279. Ibid.

280. Jung, CW 12, ¶334.

281. Neumann, "On the Moon and Matriarchal Consciousness," 99.

282. C. G. Jung, *Aion* (1968), CW 9ii, ¶426.

283. *Artis auriferae II* (1593), 248, quoted in Fabricius, *Alchemy: The Medieval Alchemists,* 182.

284. Jung, CW 9ii, ¶426.

285. Jung, CW 14, ¶670.

286. Dorn, quoted in Jung, CW 14, ¶670.

287. Jung, CW 12, ¶334.

288. von Franz, *Alchemy,* 145–146.

289. Steven Joseph, personal communication, February 1, 1991.

290. Hillman, "The Yellowing of the Work," 87.

291. Hitchcock, *Alchemy and the Alchemists,* 286–287.

292. Edith Sullwold, *Therapy with Children* (San Francisco: C. G. Jung Institute, 1975), 179. Emphasis added.

293. Hillman, "Silver and the White Earth, II," 56–57.

294. Poncé, *Working the Soul: Reflections on Jungian Psychology,* 93.

295. Richard Wilhelm and Carey F. Baynes, *The I Ching or Book of Changes,* 3rd ed. (Princeton: Princeton University Press, 1950/1967), lviii.

296. Ibid., 3.

297. Wilhelm and Baynes, *The* I Ching, 10–11.

298. Ibid., 10.

299. Pai-Chu-I, 722–846, quoted in Needham, *Chemistry and Chemical Technology,* 148.

300. Needham, ibid., 69–70.

301. Sri M. P. Pandit, *Kundalini Yoga,* 5th ed. (Madras: Ganesh, 1972), 32ff.

302. Nicole Kleinberg, personal communication, October 16, 1991.

303. Adjit Mookerjee, *Tantra Art: Its Philosophy and Physics* (Basel, Paris, New Delhi: Ravi Kumar, 1971), 33.

304. Ibid., 29.

305. Ibid., 34.

306. Ibid., 29.

307. Gershom Scholem, *Kabbalah* (New York: Dorset, 1987), 107.

308. G. William Domhoff, "Why Did They Sit on the King's Right in the First Place?" *Psychoanalytic Review* 56, no. 4 (1970), 588.

309. Charles Osgood, B. J. Suci, and P. H. Tannenbaum, *The*

Measurement of Meaning (Urbana: University of Illinois Press, 1957), quoted in Domhoff, "Why Did They Sit on the King's Right in the First Place?" 590.

310. Ibid., 590–591.

311. *The Storyteller*, Alaskan Inuit Whalebone Carving. Artist unknown. Private collection, published in Donald Kalsched, *Trauma and the Soul: A Psycho-Spiritual Approach to Human Development and Its Interruption* (London and New York: Routledge, 2013), 6.

312. Kalsched, *Trauma and the Soul*, 6.

313. Ibid., 6.

314. Robert Ornstein, *The Psychology of Consciousness* (San Francisco: Freeman, 1972).

315. Ornstein, *The Psychology of Consciousness*, 58–59.

316. Ibid., 67.

317. Jill Bolte Taylor, *My Stroke of Insight: A Brain Scientist's Personal Journey* (New York: Penguin Group, 2006).

318. Ibid., 139–140.

319. Ibid., 141.

320. Ibid., 147.

321. Ibid.

322. Ibid., 70

323. Ibid., 73.

324. Ibid., 51.

325. Ibid., 75.

326. Ibid., 74.

327. Ibid., 71.

328. Ibid., 69.

329. Ibid., 147.

330. Ibid, 141.

331. Ibid.

332. Jobes, *Dictionary of Mythology, Folklore and Symbols*, 2,1269.

333. Ibid., 1,204.

334. Henderson and Sherwood, *Transformation of the Psyche*, 46.

335. Edinger, *Anatomy of the Psyche*, 228.

336. Ehlers, "Kali," 67–78.

337. Henderson, "Shadow and Self."

338. D. W. Winnicott, "Fear of Breakdown," in *Psychoanalytic Explorations*, eds. Clare Winnicott, Ray Shepard, and Madeline Davis (Cambridge, MA: Harvard University Press, 1963/1989), 90.

339. Kohut, *The Restoration of the Self*, 104.

340. Eastwood, *Nine Windows to Wholeness*, 100–118.

341. Ami Ronnberg and Kathleen Martin, *ARAS The Book of Symbols: Reflections on Archetypal Images* (Cologne, Germany: Taschen, 2010), 392.

342. Ehlers, "The Scarab," 85–94.

343. The shamanic initiation experiences of Janet Adler, *Arching Backward: The Mystical Initiation of a Contemporary Woman* (Rochester, VT: Inner Traditions, 1995) and Malidoma Patrice Somé, *Of Water and the Spirit: Ritual, Magic and Initiation in the Life of an African Shaman* (New York: Jeremy Tarcher/Putnam, 1994) are worth reading, as are the stories of agony and ecstasy suffered by female mystics in Carol Lee Flinders, *Enduring Grace: Living Portraits of Seven Women Mystics* (New York: HarperCollins, 1993).

344. Hillman, "The Yellowing of the Work," 83.

345. Martin, "Anger as Inner Transformation."

346. von Franz, *Alchemy*, 222.

347. Ibid., 222.

348. Henderson and Sherwood, *Transformation of the Psyche*, 15.

349. Myers-Briggs Typological Inventory, https://www.myersbriggs.org/my-mbti-personality-type/mbti-basics/.

350. Elaine N. Aron, *The Highly Sensitive Person: How to Thrive When the World Overwhelms You* (New York: Birch Lane Press, 1996).

351. Judith Orloff, *Thriving as an Empath: 365 Days of Empowering Self-Care Exercises* (Boulder, CO: Sounds True Audiobook, 2019).

352. Teaching classes in dream studies and sandplay and, contributing a chapter to a book on dream studies have been wondrously enjoyable! See Lynne Ehlers, "The Ursa Major Dream" in *Integral Dreaming: A Holistic Approach to Dreams*, eds. Daniel Deslauriers and Fariba Bogzaran (Albany: State University of New York Press, 2012) 243–263; and Lynne Ehlers, "The Tao of Sandplay Therapy" in *Into the Heart of Sandplay*, eds. Dyane N. Sherwood and Betty Jackson (Oberlin, OH: Sandplay Editions, 2018), 141–154.

353. Neumann, "On the Moon and Matriarchal Consciousness," 88–89.

354. My dream describes the field work of Heifer International for ending hunger and poverty (https://www.heifer.org).

355. "Just like the great mother or wise old man, anima and animus are archetypes. In practical experience … they are images and at the same time emotions. One can speak of an archetype only when the two aspects coincide. When there is only an image, it is merely a word-picture, like a corpuscle with no electric charge. It is then of little consequence, just a word and nothing more. But if the image is charged with numinosity, that is, with psychic energy, then it becomes dynamic and will produce consequences. It is a great mistake in practice to treat an archetype as if it were a mere name, word, or concept. It is far more than that: it is a piece of life, an image connected with the living individual by the bridge of emotion. The word alone is a mere abstraction, an exchangeable coin in intellectual commerce. But the archetype is living matter." Jung, "Symbols and the Interpretation of Dreams," *The Symbolic Life,* CW 18, ¶589.

356. Philalethes, "An Open Entrance to the Closed Palace of the King," in Waite, *The Hermetic Museum,* 165, 191–198.

357. Marie-Louise von Franz, *Puer Aeternus*, 2nd ed. (Boston: Sigo Press, 1997), 5.

358. Eliot, "Burnt Norton," lines 62–67.

359. Translated from Friedrich II: Konstitution vom Maerz 1232, Hinrichtung der Ketzer in Deutschland, *Jenair Historische Arbeiten*, Herausg. von A. Cartelleiri and 'W. Judeich. Heft 6. Die Ketzerpolitik der deutschen Kaiser un Konige in den Jahren 1152–1254. Von Dr. H. Koehler, Bonn, 1913 (Aus Pfliegler, "Dokumente zur Geschichte der Kirche," Innsbruck, 1938), quoted in Jung, *ETH Seminars, 1940–1941,* 152.

360. Translated from "Conciliengeschichte," Nach den Quellen bearbeitet von Carl Joseph von Hefele. V. Bd. 2. Auflage, vermehrt und verbessert von Dr. A. Knöpfler, Freiburg, 1886 (Aus M. Pfleigler, "Dokumente zur Geschichte der Kirche," Innsbruck, 1938), in Jung, *ETH Seminars, 1940–1941,* 150–151.

361. Philalethes, "An Open Entrance to the Closed Palace of the King," in Waite, *The Hermetic Museum,* 165, 191–198.

362. I would like to acknowledge Holmyard's *Alchemy* (1957) and Martin Ruland the Elder's *A Lexicon of Alchemy* (1612/1984) as the initial inspiration for the terms as they appeared in my dissertation.

363. Eugene Monick, *Phallos: Sacred Image of the Masculine* (Toronto: Inner City Books, 1987), 102.

364. Ibid.

365. Jung, CW 7, ¶152.

INDEX

Page numbers with an *f* refer to a figure or a caption; *t* refers to a table; *n* refers to an endnote.

PERMISSIONS AND CREDITS

Permission to Quote

Excerpt from "Burnt Norton" from *Collected Poems 1909–1962* by T. S. Eliot. Copyright © 1952 by Houghton Mifflin Harcourt Publishing Company, renewed 1980 by Esme Valerie Eliot. Reprinted by permission of Houghton Mifflin Harcourt Publishing Company. All rights reserved.

Permissions for Illustrations

Images from the *Splendor Solis,* Harley MS 3469, and *Donum Dei*, Sloane MS 2560, appear by permission of the British Library © British Library Board.

Images from Herbrandt Jamsthaler, *Viatorium Spagyricum: das ist: ein increa* appear by permission of the Science Museum Group Collection © The Board of Trustees of the Science Museum. Color added to the original.

Language of Dreams (1990) and *Palimpsest* (1991), both © Susan Seddon-Boulet, appear courtesy of Eric Lawrence Boulet. All rights reserved.

Fasting Buddha, Wat Benchamabophit Dusitvanaram, Marble Temple Buddha Statues, Bangkok, Thailand, appears courtesy of Dyane Sherwood.

The *Storyteller*, Alaskan Inuit whalebone carving, artist unknown, appears courtesy of Donald Kalshched.

SOS (1914 – 1916) by Evelyn de Morgan, appears courtesy of the De Morgan Foundation © De Morgan Collection.

Credits

The Two Aspects Alchemy: the Physical and the Philosophical (Michael Maier, "The Golden Tripod," 1618, Arthur Edward Waite's *The Hermetic Museum*, "restored and enlarged: most faithfully instructing all disciples of the sopho-spagyric art how that greatest and truest medicine of the philosopher's stone may be found and held. Now first done into English from the Latin original published at Frankfort in the year 1678." Wellcome Library, CC BY 4.0)

The *Prima Materia* as Chaos (Michelle de Marolles, *Tableaux des Muses du Temple*. Paris: Nicholas L'Anglois, 1665, n.p. https://archive.org/details/dutempledesmuses00maro/page/n29/mode/2up)

Two-Headed Hermaphrodite (Michael Maier, *Symbola aureae mensae duodecim nationum,* Frankfurt: typis Antonij Hummij, impensis Lucae Iennis, 1617, 238. https://archive.org/ details/ bub_gb_87sQCxPqwrgC/page/n259/mode/2up)

Putrefactio (Georges Anrach de Strasbourg, *Prætiosissimum donum Dei*, folio 14. Paris: Bibliothèque nationale de France. Bibliothèque de l'Arsenal. Ms-975 réserve. 17th c. http:// archivesetmanuscrits.bnf.fr/ark:/12148/cc802176)

Alchemical Oven (Allison Coudert, *Alchemy: The Philosopher's Stone*, London: Wildwood House, 1980, 201)

Caught in the Grips of Manic *Rubedo* Energies (Peter Paul Rubens, detail from *The Fall of the Damned* or *Fall of the Rebel Angels*, ca. 1620, Alte Pinakothek, München)

Pairs and Quaternities (Leonhart Thurneisser zum Thurn, *Quinta Essentia*, gen. Leonhard Thurneysser, Leipzig, 1574, Wikimedia Commons {PD-US})

Two Lions Fighting, Crowned Couple Lying in a Coffin, Marriage of the King and Queen, and The Royal Son (Johannes Daniel Mylius, *Philosophia Reformata*, Germany: Jennis, 1622, n.p., 243, 224, and 300 respectively)

Slaying the Dragon, Quarreling Male and Female Wolves, Stag and Unicorn in the Wood (*Philaletha*, Basilius Valentinus, Thomas Norton, John Cremer, Nicolas Flamel, Michael Maier, Michael Sendivogius, Lambspring, Jean de Meung, and Helvetius, *Musaeum Hermeticum Reformatum et Amplificatum*, Frankfurt am Main, Germany: Apud Hermannum a Sande, 1678. https://digital.sciencehistory.org/works/5t34sk63f)

Twin Fountains (Salomon Trismosin, *La Toyson d'Or* [a later version of *Splendor Solis*], 18th century, Bibliothéque Nationale, Paris, Ms. Français 12.297, folio 14)

THE AUTHOR

LYNNE L. EHLERS, PHD, is a licensed clinical psychologist and teaching member (CST-T) of Sandplay Therapists of America (STA) and the International Society for Sandplay Therapy (ISST). She has worked with her dreams since childhood and began working with sandplay in 1977. She has served on the faculty of the Dream Studies Program and as adjunct faculty in the Sandplay Studies Program at John F. Kennedy University and as guest lecturer, visiting scholar, and associate professor at Sonoma State University. She has presented papers at dream conferences sponsored by the International Association for the Study of Dreams (IASD), and biennially at both national and international sandplay conferences since 2009. Her many articles have appeared in the *Journal of Sandplay Therapy,* and "The Tao of Sandplay Therapy" appears as a chapter in *Into the Heart of Sandplay*, edited by Dyane N. Sherwood and Betty C. Jackson (Sandplay Editions 2018). Dr. Ehlers offers sandplay, dreamwork, case consultation, and Jungian-oriented depth psychotherapy for adults in Albany, California.

CORRESPONDENCE:

Lynne Ehlers, Ph.D.
1664 Solano Avenue
Albany, CA 94707
lynne.ehlers@sbcglobal.net
(510) 388-7679

55802318R00136